Kennedy versus Lodge

Kennedy

versus **Lodge**

The 1952
Massachusetts
Senate Race

Thomas J. Whalen

Foreword by Robert Dallek

Northeastern University Press
BOSTON

Northeastern University Press 2000

Library of Congress Cataloging-in-Publication Data
Whalen, Thomas J.
    Kennedy versus Lodge : the 1952 Massachusetts Senate race /
  Thomas J. Whalen ; foreword by Robert Dallek.
      p. cm.
    Includes bibliographical references (p.) and index.
    ISBN 1-55553-462-7 (cloth : alk. paper)
      1. Massachusetts—Politics and government—1951– 2. Kennedy, John F. (John Fitzgerald), 1917–1963. 3. Lodge, Henry Cabot, 1902– 4. Elections—Massachusetts—History—20th century. 5. United States. Congress. Senate—Elections, 1952. I. Title.

F71 .W49 2000
324.9744'043—dc21   00-033235

Illustration on title page reproduced courtesy of Paul Szep, *The Boston Globe*

Designed by Gary Gore
Composed in Galliard by Graphic Composition, Inc., in Athens, Georgia. Printed and bound by The Maple Press Company in York, Pennsylvania. The paper is Sebago Antique Cream, an acid-free sheet.

MANUFACTURED IN THE UNITED STATES OF AMERICA
04 03 02 01 00   5 4 3 2 1

For my mother

Contents

Foreword

John F. Kennedy's election to the U.S. Senate in 1952 has puzzled historians. How did a three-term congressman defeat the Boston Brahmin incumbent Henry Cabot Lodge? Lodge had won three landslide elections to the seat, most recently in 1946, when he defeated David I. Walsh, a popular Irish Catholic politician. Moreover, 1952 was a decisive Republican year: Dwight Eisenhower defeated Adlai Stevenson in Massachusetts for the presidency by a large margin, and the incumbent Democratic governor Paul Dever lost to his Republican opponent, Christian Herter, by fourteen thousand votes. Kennedy's seventy-thousand-vote advantage over Lodge begs for explanation. The idea that JFK's standing as a first-generation Irish Brahmin made the difference in putting him across is, as Thomas Whalen shows, insufficient explanation.

Whalen's book will now stand as the definitive study of this subject. His use of primary sources, and his analysis of the Kennedy and Lodge campaigns and of the vote tally give us the most thorough study of this crucial election, which propelled John Kennedy toward the White House. Whalen's use of the Lodge papers in the Massachusetts Historical Society is particularly useful in helping us understand the dynamics of the contest. Most historical subjects are revisited by different generations of scholars. But Whalen's monograph will likely be the last word on the Kennedy-Lodge election. It is difficult to imagine that anyone will find new materials or much new to say beyond what Whalen tells us in this book.

The appearance of this monograph marks the debut of a promising political historian. It is gratifying to see that political history is alive and well and seems likely to flourish among the next generation of historians such as Tom Whalen.

ROBERT DALLEK

Acknowledgments

I would like to thank those special individuals who helped make this book a reality.

To begin with, I want to single out my late father, Herman T. Whalen, who instilled in me a love of history and a belief that the world can be made a better place if only one tries. I miss him dearly.

My mom, Mary Anne Whalen-Spinale, and my stepfather, Joseph Spinale, helped me in ways beyond words or feelings. They believed in me and were always there to offer good cheer and encouragement. They never gave up on me, and I love them dearly for it.

Dan Hammond and Chris Callely, the other two-thirds of the "Three Musketeers," kept my enthusiasm high and offered invaluable suggestions on how to improve the final manuscript. I am forever indebted to them. They are the best friends anyone could have.

Andrew Bunie displayed tireless patience and good humor. I never could have done it without him. Thomas O'Connor was terrific as always and reminded me once again what a great historian and person he is. Mark Gelfand contributed helpful insights and criticisms.

Tracy Vitolo was like a Rock of Gibraltar in supporting me, as were Joe King and Mike Feloney. John Weingartner, my editor, did a terrific job in guiding this project through to completion.

A special debt of gratitude is owed James MacGregor Burns, who took time off from a busy schedule to review an early draft of my work. He was extremely generous in his praise and was gracious enough to permit me to quote from an unpublished interview he had had with John F. Kennedy in 1959. He was an inspiration.

Equally helpful were Ralph Martin, Christopher Matthews, and Clay Blair, who allowed me access to the interviews and research materials they used for books on Kennedy. They have my highest regard.

Special thanks to the staffs of the John F. Kennedy Library, the Massachusetts Historical Society, the American Heritage Center, the Boston Globe Archives, and Boston University Special Collections for providing a professional and friendly atmosphere in which to conduct my research.

I would also like to single out the assistance of Fran Coen, Paul Lydon, Maura Porter, William Johnson, Ed and Judy Fierros, Donald and Gayle Clemenzi, Joe Powers, Steve and Jodie Blumenkrantz, Mary Allston-Hammond, Scott Ferrara, Ronald Whealon, Alan Goodrich, Mike Case, Judge Joseph I. Dever, Amanda Kennedy Smith, Robert Healy, Maxwell Rabb, Henry Sears Lodge, Fred Hammond, Jeremiah Murphy, Herb Kenny, James Sullivan, Anna Mae Arsenault, Robert Capeless, and Nigel Hamilton.

Kennedy versus Lodge

A Decisive Moment

D U R I N G a 1962 plane trip to Minneapolis, Minnesota, for a political fund-raiser, President John F. Kennedy suddenly turned to his traveling companion, trusted friend, and political advisor Dave Powers, and asked, "Dave, what was my vote against Henry Cabot Lodge [Jr.] in 1952?" Powers, who had been with Kennedy since the beginning of his political career in 1946, was not caught off-guard by the question. "1,211,984," Powers told the chief executive. When the president asked what Lodge's tally had been, Powers again had the figure memorized. "1,141,247," he replied. The ritual had been repeated several times over the previous decade, but for the first time the president carefully wrote down the figures Powers gave him on a piece of paper. After doing some quick arithmetic, the president finally asked, "Dave, what did you say my plurality was?" "70,737, Mr. President," Powers answered. "You know, you're right. For ten years I thought you were throwing numbers at me," Kennedy exclaimed as the significance of his early political triumph finally sank in.[1]

On November 4, 1952, John F. Kennedy defeated incumbent Henry Cabot Lodge Jr. to become only the third Democrat in history elected to the U.S. Senate from Massachusetts. It was a decisive moment in Kennedy's political career. After his victory in that contest, Kennedy went on to gain national prominence as a contender for the vice-presidential nomination at the 1956 Democratic National Convention and as a Pulitzer Prize–winning author the following year for the book *Profiles in Courage,* "a group of biographical essays about a group of politicians willing to defy the clear sentiment of their constituents."[2]

In 1958 Kennedy won election to the Senate by 874,608 votes, then the largest margin in Bay State history, and immediately set his sights on a presidential run in 1960.[3] Beating out a crowded Democratic field that included senators Lyndon B. Johnson of Texas and Hubert H. Humphrey of Minnesota, Kennedy secured his party's presidential nomination on the first ballot. In what turned out to be the closest presidential election of this century, Kennedy bested his Republican opponent, Richard M. Nixon, by a margin of .2 percent of the popular vote to become the youngest man and only Roman Catholic elected to in the Oval Office to date.

Had Kennedy lost in 1952, it is likely that his political career would have ended right there, and the so-called Kennedy political dynasty would have been over before it had actually begun. Only by beating Lodge, arguably one of the most prominent names in American politics in the early 1950s, did Kennedy become, in the words of the presidential historian James N. Giglio, "a nationally known figure and a dominant Democrat in his state."[4] Such political credibility was essential for Kennedy's successful run at the White House eight years later.

For Lodge the 1952 Massachusetts Senate election was an equally decisive moment in his political career. Had he been able to fend off Kennedy's challenge, he would have in all likelihood emerged as one of the most powerful political figures in the country. By 1952 he already held important seats on the Senate Foreign Relations and Armed Services committees, and was second only to Robert A. Taft of Ohio in terms of party seniority. When Taft died the following year, Lodge stood a good chance of succeeding him as Senate majority leader. Even if Lodge had not become majority leader, his political influence still would have been great because Dwight D. Eisenhower, the man whose presidential campaign he managed through the 1952 Republican National Convention, was now sitting in the Oval Office.

Assured of at least six more years in the Senate, Lodge might then have maneuvered for the top spot on the GOP national ticket in 1960. His moderate voting record, rugged good looks, fine war record, and well-known family name were strong campaign assets. Add to this President Eisenhower's well-publicized unease with Nixon as the Republican standard-bearer, and it is not inconceivable that the GOP nomination might have been his. Whether Lodge could have gone on to win the general election is unclear, but it is interesting to note that during the 1960 presidential race, national polls indicated that Lodge, the Republican vice-presidential candidate, was more popular among

American voters than either Kennedy or Nixon. "If Lodge got by [in 1952], he'd have been your president," irascible Kennedy aide Patrick (Patsy) J. Mulkern told interviewer Ed Martin in 1964. "He would have won that presidential fight."[5]

But Lodge didn't win in 1952. In fact, he never held elective office again, despite the vice-presidential attempt in 1960 and as a Republican presidential hopeful in 1964. Instead, he served the remainder of his years in public life in a series of appointive offices, starting with his posting as the U.S. representative to the United Nations in 1953. Indeed, no member of the Lodge family ever held elective office after Connecticut governor John Davis Lodge, Henry's younger brother, lost his reelection bid in 1954.

This was a far cry from 1916, when the Kennedys and Lodges first squared off against one another. Then four-term incumbent Henry Cabot Lodge Sr., Lodge's paternal grandfather, edged former Boston mayor John "Honey Fitz" Fitzgerald, Kennedy's maternal grandfather, by thirty-three thousand votes to become the first U.S. senator in Massachusetts history elected by popular ballot under terms of the Seventeenth Amendment. Running under the campaign slogan "The case of the people of Massachusetts against Henry Cabot Lodge," Fitzgerald portrayed his opponent as a "cold and narrow aristocrat" who was out of touch with the needs of average citizens.[6]

To prove his point, Fitzgerald took out half-page newspaper ads showing that Lodge had opposed such popular measures as the Federal Workmen's Compensation Act and direct elections of senators. "Henry Cabot Lodge has been in the political life for [forty] years," Fitzgerald claimed, "and I would challenge any man in this community to name a single constructive act that bears his name that has marked progress to humanity or to the state of Massachusetts. His career shows a singular lack of touch with the people—in fact, he emphasi[z]es this idea when in his autobiography he says he was educated in private schools and the word 'private' has been closely related to him all his life, because it is for private interests that he has stood during his career."[7]

Lodge did not appear to be fazed by these assaults. Supremely confident in his own reelection, he refused to get into a public debate with Fitzgerald over the issues he raised. He was either unwilling or unable to see the political toll Fitzgerald's charges were having on his own heavily favored candidacy.

Lodge did himself a further disservice when he attacked President Woodrow Wilson for considering the inclusion of a "weakening postscript" to a protest note the United States had sent the German government over the sinking of the *Lusitania*. A baseless charge, Lodge was forced to admit his error, but not before Fitzgerald denounced him as a partisan opportunist. "I hope for the honor of Massachusetts that Senator Lodge will withdraw his statements," Fitzgerald lectured. "He must remember that when he attacks the President of the United States he is not attacking Woodrow Wilson, the Democrat, he is attacking Woodrow Wilson, President and representative of hundreds of millions of people, at a time when the honor of his office should remain unsullied and when he should have the backing of every one of his people."[8]

Thanks in part to this political gaffe and Lodge's lack of attentiveness as a campaigner, Fitzgerald nearly pulled off an upset on election day. He outpolled all other Democratic candidates in Boston, including President Wilson, and captured 47 percent of the vote overall.[9] What saved Lodge from defeat was his strong showing in the rural areas where state Republicans had received most of their support since the mid-nineteenth century.

By winning thirty-six years later, John Kennedy had, in the words of his mother, Rose Fitzgerald Kennedy, "evened the score" with the Lodges in a family political duel that would span nearly half a century and not conclude until 1962, when Edward M. Kennedy defeated George Cabot Lodge, Henry Cabot Lodge Jr.'s son, for his brother's old Senate seat.

The 1952 Massachusetts Senate race marked the climax to a rivalry, ultimately changing the course of politics in the Bay State as well as producing the thirty-fifth president of the United States. It is for these reasons that the election, which the political scientist James MacGregor Burns has described as "one of the most significant of the postwar years," warrants closer examination.[10]

Two Households,
Both Alike in Dignity

J OHN F. KENNEDY and Henry Cabot Lodge Jr. had much in common. Both graduated cum laude from Harvard and published books advocating greater military preparedness for democracies in the era before World War II. Both entered newspaper journalism but gave up the profession to pursue public office. Each volunteered for combat duty during World War II and were decorated for heroism on the battlefield, Kennedy in the South Pacific and Lodge in Europe. They were tall, handsome men born and reared in an atmosphere of wealth and privilege, coming from families with distinguished political pedigrees.

While the two men had many similarities, they nevertheless differed in some critical aspects. Lodge, fifty, was fifteen years older than Kennedy and had a personality that best can be described as cold and aloof. "He wasn't the type of person you approached too easily," a 1952 campaign aide, James Sullivan, recalled. "He had a gracious manner, a certain remoteness. . . . He wouldn't put his arm around you and say, 'Let's go out for a beer,' or something like that. No way." Though something of a loner himself in private life, Kennedy was more friendly and outgoing in public. "He had that marvelous quality of making you feel that you were his special friend," remembered Camman Newberry, a longtime Kennedy associate who, ironically, was Lodge's 1952 administrative assistant. "Now there's the mark, I think, of a real true politician in the best sense of the word."[1]

Whereas Lodge was the product of a centuries-old, tradition-laden Yankee lineage, Kennedy was only two generations removed from Irish immigrant status. "The Kennedys might be of Boston society," journalist Fletcher Knebel once shrewdly observed. "The Lodges were Boston society." The difference was not insignificant. While the Lodges encountered little difficulty in joining the best social clubs or vacationing at the most exclusive summer resort towns, the Kennedys for many years struggled to achieve full social acceptance. They were Irish Catholic and, as such, had to contend with the traditional prejudices that had predominated against their culture and religion for decades. "I was born here," Joseph P. Kennedy complained. "My children were born here. What the hell do I have to do to be an American?" Years later John Kennedy would echo his father's sentiments when he told a close friend that no Irish Catholic could ever belong to the Somerset Club, a traditional stronghold for Boston's Brahmin class. "If I moved back to Boston even after being President, it would make no difference," he said.[2]

On the surface, both candidates over several years had maintained cordial relations with one another. According to Pulitzer Prize–winning journalist and onetime Kennedy family confidant Arthur Krock, Kennedy even looked upon Lodge as his "ideal" for a public servant, when he was studying government at Harvard and Lodge was a first-term U.S. senator. As a freshman congressman, he continued to be respectful of Lodge and once even reprimanded an aide for making a tactless comment about the Republican while in the latter's presence. "I made a faux pas," remembered former Kennedy staffer William "Billy" Sutton. "I said to [Lodge] that day, 'Well, I see the day I think that we'll be chasing you down these dark alleyways [on Capitol Hill] for your seat.' Jack got very mad at me. He said, 'You shouldn't have said that. He's a nice guy.' I said, 'It's politics and you'll run against him.'"[3]

The young Democrat's respect for Lodge also spilled over into legislative matters. When he needed a Senate cosponsor for a bill he was introducing in the House to aid Latvian refugees, he turned to Lodge for help. "If you could see your way clear to reintroduce the companion bill in the Senate, I shall be most grateful," Kennedy wrote the Republican lawmaker. "I will be only too happy to sponsor a Senate bill on behalf of the Latvian refugees which would be a companion bill to the one which you are sponsoring in the House," came the reply.[4]

Similarly, Lodge was not deficient in showing his own respect for Kennedy. As senator, he publicly lauded Kennedy for his reported heroics as a PT-boat commander in the South Pacific during World War II. "I think of Lt. Jack Kennedy of Massachusetts, son of our former Ambassador to Great Britain, whose PT-boat was cut in two by a destroyer, who drifted [eighteen] hours on the hull, and finally reached a small island," Lodge remarked in a

July 7, 1943, speech that was later published in the *Congressional Record*. "Every night that young man would swim out to the channel, and, supported by his life preserver, would signal with a flashlight all through the night to attract the attention of an American boat. He finally succeeded, and thus, by means of his brave conduct, the other members of his crew were saved."[5]

Lodge also proved solicitous of his future political opponent in times of personal tragedy. When Kennedy's second-oldest sister, Kathleen, the widow of British nobleman William Hartington, the duke of Cavendish, died in a plane crash in the spring of 1948, the Republican lawmaker was quick to send off a warm letter of condolence. "This letter is for your family as well as for yourself personally and seeks to express some of the very deep sympathy which I feel for you all in the death of your sister," Lodge wrote Kennedy.[6]

Despite such overt gestures of cordiality, there were times that Kennedy and Lodge did not see eye to eye politically. One glaring example involved the Taft-Wagner-Ellender Housing bill, which was designed to provide low-cost housing for returning veterans of World War II. Kennedy, who strongly supported the measure, became privately incensed when Lodge helped bottle up the legislation in Senate committee. "So I don't think that Jack had much love for Lodge, I mean political love," Billy Sutton claimed.[7]

Lodge also had several dealings with Joseph P. Kennedy Sr. over the years, one of which occurred in 1938 when the then newly appointed ambassador to the Court of St. James approached him about a scheme to do away with the traditional practice of presenting American debutantes to the king and queen. The senior Kennedy had privately complained that the practice was personally degrading and detracted from his duties as ambassador.

Between them, the two Harvard graduates devised a plan, whereby Lodge agreed to write a letter to Kennedy formally asking him to arrange a presentation for a local debutante. Kennedy, in turn, agreed to write back to Lodge saying that such an arrangement would be impossible given the heavy demands of his position. Lodge would then make Kennedy's letter public and announce his enthusiastic endorsement of the ambassador's decision, thus ensuring positive publicity for both figures.[8]

Everything went according to plan except for the last part. Kennedy's letter rejecting Lodge's request was somehow leaked to the press before Lodge had a chance to respond. While Kennedy received praise within American and British circles for ending an archaic ritual for the socially ambitious, Lodge became the "goat" of the affair. "To his chagrin, the senator was put in the pos-ition of being soundly rebuked by the Ambassador," a *Boston Post* editorial later commented. Though no final determination has ever been made concerning the origin of the press leak, Kennedy bristled at suggestions it came from him. "I quite agree that Cabot was against the idea of presentations, but the facts are not quite as you present," Kennedy wrote *Post* city editor Edward J. Dunn, "and my own belief is that there wasn't any attempt to make him a goat, but there were leaks in America that embarrassed the whole situation."[9]

If Lodge felt Joseph Kennedy had been the orchestrater of his public humiliation, the Massachusetts Republican never let on. In 1942 he accepted an undisclosed amount of financial help from the elder Kennedy in fending off a challenge by New Deal congressman Joseph E. Casey of Canton for a second Senate term. "I was quite active in the fall campaign," Kennedy noted cryptically to a friend a few months after the election.[10]

Kennedy had given the aid as a result of a personal falling-out he had with President Franklin D. Roosevelt. He felt the Democratic president had largely ignored him as ambassador to Great Britain because of his isolationist views. Moreover, Kennedy resented how Roosevelt preferred bypassing him in communicating important diplomatic messages to the British Foreign Office. Since Casey was Roosevelt's hand-picked candidate of choice, Kennedy thought it would be satisfying from the standpoint of personal revenge to see the New Dealer go down in defeat.[11]

At first Kennedy tried to torpedo Casey's campaign by running his seventy-nine-year-old father-in-law, John F. Fitzgerald, the former mayor of Boston, against him in that fall's Democratic primary. But when Casey beat back Fitzgerald's challenge, 106,000 to 82,000, Kennedy turned his attention and considerable checkbook to Lodge.[12]

Regardless of the underlying motive, Lodge did not seem to forget the Kennedy family patriarch's generosity. When Kennedy evinced an interest in the late 1940s in becoming a member of the Hoover Commission, a bipartisan body charged with recommending ways to reorganize the executive branch, Lodge intervened successfully on his behalf. "I feel that you know that I am very appreciative of your interest in having me named to this Commission," Kennedy wrote Lodge. "It was a very nice thing for you to have done and I am grateful for your thought."[13]

Little did Lodge know that this would be the last political favor a Kennedy would ask of his family. By the eve of 1952 the battle lines were being clearly drawn between the two famous political clans. At stake was not only Lodge's Senate seat but also the honor of two families. Did Kennedy possess the necessary political skills to, as his mother would later say, "even the score" with the Lodges? This issue dominated political discourse in Massachusetts over the

Boston mayor John "Honey Fitz" Fitzgerald takes in a football game on a chilly fall day in 1913. Honey Fitz would miss out on his bid to unseat Henry Cabot Lodge Sr. from his U.S. Senate seat three years later. Courtesy of the Boston Public Library, Print Department.

next twelve months. "Two households, both alike in dignity," an irreverent newspaperman wrote of the looming clash, while quoting the opening lines of William Shakespeare's *Romeo and Juliet*.[14] Yet it took more than dignity to win in politics, and Lodge's Democratic challenger fully understood this fact. His life's experience did not permit him to think otherwise.

John F. Kennedy was born on May 29, 1917, in Brookline, Massachusetts, the second oldest of nine children of Irish Catholic parents. His father, Joseph P. Kennedy, was a Harvard-educated business entrepreneur on his way to making the first of many millions on Wall Street and in Hollywood. His mother, Rose Fitzgerald Kennedy, was the daughter of former U.S. congressman and Boston mayor John F. "Honey Fitz" Fitzgerald, one of the most colorful Irish American politicians of the early twentieth century.

Although he once claimed in an interview to have been raised in a "real third rate district" (in actuality, Brookline was an upper-middle-class community), John Kennedy did not lack for any material comforts growing up. Indeed, he dressed in the finest clothes, attended the best schools, and was driven around town by a chauffeur. Emotionally, his needs were tended to by his mother. "She's not as forceful as my father," he later recalled, "but she was the glue." If Kennedy fell ill or needed a shoulder to cry on, Rose would invariably be there for him providing comfort and good cheer. "She was deeply religious, highly devout," he explained. "She wasn't interested in politics so much [but she] was interested in things like the Pilgrims' landing at Plymouth Rock, things like that."[15]

While Rose's influence was unquestionably strong, it still did not compare to that of Joseph P. Kennedy, whom many regarded as the "architect" of his children's lives. Proud, ambitious, overbearing, and unscrupulous, the "Founding Father" exerted a "savage domination" over his sons and daughters. "I don't think you can have nine children in a house without there being some rigid authority," John Kennedy later commented, "and I think my father supplied that. But not unnecessarily so, and I think it did us all good."[16]

Not everyone agreed with this assessment. "He disciplined Jack like a Jesuit," complained Boston friend Norman MacDonald. "When the father was around, Jack couldn't invite any of his friends he wanted to their summer home in Hyannis Port. He had to submit a guest list and schedule to his father, and could invite only people who were useful."[17]

Viewing his children as extensions of himself, Joseph P. Kennedy sought to instill in them a burning desire to succeed. "The father particularly laid it on hard trying to make the boys, and the girls, excellent in something," Supreme Court Justice William O. Douglas later recalled, "whether it was touch football, or tennis, or boating, or something else." Sometimes the emphasis on competition bordered on the extreme. When his eldest son, Joe Junior, lost a sailboat race one summer, his father ordered a new mainsail be made that was nine inches longer than the rules of competition allowed. The notion of fair play did not enter into the equation. All that mattered was Joe Junior winning his next race. "For the Kennedys," Joseph Kennedy once said, "it is the castle or the outhouse—nothing in between."[18]

This obsession with winning stemmed from a deep-seated sense of personal frustration. Barred from entering Brahmin society on account of his Irish Catholic heritage ("When are the nice people of Boston going to accept us?" his wife asked an aquaintance), the elder Kennedy vowed his children would be accepted into elite circles. To this end he packed up his family and moved them to toney Riverdale, New York, in an attempt to "show" his supposed Brahmin betters he needed neither their acceptance nor approval.[19] Not satis-

PT-109 skipper John F. Kennedy at the helm. Kennedy's displayed heroism after his ship had been cleaved in half by a Japanese destroyer on the night of August 1, 1943, earned him national acclaim. Courtesy of the John F. Kennedy Library.

fied with having his children receive a public school education, he sent them off to select boarding schools where they could rub elbows with other sons and daughters of the rich and famous.

If there was a model for what Joseph Kennedy wanted his children to become, one could look no further than Joe Junior. Tall, handsome, athletically gifted, and smart, the eldest son represented the "best and the brightest" of the Kennedy clan. In him Joe Senior invested all his hopes and dreams. "Joe [Junior] was the one," recalled a family friend; "he was always the anointed politician. Always."[20]

In contrast, John Kennedy was the proverbial runt of the litter. Thin, bookish, and sickly, the future president of the United States did not cut a particularly striking figure. "He was too slight, too frail, too brittle to make the varsity in any contact sport," recalled one prep school instructor. "He tried them all only to wind up with broken fingers, wrists or ankles or whatever.

Through both school and college he was frustrated by his failure to measure up to his older brother, but he never stopped trying." More times than not, however, these efforts proved unsuccessful. "My brother is the efficient one in the family," young Jack conceded, "and I'm the boy who doesn't get things done. . . . If my brother were not so efficient, it would be easier for me to be efficient. He does it so much better than I do."[21]

To compensate for these perceived shortcomings and carve out his own sense of identity, Kennedy became something of an "archetypal rebel." At Choate School in Wallingford, Connecticut, for instance, he specialized in having fun and antagonizing the school's administration. "Well, I have two things to do," complained headmaster George St. John to Joseph P. Kennedy Sr. "One to run the school, another to run Jack Kennedy and his friends."[22] Indeed, so unruly did Kennedy's behavior become that he came within a hair of being permanently expelled.

The precipitating incident involved the formation of a clandestine student prankster group known as the Mucker's Club. So named for the term St. John used to describe undisciplined boys, the group flourished on the all-male campus, threatening even to surpass the popularity of the football team. "Why were we so devilish?" remarked one member. "Maybe we didn't like to be structured. Each of those guys had a pretty darn good sense of humor. Jack had a very, very keen wit. We just liked fooling people. . . . We were just nonorganization in some ways."[23]

Concerned that the "Muckers" were undermining his authority as headmaster, St. John rounded up the club's ringleaders, including Kennedy, and proceeded to inform them that they were no longer welcome as students at the school. "I don't blame him," remarked "Mucker" Maurice Shea years later. "He thought we were not quite the boys he wanted to have the stamp of Choate on." Only through the timely intercession of Joseph P. Kennedy, who reportedly made a generous financial contribution to the school, were the future Massachusetts politician and his friends able to avoid expulsion. "If that crazy Mucker's Club had been mine," the elder Kennedy told his son, "you can be sure it wouldn't have started with an M."[24]

Despite such levity, Joseph Kennedy was disturbed enough by the affair to pen his son the following warning: "Don't let me lose confidence in you again because it will be pretty nearly an impossible task to restore it—I am sure it will be a loss for you and a distinct loss for me." Thus chastened, John Kennedy spent the remainder of his Choate career staying out of trouble and improving upon his mediocre academic record. Still, he could not resist the temptation of pulling off one final prank. As class elections got under way, he convinced friends to stuff enough ballot boxes on his behalf to become "Most Likely to Succeed."[25]

Upon graduation from Choate in 1935, Kennedy entered Princeton University, but a hepatitis attack forced him to leave the school after only six weeks of classes. By attending the prestigious Ivy League institution, the former "Mucker" had hoped to escape the shadow of his older brother, Joe, who had become a star student athlete at Harvard. It didn't work out that way. News of his brother's triumphs continued to reach him at Princeton, thanks to letters from old Choate schoolmates and family members. "I always had the problem of my older brother," he later admitted to biographer James MacGregor Burns.[26]

Determined to match his brother's success, Kennedy gave in to pressure from his father to matriculate into his alma mater. "Jack," Joseph P. Kennedy wrote a Harvard dean at the time, "has a very brilliant mind for the things in which he is interested, but is careless and lacks application in those in which he is not interested. This is, of course, a bad fault."[27] As if to prove his father's point, the younger Kennedy spent most of his freshman year pursuing the two activities he enjoyed the most: socializing and playing football. While he could hold his own against his brother in the former, he did not stand a chance against him in the latter.

"Joe was physically more rugged," remembered Torbert MacDonald, Kennedy's Harvard roommate and later a U.S. congressman. "Jack played [junior varsity] offensive end and was a very good pass receiver. He had great desire, wanted to play very much, but his physical makeup was not that of an end who could block tackles which in those days were the biggest defensive linemen that the opponent ever had. His greatest success was in catching passes, shall we say."[28]

Indeed, it wasn't until his sophomore year that Kennedy's intellectual curiosity became aroused. Although his grades showed scant improvement, he began to read more and ask questions about the world around him. "I don't know what to attribute it to," he later told a journalist. "No, not professors. I guess I was just getting older. . . . It was during my junior year that I went to England for six months, which meant taking six courses as a senior and hard work. I had to work like hell."[29]

He took a semester off and went to England with his father, the ambassador to the Court of St. James appointed by President Franklin Roosevelt. FDR had made the move on strictly political grounds; he wanted to shore up support within his Irish Catholic constituency. This cold reality did not appear to bother the elder Kennedy, however. "The office," surmised historians David

Burner and Thomas R. West, "would make him the social superior of Boston's 'best people'; it was an achievement by which one generation of Kennedys could extend the reach of the next."[30]

The Kennedys did, in fact, for a time become the toast of London society, and while young Jack shared in the excitement of the seemingly endless rounds of embassy parties and royal galas, he spent an equal amount of time familiarizing himself with the problems that would soon plunge the Continent into World War II. "It was a great chance to go because it was certainly Europe on the eve," he later told an interviewer, "and the tempo was heightened because of it. It was a great opportunity to see a period of history which was one of the most significant."[31]

What he observed in Europe was later incorporated into his senior thesis, "Appeasement at Munich," which earned him magna cum laude honors. The 150-page study, an analysis of the reasons why British prime minister Neville Chamberlain "appeased" German leader Adolf Hitler at the Munich Conference of 1938, placed heavy emphasis on the role public opinion played in determining national policy. Arguing that the overwhelming pacifist sentiment of the country forced Chamberlain to make unwise concessions to the Nazi dictator, he proceeded to exonerate the British leader of any blame. He concluded that the Munich Pact, which pledged British acquiescence to Germany's seizure of the Sudetenland from Czechoslovakia, was inevitable given the conditions of democratic government. Although there were some reservations about the quality of the writing, Kennedy's thesis advisor, Henry A. Yeomans, determined that, on the whole, the work represented "a laborious and intelligent discussion of a difficult question."[32]

Pleased by his son's effort and the thesis's mirroring of his own sympathetic attitude toward Chamberlain, Joseph P. Kennedy sent a copy to Pulitzer Prize–winning columnist Arthur Krock of the *New York Times*. Finding the author's argument persuasive, the longtime Kennedy family friend recommended the work be refashioned into a book. "I was an editor, an advisor," Krock later admitted to Kennedy biographer Clay Blair, "and I may have supplied some of the material as far as prose is concerned, but it was [Kennedy's] book. So we got it published and you know the rest."[33]

Retitled *Why England Slept,* a clever take on Winston Churchill's widely acclaimed *While England Slept,* the book soared to the top of most national best-seller lists. But things were not as they appeared. Fearing poor book sales would reflect badly on his son's budding literary reputation, the elder Kennedy clandestinely purchased hundreds of copies to give the impression the work was a runaway success. "You would be surprised how a book that really makes the grade with high-class people stands you in good stead for years to come," the ambassador wrote his author-son.[34]

After his graduation from Harvard in June 1940, John Kennedy spent the next year and a half largely adrift and unfocused. He enrolled at Stanford University in California to do graduate work in business and political science, but the slow pace of academic life bored him. Putting aside his studies, the wealthy Ivy Leaguer spent most of his time visiting popular beachfront hideaways and dating socially eligible Stanford coeds. Only occasionally did the outside world intrude upon his thoughts. That occurred in December 1940, when his father sought his advice on a radio speech he intended to give on American neutrality. A staunch isolationist and defeatist ("I'll bet you five to one—any sum—that Hitler will be at Buckingham Palace in two weeks," he once told an aide during this period), the now former ambassador sought to keep America out of World War II.[35]

Although he had expressed support of his father's isolationism as a college undergrad, even going so far as advocating "considerable concessions to Hitlerdom" in an unsigned *Harvard Crimson* editorial, John Kennedy had in the interim experienced a political transformation. Reasoning that a triumphant Nazi Germany in Europe would endanger the security of the entire Western Hemisphere, the future commander in chief urged his father to back policies aimed at militarily propping up a besieged Great Britain. "We should see," he wrote, "that our immediate menace is not invasion, but that England may fall—through lack of our support."[36] Adhering to his son's advice, Joseph P. Kennedy came out in favor of the Lend-Lease Act, which empowered the president to sell or lend defense materials to Britain and her allies.

When American entry into the war became more likely in 1941, John Kennedy decided to sign up for military duty. Again, as was the case with his decision to enter Harvard, sibling rivalry played a key role. Envious of his brother Joe's acceptance into the prestigious U.S. Naval Aviation program, the ex-ambassador's son tried to enlist in both the army and navy, but a bad back brought on by an earlier football injury convinced service officials that he lacked the physical health to be inducted.

Unwilling to see Joe Junior have a monopoly on all the military glory, he got his father to arrange for a second navy physical, this time with a friendly doctor the elder Kennedy knew.[37] The ruse worked; he passed the examination without difficulty and received an ensign's commission in the U.S. Naval Reserves. Several weeks later, while returning from a regular Sunday morning touch football session with friends, he heard the news of the Japanese attack on Pearl Harbor. His life, as well as the lives of millions of other Americans, would never be the same.

Kennedy's naval career began with an unglamorous desk job at the Office of Naval Intelligence in Washington, D.C. His assigned duties involved preparing a daily intelligence bulletin for the secretary of the navy and other top officials. "We never dealt in anything higher than 'secret,'" remembered one contemporary, "and if we had code-breaking information, it came to us disguised, so we didn't know its source." Bored by the tedious work, the junior officer persuaded his father to "pull strings" and get him transferred to sea duty.[38] Freed from the drudgery of intelligence work, Kennedy entered midshipman's school at Northwestern University, where he signed up for patrol torpedo boat duty. Otherwise known as PT-boats, these small but maneuverable craft had gained considerable publicity at the start of the war for whisking General Douglas MacArthur off to safety during the Japanese invasion of the Philippines.

Lured by the hype, Kennedy, along with several other Ivy Leaguers with sailing or yachting experience, could not resist the temptation of commanding so glamorous a vessel. Assigned to the Solomon Islands of the South Pacific, the now lieutenant junior grade got more action than he could have reasonably expected. On the night of August 1, 1943, Kennedy's boat, the PT-109, was sliced in two by a Japanese destroyer while on a routine patrol in the Blackett Strait. "How it felt?" the junior officer later mused. "I can best compare it to the onrushing trains in the old-time movies. They seemed to come right over you. Well, the feeling was the same, only the destroyer didn't come over us, it went right through us."[39] Two crewmen lost their lives in the crash while another, forty-one-year-old machinist Patrick McMahan, was badly burned.

Thrown into the sea by the impact of the collision, Kennedy cajoled the surviving thirteen members of his crew into swimming to a nearby atoll about three and a half miles away. "I have nothing to lose," he told them, "but some of you have wives and children, and I'm not going to order you to try to swim to that shore. You'll have to make your own decision on that."[40]

With Kennedy leading the way, all of his men arrived safely on the deserted atoll. "During the week we spent on the island," he later recounted, "the men never beefed as they did when a request for going to town in the states was refused them. I never could praise them enough." The feeling was mutual. "Kennedy was the hero," remembered crew member Charles "Bucky" Harris. He "saved our lives. I owed him my life. If it wasn't for him I wouldn't be here—I really feel that."[41]

What prompted such praise was the extent to which Kennedy was willing to place his own life at risk for the sake of his men. In a desperate attempt to signal a passing PT-boat, the young lieutenant swam out to an island passage with a blinking lantern in one hand. "In the first place," recalled a fellow survivor, "it was a hell of a long way out to the passage. He'd go out there and float. Now in my mind if the boats had seen a light in the water, they'd have blown the light out of the water!"[42]

After several failed attempts, including one in which his men had given him up for dead, the former Harvard athlete stumbled across some friendly natives who agreed to alert Allied authorities about the whereabouts of him and his crew. The now legendary message he gave them to deliver was written on the husk of a green coconut and read as follows: "NAURO ISL NATIVE KNOWS POSIT HE CAN PILOT 11 ALIVE NEED SMALL BOAT KENNEDY."[43]

In the immediate aftermath of his rescue, Kennedy tried to downplay any talk of being a hero. "None of that hero stuff about me," he curtly informed one reporter interviewing him about the incident. "Real heroes are not the men who return but those who stay out there like plenty of them do, two of my men included."[44] His reluctance to see himself in this light was understandable.

Though he displayed great courage and personal leadership in keeping his men together following the sinking, he had nonetheless showed questionable command judgment in allowing his ship to be sunk in the first place. Indeed, he had only one of his three engines engaged when the Japanese destroyer was spotted, making escape a highly unlikely prospect. "Kennedy," a naval commander later remarked, "had the most maneuverable vessel in the world. All that power and yet this knight in white armor managed to have his PT-boat rammed by a destroyer. Everybody in the fleet laughed about that."[45]

Such ridicule, however, did not prevent Joseph P. Kennedy from successfully lobbying Undersecretary of the Navy James Forrestal into awarding his son the Navy and Marine Corps Medal for valor. "Unmindful of personal danger," Forrestal's citation read, "Lieutenant Kennedy unhesitatingly braved the difficulties and hazards of darkness to direct rescue operations, swimming many hours to secure aid and food after he had succeeded in getting his crew ashore."[46]

Picking up on this heroic theme, the *New Yorker* magazine commissioned future Pulitzer Prize–winning author John Hersey, a personal friend of the Kennedy family, to write about the PT-109 affair for a mid-1944 issue. Entitled "Survival" and later republished in a condensed form for the more widely circulated *Reader's Digest,* the article depicted John Kennedy in Heming-

John F. Kennedy conferring with his father, former Ambassador to the Court of St. James Joseph P. Kennedy, in Hyannis Port in June 1946. Proud, ambitious, over-bearing, and unscrupulous, the elder Kennedy exerted a "savage domination" over his sons and daughters. Courtesy of the *New Bedford Standard-Times*.

wayesque terms: "He thought he had never known such deep trouble. . . . His mind seemed to float away from his body. Darkness and time took the place of a mind in his skull. For a long time he slept, or was crazy or floated in a chill trance." For his part, the now famous junior officer felt uncomfortable about such embellishment. When he became president two decades later, he confided to a friend that the entire PT-109 episode was "more fucked up" than his efforts to unseat Fidel Castro in Cuba.[47]

To put the incident behind him, Kennedy took command of another vessel, the PT-59, before back troubles and a bout with malaria sidelined him permanently from active duty. It was while recovering from these ailments that he learned of his older brother Joe's death in a top secret mission over the skies of Europe. The news extracted a tremendous emotional toll on himself and his family, in particular Joseph P. Kennedy, who had previously informed anyone within earshot that he fully expected his eldest son to become president of the

United States someday. "You know," the ambassador wrote an acquaintance, "how much I had tied my whole life up to his and what great things I saw in the future for him. Now it's all over."[48]

Following his discharge from the navy in 1945, John Kennedy briefly toyed with the idea of becoming a journalist. Taking advantage of his father's friendship with conservative newspaper publisher William Randolph Hearst, the twenty-six-year-old war veteran landed a special correspondent's job with the Hearst-owned *Chicago Herald American*. Though he was a cub reporter, his family connections were such that he received one of the paper's choice assignments, covering the charter conference of the United Nations in San Francisco.

While stylistically flat and redundant, his U.N. dispatches nonetheless showed flashes of a lively intellect. "There is an impression," he wrote, "that this is the conference to end wars and introduce peace on earth and good will towards nations—excluding, of course, Germany and Japan. Well, it's not going to do that." Citing Russian fears of a "German comeback" as the main obstacle to peace, Kennedy argued that it would be naive to think the ruling communist regime would not shore up its European borders as a hedge against another invasion. "They feel they earned this right to security," he concluded.[49]

Although he found newspaper work intellectually stimulating, Kennedy could not shake the feeling he was but a mere observer of great events. "He told me," recalled personal friend and journalist Charles Bartlett, "that the reason he decided to get out of the newspaper business was that he felt it was not effective; he wanted to be in something more active."[50] Indeed, politics appeared to offer the kind of "effective" public involvement he was looking for. With the encouragement of his father, who privately relished the idea of his son's picking up the political torch for his fallen brother Joe, Kennedy began casting about for a public office for which to run.

His opportunistic gaze eventually fell upon a U.S. House of Representatives seat in the Eleventh Congressional District of Massachusetts, a predominantly working-class Irish and Italian area that embraced Cambridge and portions of East Boston, Charlestown, Somerville, and Brighton. What made the seat so attractive to Kennedy was the fact that his Democratic family already had a well-established political base there, thanks largely to John "Honey Fitz" Fitzgerald, who had represented the district in Congress at the turn of the century.

Nevertheless, there was one potentially troublesome obstacle in the way: James Michael Curley. As the popular incumbent congressman, the former Boston mayor was in a position to do enormous damage to Kennedy's candidacy, possibly even defeat it, were he to seek reelection. To prevent such a scenario, a way had to be found to ease Curley out of the picture. As he would at various other critical stages in his son's political career, Joseph P. Kennedy stepped in to provide a solution. In exchange for a pledge not to run, the elder Kennedy gave the aging Democratic leader "somewhere in the neighborhood of $100,000" to pay off long-standing personal debts.[51]

With the Curley threat thus neutralized, John Kennedy was free to announce his candidacy for Congress on April 22, 1946. The "temper of the times," he declared in his opening campaign statement, "imposes an obligation upon every thinking citizen to work diligently in peace as we served tirelessly in war."[52] Such an appeal found resonance among returning veterans, many of whom lived in the run-down triple-decker tenement houses that so dominated the main thoroughfares of the district. They had survived one of the bloodiest conflicts in American history and were now looking for public leaders who could best represent their views and interests.

As a famous war hero, Kennedy had the distinct advantage of being able to relate to them and they with him. "You just thought this fellow would be a good representative, the kind of fellow you'd like to have in politics and you wanted to help," recalled one veteran. In what became known as the "Year of the Veteran" in American politics, the young candidate made a special point of bringing up issues that most concerned potential veteran voters: affordable housing, jobs, and a strong national defense. "We must work together," he insisted. "We must recognize that we face great dangers. We must recognize how interdependent we are. We must have the same unity that we had during the war."[53]

He recruited local veterans to go door to door on his behalf within their respective communities. "We just told them: here was an educated guy who was going to dedicate his life to do all he could for humanity and for the good of the people; and he was fearless, courageous, and had ability," remembered volunteer veteran Charles Garabedian of Charlestown.[54]

Despite Kennedy's obvious popularity among veterans' groups, many seasoned political observers did not give him much of a chance to advance beyond a crowded Democratic primary field of nine other candidates. "The first time I saw Jack Kennedy," then–State Representative Thomas P. "Tip" O'Neill of Cambridge recalled, "I couldn't believe how this skinny, pasty-looking kid was a candidate for anything." Indeed, Michael J. Neville, the popular Cambridge mayor and state representative, was considered by some a "lead pipe cinch" to win the primary.[55]

But such assessments failed to take into account the young Democrat's unique appeal as a politician. "He came upon the scene when people were subconsciously looking for a new type of candidate," Kennedy's Harvard classmate and Cambridge worker Anthony Gallucio contended. "And Jack fitted into this. He had the naive appearance, he had the shock of hair that fell over his forehead. He was a multimillionaire who was very humble. As people would say, this fellow is not the kind who would steal [as Curley did]."[56]

Though he initially disliked the glad-handing that went along with traditional campaigning, he soon learned that a ready smile, a kind word, and the ability to listen could disarm even the greatest of skeptics. Indeed, Joseph P. Kennedy was taken aback by the ease with which his son went one-on-one with voters. Standing across the street from him one day in East Boston, the ambassador voiced surprise at the sight of the Harvard-Choate product conversing with a group of "hard-boiled guys" on the corner. "I remember saying to the man who was with me," Kennedy later reminisced, "that I would have given odds of five thousand to one that this thing we were seeing could never have happened. I never thought Jack had it in him."[57]

Logging upward of eighteen hours a day campaigning, John Kennedy simply outworked and outhustled his opponents, many of whom were not expecting such an effort. "The pros in the district thought of him as a millionaire's son," remembered David Powers, a popular service veteran hired by the candidate to oversee campaign activities in his native Charlestown, "and they wondered how he could get longshoremen and freight handlers and truck drivers—people who worked for a living—to vote for him. He just climbed more stairs and shook more hands and worked harder than all the rest combined. . . . He not only wanted to win, he wanted all the votes—that's what made him great." Still, more than a good work ethic was present in the young candidate's drive toward a congressional seat. "You know," remarked Tip O'Neill, "you can be a candidate, you can have the issues, you can have the organization, but money makes miracles and money did miracles in that campaign. Why they even had six different mailings . . . nobody had any mailings in that district."[58]

Evidence of Kennedy money was everywhere. Posters and billboards emblazoned with the campaign slogan "The New Generation Offers a Leader" blanketed the district. Pathé newsreel photographers were recruited by Joseph P. Kennedy, a former Hollywood movie producer, to shoot footage of the young candidate in action, which was then "shown in theaters in the Boston area a few nights before the election." Reprints of the *Reader's Digest* version of John Hersey's PT-109 article, trumpeting the wartime heroism of the Democratic hopeful, were distributed by the thousands. Even the courageous image of Kennedy's deceased older brother was evoked when the candidate, in a widely publicized move before the general election, presented the Boston archdiocese with a check for $650,000 to build the Joseph P. Kennedy Jr. Memorial Hospital in Boston.[59]

But the most glaring example of all concerned the financing of a "second Joe Russo" candidacy to split the vote of a popular Italian American undertaker of the same name who was also seeking the Democratic nomination. The Kennedys "must have been afraid," concluded Mark Dalton, a well-respected Cambridge attorney tapped to manage the Kennedy campaign; "with Joseph Russo on the ballot and the only Italian candidate on the ballot, there was a possibility that every Italian in the district would vote for Joe Russo."[60]

The "other Joe Russo" was, in fact, a twenty-seven-year-old custodian who lived in Boston's West End. According to this Russo, "a couple a wise guys" representing the Kennedy family approached him one day about declaring a run in return for some modest financial considerations. "They gave me favors," he later confessed to a journalist. "Whatever I wanted. I could of gone in the housing project if I wanted. If I wanted an apartment, I could of got the favor. You know."[61]

Primary day, June 18, brought more shenanigans. The Kennedys "approached a number of large families and promised them fifty dollars in cash to help out at the polls," Tip O'Neill later recalled. "They really didn't care if these people showed up to work. They were simply buying votes, a few at a time, and fifty bucks was a lot of money." Not even the transportation of voters to the polls escaped the notice of the Kennedy operation. "Every car or cab that was for hire [in the district] was taken, carrying voters for the Kennedys," Democratic rival Mike Neville complained. All told, a then-staggering three hundred thousand dollars was believed to have been spent on the congressional campaign.[62]

In the end, John Kennedy may not have needed to go to such lengths to secure victory. His war hero status, boyish charm, and winning personality were probably enough to ensure success. As it was, he outpolled his closest primary challenger, Neville, nearly two to one. In the general election, which was a perfunctory affair given the largely Democratic makeup of the district, Kennedy bested his Republican opponent, Lester W. Bowen of Somerville, by an even greater margin, with 79.7 percent of the vote.[63]

Initially skeptical lawmakers could not help but be impressed by this showing. "There were tough parts of that district, but Jack Kennedy showed he had what it takes to be successful in politics," O'Neill observed afterward. "Sure, he was different from a lot of voters. But he came up, shook their hands, looked them in the eye and talked about problems in the area. They respected him for that. Eventually, many of them loved him for it."[64]

John F. Kennedy seeking the women's vote in his early political career. "He had what we called a warm hand and the
women would melt when he looked in their eyes," former
Speaker of the House Thomas P. O'Neill once observed.
Courtesy of the Boston Public Library, Print Department.

As a freshman congressman, Kennedy struck many political observers as a
"fish out of water." He was late for meetings, tardy in his paperwork, and often sloppy in personal appearance. He would think nothing of showing up for
a vote on the House floor in a pair of sneakers. "You know we were simply
worms over there," he later told biographer James MacGregor Burns. "The
only importance for [a] Congressman is to his district, but you know to be
honest with you, not for publication, I could not name the members of the
House Foreign Affairs Committee or anything."[65]

Even sympathetic family friends such as Supreme Court Justice William O. Douglas found it difficult to give him high performance marks. "He never seemed to get into the mid-stream of any tremendous political thought, or political action, or any idea of promoting this or reforming that—nothing," Douglas recalled. Instead, the young Democrat appeared content to fritter his time away in the pursuit of personal pleasure. Cocktail parties, one-night stands, and touch football games filled his calendar and became his raison d'être. "We had laughs in those days," admitted administrative assistant William Sutton. "Always plenty of laughs."[66]

Accounting for this frivolous behavior was Kennedy's own awareness that he probably would not live out a normal life span. In September 1947, on a visit to England, the Massachusetts lawmaker collapsed and was diagnosed with Addison's disease, a potentially fatal illness marked by a failure of the body's adrenal glands and resulting in extreme weakness, loss of weight, low blood pressure, and gastrointestinal disturbances. "That young American friend of yours, he hasn't got a year to live," a physician informed Pamela Churchill, the former British prime minister's daughter-in-law, after the latter had brought the stricken World War II veteran to the London Clinic.[67]

Making matters worse, Kennedy reinjured his back around this time, causing episodes of near-disabling pain. "I remember playing golf with him and you'd always have to tee his ball up for him," revealed personal friend Camman Newberry. "It was too painful for him to lean over and tee it up himself. And also [I had to] take the ball out of the cup for him and things like that. He suffered a great deal with that back and never talked about it very much."[68]

Kennedy had good reason not to discuss his poor physical condition openly. Had word leaked out, questions would have been inevitably raised about his fitness to remain in public office. As it was, his congressional staff had a hard enough time explaining away his frequent absences from official duties.

When the Bay State Democrat was originally hospitalized in London for Addison's disease, a cover story was released saying that Kennedy was suffering from a war-related injury and that he could be expected to be up and about in no time. "The word was given that he'd had some kind of attack from swallowing sea water and oil" during the war, *Washington Times Herald* reporter Frank Waldrop later said of the 1947 incident. "I guess the truth was it was the onset of the Addison's."[69]

Concerned that his son's responsibilities as congressman were too physically taxing given his precarious state of health, Joseph P. Kennedy gave serious thought to setting him up as a major league baseball executive. "He's got this son, John, who is brilliant in politics, but has physical problems," Brooklyn Dodgers president and general manager Branch Rickey reportedly told business associate Walter O'Malley, after the former had been approached by the ambassador about purchasing his share of the ballclub. "Mr. Kennedy thinks running the Dodgers could be the greatest outlet in the world for him." A baseball career was not in the works for the former Harvard athlete, however. "It might have been Jack Kennedy, president of the Dodgers, but Joe rejected the deal when he found he'd face an unhappy minority stockholder in myself," O'Malley later claimed.[70]

A more plausible explanation is that John Kennedy no longer had the need to seek less strenuous employment. In the late 1940s the Mayo Clinic discovered that artificially produced corticosteroid hormones, or cortisone, implanted on the thigh could significantly extend the life expectancy of those afflicted with Addison's. Thus, by integrating this "miracle drug" into his daily regimen, Kennedy was able to upgrade his health dramatically as his appetite, strength, and stamina improved.[71] Though the prospect of premature death still remained a possibility, the apparent success of the cortisone treatment gave him hope that he could maintain a vigorous public and private life without serious medical consequences.

With a new lease on life, Kennedy was able to concentrate as never before on his fledgling congressional career. He took greater interest in his work, read up on issues, and showed increased self-confidence. Acquiring the reputation of an independent thinker, the Massachusetts lawmaker also regularly angered many of his Democratic colleagues by refusing to toe the traditional party line. "Jack thought for himself," noted his Washington office secretary, Mary Davis. "He stood on his own two feet."[72]

Nowhere was this individualistic approach more evident than when Kennedy publicly lambasted American Legion officials in 1949 for failing to support affordable housing legislation. "The leadership of the American Legion has not had a constructive thought for the benefit of this country since 1918!" he thundered.[73] House Democrats, fearful that Kennedy's intemperate remarks about a celebrated patriotic organization would reflect unfavorably upon themselves, wasted little time in denouncing the attack. The legion was a great American institution, they claimed, and the Bay State congressman had no business deriding its character.

For his part, Kennedy remained studiously unrepentant. "Well, Ted, I guess we're gone," he told administrative assistant Ted Reardon with a laugh. "That finishes us down here." Despite such dire predictions, the hero of the South Pacific suffered no serious political damage. Mail from veterans, in fact, ran ten to one in favor of his bold stance. Observed historian James MacGregor Burns, "The short-run effects of defying the Legion were negligible; in the long run, Kennedy's action showed that political daring might have more advantages than disadvantages."[74]

Such daring, however, had its limits. Acutely aware that his district was primarily blue collar in makeup, Kennedy tried to cast his votes in the House accordingly. He, for instance, favored an extension of social security benefits, a higher minimum wage, expanded public housing, and a national health program for the underprivileged. He also made a point of opposing efforts to eliminate rent control and to reduce the federal subsidy for school lunches. "When I first went into Congress in 1946," he later explained, "I represented a district that was very poor in Massachusetts. We had many problems, housing [for example]. Many families were in need of assistance. Therefore, my viewpoint on the necessity of social legislation came really pragmatically through just observation."[75]

In foreign affairs, Kennedy was a committed cold warrior. Agreeing with the Truman administration's assessment that the Soviet Union needed to be contained militarily, he supported military aid to Greece and Turkey, the Marshall Plan, and the establishment of the North Atlantic Treaty Organization (NATO). Where he differed from the Democratic administration was in the prosecution of the Cold War. He thought more needed to be done, especially in East Asia, to prevent the "onrushing tide" of communism from engulfing the world. To this end he was an outspoken advocate for a strong military, even going so far as to lecture his fellow legislators on not allocating enough money for national defense.[76]

Kennedy's brashness was not confined to the halls of Congress. In Massachusetts he had frequent run-ins with influential political figures such as John McCormack of South Boston. The senior Bay State representative, second only to Texan Sam Rayburn in the House of Representatives' Democratic hierarchy, McCormack represented "the type of earlier Massachusetts Irish politician who was self-made and had worked his way up the political pecking order." Kennedy, however, viewed him as a stodgy, self-important windbag who was unwilling to share the spoils of his office. "I had several fights with him," Kennedy later recounted. "You know, he hogged all the patronage. He wouldn't give us anything."[77] That McCormack was reluctant to aid Kennedy is not surprising.

In 1947 Kennedy rebuffed the senior lawmaker's efforts to get him to sign a petition of clemency for James Michael Curley, the four-time Boston mayor who was serving out a sentence for mail fraud in a federal penitentiary in Danbury, Connecticut. "Well, [McCormack] was sore as hell at me afterwards," Kennedy later admitted.[78] But Kennedy simply could not bring himself to support Curley, the kind of back-slapping "old school" politician he personally abhorred.

Curley invoked an earlier, seamier era of Boston politics, when elections were determined in smoke-filled back rooms by men dressed in pearl-gray fedoras and Chesterfield coats with black velvet collars. Kennedy eschewed these traditional outer trappings by presenting himself as a morally upright, clean-cut professional who was more in tune with the issues of the "atomic age" than with some bygone era. In other words, he was "no Irish political hack." Observed Tip O'Neill, "It was said that Jack Kennedy was the only pol in Boston who never went to a wake unless he had known the deceased. He played by his own rules."[79]

Voters from the Eleventh District did not seem to mind this departure from traditional Massachusetts ward politics; they returned Kennedy to office by overwhelming margins in 1948 and 1950. In fact, so strong was the young politico's standing in the district that the local Republican Party was unable to find a candidate willing to run against him in 1948. Accounting for this enormous popularity was the Democrat's continued war hero status, his charming public persona, and his willingness to support issues that were dear to the hearts of his working-class constituents such as public housing and social security. To them he simply represented "a young man of distinction."[80]

Yet political success could not quell Kennedy's growing dissatisfaction with House life and its stifling seniority system. Indeed, he began entertaining serious thoughts about seeking higher statewide office in 1952. "I think that he felt hemmed in by the committee chairman tradition and [the lack of] opportunity to make an impact on the floor," remembered one close aide. "This was not the organization which he visualized as the one [in which] he wanted to spend most of his political life."[81]

Not even the possibility of defeat seemed to faze him. "I would rather run for Governor or the Senate and lose, and take the shot than go back and serve another term as a Congressman," he admitted. Compounding his unhappiness was seeing political contemporaries such as Richard Nixon of California and George Smathers of Florida move on to the Senate after relatively brief stays in the House. "The last thing he wanted now was to be left behind while Nixon and Smathers strode Capitol Hill as U.S. Senators," Kennedy biographer Chris Matthews has concluded.[82]

Equally significant was the influence of Joseph P. Kennedy. The family patriarch's lifetime ambition had been to see his eldest son, Joe Junior, reach the

White House. With the latter's untimely death during World War II, however, the "Founding Father" had to amend his plans. "When [Joe Junior] died, I took his place," John Kennedy later explained. "If something had happened to me, Bobby would take my place. If something happened to Bobby, Teddy would take his place."[83] Realizing that the chances of someone attaining the presidency directly from the House were remote, the ambassador urged his second son to seek the Senate or the governorship. Either way, he figured, the higher-profile position would act as a springboard to the Oval Office.

But moving up to the next rung of the political ladder would be no easy task. Though popular in his own congressional district, John Kennedy was still a relatively unknown figure outside of Boston. Tellingly, a Williams College study, in one of the few polls taken, later revealed that only 35 percent of the eligible voters in Pittsfield, an industrial city in far western Massachusetts, even knew who Kennedy was by the summer of 1952.[84] Further complicating matters was the fact that Kennedy's most likely rivals for statewide office in this presidential election year, incumbent Democratic governor Paul Dever and three-term Republican senator Henry Cabot Lodge Jr., were proven vote getters with enviable records of public service dating back over two decades.

Of the two, Lodge represented by far the more formidable opponent. "When you've beaten him," Joseph Kennedy told his son, "you've beaten the best. Why try for something less?" Indeed, aside from having one of the most widely respected names in Massachusetts politics, Lodge possessed a substantive record of achievement in the Senate to go along with a handsome face and a fine speaking voice. "This was a toughie," Kennedy campaign publicist John Galvin later confessed. "This guy had—well—what didn't he have? [He] had . . . great Irish support [and] a good service record."[85]

Yet Kennedy was not without his own unique advantages as a candidate. Young, rich, and attractive, he had the money, looks, and charisma to mount an effective statewide challenge. More importantly, he was also the beneficiary of a dramatic political transformation that had taken place in Massachusetts in the years immediately following World War II. The state went from being predominantly Republican to predominantly Democratic in the span of half a decade.

The year 1948 marked the turning point. In this crucial presidential election year, state Democrats, like the party's national standard-bearer, Harry S. Truman, were not expected to fare very well, as the GOP was expected to build on the gains it had achieved in 1946, when the Republicans had swept to victory in the House and Senate. "This air of uncertainty stemming from Truman's seemingly weak position in his bid for reelection in 1948 appeared to induce a defeatist air in the state Democratic Party," notes Massachusetts political historian Alec Barbrook.[86]

To be sure, Republicans had managed to dominate the local political scene for most of the century, and there seemed to be no compelling reason to suspect that their electoral reign would end. Yet come November, all Democratic candidates for the top five constitutional offices—governor, lieutenant governor, secretary of state, auditor, and attorney general—registered decisive wins. Traditional areas of GOP voting strength such as Boston's Ward Twenty (West Roxbury–Roslindale) made history by going Democratic in a presidential election year.[87] In the state legislature, Democrats picked up four Senate seats and twenty-six House of Representatives seats, giving them a majority in the lower chamber for the first time ever.

In retrospect, the 1948 victory was no fluke. State Democratic leaders such as John McCormack and Tip O'Neill had built a formidable campaign organization to provide financial assistance, free advertising, and informational services to Democratic candidates in contested Republican districts across the commonwealth. "Everything was run from Boston," recalled O'Neill. "If we didn't like the way you were handling your campaign, we came to your town, took your mailing list down to Democratic headquarters, had the envelopes stamped and addressed, put on the stamps, and then brought all the letters back to your town and mailed them ourselves. . . . Above all, we left nothing to chance."[88]

With a "fighting fund" of twenty-six thousand dollars, of which John Kennedy contributed one thousand dollars, prospective Democratic candidates, mostly young men new to politics, were supplied the necessary "seed" money to launch their campaigns. "Today, that kind of money couldn't pay for a single billboard," O'Neill opined in 1987. "And even then it was a ridiculously low figure." Nevertheless, the amount was sufficient for Democratic purposes in 1948.[89]

Another contributing factor to the Democratic victory was the presence of several high-profile referendum questions on the ballot. The most controversial was referendum no. 4, which called for the repeal of the Massachusetts statute barring doctors from disseminating birth control information to their patients. Alarmed by the prospect of women using "unnatural" birth control techniques, the Roman Catholic Church led by Archbishop Richard J. Cushing mounted a massive public relations campaign against the proposal.[90]

The product of a middle-class family from South Boston, Cushing was an enormously popular figure among Bay State Catholics. His earthy humor, disarming charm, and spontaneity were in marked contrast to his predecessor, the austere William Henry Cardinal O'Connell, who earned the sobriquet "Gang-plank Bill" for his frequent trips to the Bahamas during the Great Depression. Though reluctant to openly assert himself politically ("The Archbishop of Boston has a great deal of power, provided he doesn't use it," he once said), Cushing nevertheless did not shy away from advancing causes he believed in such as anticommunism and opposition to birth control. "In a Democracy," he lectured his flock, "it is not enough to be right. You can be right and suffer the bitterness of seeing victory go to those who are wrong but numerous."[91]

To ensure that the latter did not occur, Cushing enlisted the aid of former Boston mayor Frederick W. Mansfield in organizing an "anti–baby bill" com-mitee, whose task it was to inform Catholic voters, through the use of sophis-ticated advertising techniques such as spot radio commercials, newspaper ads, and billboards, about the immorality of the referendum question. The not-so-subtle implication was that in order to be a good Catholic, one had to vote against the proposal. As if on cue, Catholics turned out in record numbers on election day to defeat the referendum question decisively.[92]

Since Catholics tended to vote Democratic, the percentage of Democrats casting ballots in that election was "unusually high," thereby giving Demo-cratic candidates an unexpected edge over their Republican opponents.[93] This electoral trend was enhanced by a large labor union turnout, courtesy of a right-to-work referendum on the ballot that was ultimately defeated. The union rank and file had traditionally been strong supporters of the Demo-cratic Party, and 1948 represented no exception.

Finally, Republicans had been steadily losing their political grip on the state over the previous two decades. Since 1928 Massachusetts had voted Dem-ocratic in every presidential election. Two years before the start of this elec-toral streak, former Democratic governor David I. Walsh of Clinton had cap-tured a U.S. Senate seat by putting together a "victory" coalition of Catholics, blue-collar workers, and disillusioned Republicans with an "independent" turn of mind. "There is a potential Democratic strength in the Common-wealth which needs only skillful Democratic leadership to become formi-dable," the conservative *Springfield Republican* commented at the time.[94]

In the late 1930s and early 1940s, local Democrats, buoyed by the popu-larity of President Franklin Roosevelt's New Deal social programs and disaf-fection over the perceived "stand pat" policies of the Republican Party, began moving into the lower state constitutional offices. Although Republicans maintained solid control over the state legislature, the electorate was becom-ing increasingly more liberal in political outlook and Catholic in makeup. In-deed, persons of Catholic faith constituted 48.4 percent of Massachusetts's total population by 1950.[95] The latter development was particularly significant given the traditional Catholic affinity for the Democratic Party.

Yet state Democrats were unable to exploit this trend during the late depression and World War II owing to factionalism within their own party. Indeed, the two most influential Democrats in the state, David I. Walsh and James Michael Curley, were longtime bitter rivals who did not see any political advantage to be gained from cooperating with one another. As a result, the party was, in the words of Massachusetts political historian J. Joseph Huthmacher, "left rudderless, except for its quadrennial mobilization behind the Democratic presidential nominee."[96] Not until 1948 would state Democrats possess the unity, issues, and organization to reverse this propensity for self-destruction.

In order, then, to win a statewide contest against Henry Cabot Lodge Jr. in 1952, Kennedy needed to hold on to this Democratic base as well as attract a sizable portion of the independent vote, which tended to go Democratic in Massachusetts. But given Lodge's strong showings in Democratic wards across the state in previous senatorial outings against James Michael Curley, Joseph E. Casey, and David I. Walsh, this proposition seemed problematical at best. For in Lodge, Kennedy faced an opponent who had the ability to attract the support of persons of either party, regardless of his own GOP affiliation. To understand this wide-ranging appeal, one needs to examine the formative events that helped shape the Republican lawmaker's life and noteworthy political career.

Chapter **TWO**

Striking High

HENRY CABOT LODGE JR. was born on July 5, 1902, in his grandfather's home along the cold, rocky shores of Nahant, Massachusetts, which Lodge once described as sticking out "like a finger toward Europe some ten miles north of Boston."[1] The oldest of three children, he was heir to one of the most famous names in American politics. No fewer than five family members had served in the U.S. Senate, dating back to the early days of the republic.

His grandfather, for whom he had been named, was the confidant of President Theodore Roosevelt and became chairman of the powerful Senate Foreign Relations Committee at the end of World War I. A conservative at heart, the "Old Senator," as his family and friends fondly called him, championed protective tariffs, the gold standard, and literacy tests for immigrants. He is best remembered for his leadership role in defeating President Woodrow Wilson's proposed League of Nations.[2]

When Lodge's father, the minor poet George Cabot Lodge, died of an apparent heart attack in 1909, Henry Cabot Lodge Sr. became his surrogate father. Apart from his mother, former Washington society belle Mathilda Elizabeth Frelinghuysen Davis, whom he credited with providing warmth, encouragement, and emotional support, Lodge's greatest influence in these formative years was his grandfather.

In the elder Lodge, Cabot, as he was known to friends and relatives, had a stern taskmaster who demanded hard work and excellence in all endeavors. When he performed poorly in geometry and Greek while prepping at the Middlesex School in Concord, Massachusetts, the grandfather offered little sympathy. "It would be a terrible disappointment for me if you should fail any of your Harvard examinations," he wrote his grandson in 1919. "You must learn to use your mind and if you apply your mind to geometry and Greek you can perfectly well master them both and pass exams in both, and I look to you to do it."[3] Chastened by the thought of earning his grandfather's displeasure, Cabot redoubled his efforts and was eventually able to pass all his entrance tests.

The message had then, as always, been received without argument or complaint. Yet prodding his grandson to get into Harvard was one thing, badgering him about poor grammar while recovering from a minor bout of influenza was another. "I am happy to think you are getting over it entirely," the Bay State lawmaker wrote in 1922. "Now let me say to you there is one thing in your letter which gives me absolute pain and that is the way you use 'will' for 'shall.' I beg you to get over that."[4]

Howsoever petty or insensitive these words now appear, there is no denying that the younger Lodge had a deep, abiding affection for his grandfather and vice-versa. That such an emotional bond existed is evidenced by a letter Cabot penned his grandfather in March 1924, some eight months before the latter's death. "I certainly try and hope," he vowed, "that someday through my work I shall be able to give any children which I may have an advantage, such as you have given me. There is nothing like striking high."[5]

Aside from instruction on proper usage and academics, Henry Cabot Lodge Sr. also schooled his grandson in politics. "The discussion of political topics was one of the first things I can remember," Cabot later remarked. "A haze of cigar smoke and the emphatic utterance of such words as 'caucus,' 'committee' or 'campaign'—words which were then incomprehensible to me—are vividly impressed on my mind." As a teenager, the junior Lodge spent many a late night in his grandfather's book-lined study in Washington, D.C., reviewing the great issues of the day with the aging patriarch. "As you know my grandfather was pleased when I began to take an interest in public affairs," he once told a reporter. "His own sons took no interest whatsoever in politics and it was his hope that I might carry on in this field."[6]

On most political issues, Cabot not surprisingly shared the same conservative views as his grandfather. He touted the efficacy of the American free enterprise system, downplayed social reform, and cited the supposed need for increased duties on foreign manufactures. Regarding U.S. entry into the League of Nations, he staunchly opposed the idea. Nor was he shy about expressing these opinions. When noted Harvard English professor Charles T. Copeland publicly denounced the senior Massachusetts senator for his anti-League

stand, the younger Lodge sought out the academic for a one-on-one confrontation. "Professor Copeland, I am Senator Lodge's grandson," Cabot
chastised him before a student gathering. "I think you have done him a great
injustice and I want you to know I resent your unfair criticism of him."[7]

After graduating from Harvard with honors in 1924, Lodge found in journalism an outlet for his interest in politics. Again, his grandfather played a decisive role in shaping his future. As the holder of a Ph.D. in political science
from Harvard and the author of such scholarly works as *The Life and Letters of
George Cabot, Alexander Hamilton,* and *A Short History of the English Colonies
in America,* Henry Cabot Lodge Sr. believed the ability to turn a well-phrased
sentence was "at least the equal of the [study of] law as training for political
life."[8] Making use of family and political connections, the Bay State lawmaker
landed Cabot a general assignment reporter's position on the staid *Boston
Evening Transcript,* the paper of record for the city's ruling class.

The "Old Senator," Henry Cabot Lodge Sr., relaxing on the front porch of his Nahant, Massachusetts, home. "I certainly try and hope," Henry Cabot Lodge Jr. once
wrote his grandfather, "that someday through my work I shall be able to give any
children I may have an advantage, such as you have given me. There is nothing like
striking high." Courtesy of the Massachusetts Historical Society, Boston.

Specializing in human interest features as a cub reporter, Cabot wrote articles on such mundane topics as the frequency of phone usage in the Boston area. "The day starts and ends with the telephone, and anything which disturbs the equilibrium of a community, be it the murder of a crown prince or the preparation for a church sociable, is reflected in its use."[9] Seeking more challenging work, in the late 1920s he moved on to the Republican *New York Herald-Tribune,* where he established himself as a competent news editor.

During this period Cabot also spent a considerable amount of time courting his future wife, Emily Sears, an heir to the famed Sears shipping fortune. Bright, witty, and reserved, Emily provided the emotional ballast Lodge needed to weather the stormy political seas he would navigate in the years ahead. The two had met at a dance in Boston in 1924, and while the Ivy Leaguer impressed the young socialite with his ruggedly handsome looks and distinguished family pedigree, his intellect evidently left something to be desired. "Well, I thought he was a little slow [intellectually]," Emily puckishly told television interviewer David Brinkley in 1960.[10] She soon revised her opinion, however, and began a courtship that lasted over two years. They were married on July 1, 1926, at St. Peter's Episcopal Church in Beverly Cove, not far from where Emily's parents had a summer home. The union would eventually produce two sons, George Cabot in 1927 and Henry Sears in 1930.

When the Old Senator passed away in November 1924, expectations were strong that Cabot would carry on in his footsteps. But he was hesitant about entering politics. Though interested in political office, Lodge viewed himself as too young and inexperienced to run. Adding to his discomfiture was the witnessing firsthand of his grandfather's political eclipse at the 1924 Republican National Convention in Cleveland. Upset that the elder Lodge had helped enact a soldiers' bonus bill over the veto of President Calvin Coolidge, an old Bay State rival, party chieftains saw fit to punish the previous convention's chairman and keynoter by demoting him to ordinary delegate status. The Old Senator had perhaps sealed his fate four years earlier when he condescendingly dismissed Coolidge's budding presidential aspirations as unlikely, given the latter's humble Yankee roots. "No man who lives in a two-family house is going to be President," Lodge sniffed.[11] These words would soon come back to haunt him.

Young Cabot never forgot the calm manner in which his grandfather bore this humiliation, but the episode left enough of a sour taste in his mouth to discourage any early entry into politics. Accordingly, he waited until 1932 before throwing his hat in the ring, by which time he was thirty, with eight years of professional journalism under his belt to go along with a collection of essays on America's then-woeful state of military preparedness.

Published in part as a response to the worldwide depression and the growing fear of fascism and totalitarianism, *The Cult of Weakness* (1932) can best be
described as Lodge's *Why England Slept*. Like Kennedy, Lodge sought to convey the message that a democracy such as the United States could not survive
if the doctrine of "peace by unpreparedness" prevailed on issues dealing with
national security. "We may wonder still further," he wrote, "whether we are not
standing face to face with a veritable cult of weakness in matters of public concern which has us permanently in its grip—a cult which is all the more dangerous, because it is not conscious."[12]

To correct the situation Lodge advocated a public policy that valued military preparedness over extreme pacifism. "No doubt," sympathetic Lodge biographer Anne Blair has concluded, "the views of his grandfather, who had
died eight years earlier, were the chief influence on his thinking at the time."
Indeed, Lodge faulted deceased former president Woodrow Wilson, his grandfather's political nemesis, for popularizing the supposedly false notion that
peace can be attained through collective security arrangements among nations
rather than by individual military might.[13]

Whether it was this disrespectful tone toward a fallen wartime leader or
the dour-sounding title, *The Cult of Weakness* sold only 350 copies despite
mostly favorable reviews.[14] The work later became a source of personal embarrassment to Lodge when he became a strong supporter of collective security in the post–World War II period.

The autumn of 1932 marked Lodge's formal entry into politics. He won
election by fourteen hundred votes as a Republican state representative from
Beverly, one of the most affluent and staunchly conservative communities in
Massachusetts. Running on a platform that called for the elimination of wasteful government spending, which appealed to many of his parsimonious Yankee constituents, he mounted an energetic door-to-door campaign throughout the city. Little mention was made of the depression or President Herbert
Hoover. Lodge shook hands, addressed local civic groups, attended house parties, and kept an index card file on every registered voter he met. "As John F.
Kennedy would learn several years later," one study later concluded, "the
youthful Yankee found that a good organization, personal contact, hard work,
and a respected family name were almost unbeatable ingredients for getting
ahead."[15]

The four years Lodge spent as a legislator on Beacon Hill (he was reelected
in 1934) coincided with a massive social and economic upheaval taking place
in Massachusetts and across America. Unemployment soared, poverty spread,
and thousands of families became uprooted. After a decade of unparalleled

prosperity and abundance, the Great Depression ushered in an age of economic scarcity and hardship. Voters nationwide no longer wanted laissez-faire government; they demanded activist solutions to their plight.

Although Lodge represented a district that frowned upon an expanded government relief role, his subsequent record in the state legislature indicates that he was in harmony with the prevailing political mood of the country. He was a strong backer of President Franklin D. Roosevelt's National Industrial Recovery Act, which established minimum wages and maximum hours for workers, as well as providing public sector construction jobs for the unemployed. He also lobbied Massachusetts governor Joseph B. Ely to enact a short-term moratorium on home mortgage foreclosures, supported legislation abolishing child labor and improving industrial workplace conditions, and opposed a proposed sales tax on the grounds it would hurt struggling working families. "The economic system should be changed to provide a better distribution of wealth," the freshman legislator informed his constituents in 1933, "although I'm against any system which [favors] the lazy and spendthrift at the expense of the industrious and the thrifty."[16]

What prompted him to take these fairly liberal stands is open to speculation. According to friendly biographer William J. Miller, Lodge grasped immediately the fundamental "social upheaval" taking place. "Rather than oppose needed changes," Miller argues, Lodge "felt that the true role of a conservative was to give change a sound and coherent structure."[17]

A more likely explanation is that he received a dose of political reality. The young Republican may well have preferred to have things remain as they were in his grandfather's day, but he was politically astute enough to realize that new circumstances now made that impossible. To think otherwise risked public disapproval or, worse, a bar against attaining higher political office. "My conception of policy is always a blend of what I think is desirable and what I think is possible," he once wrote a constituent. "Maybe I think too much of the latter." Thus, Lodge embarked on a political journey that took him from being a conservative in his grandfather's image to being what he later described as a "practical progressive."[18] Pragmatism became his political compass, and it pointed to an open U.S. Senate seat in 1936 when the Democratic incumbent, Marcus Coolidge, died.

Lodge's initial decision to run for the Senate raised many eyebrows around the state and from within his own party. He was only thirty-four, the same age John Kennedy was when he ran for U.S. senator in 1952, and his youthfulness, liberal political stands, and inexperience offended many conservative state GOP leaders such as Joseph Martin, the future Speaker of the U.S. House of Representatives, and John H. Haigis, the Republican nominee for governor that year. "I have a feeling that the group . . . thinks me too young," Lodge wrote his mother early in the campaign. "I don't think any of these men can defeat me, but if they do, I can guarantee that they will get plenty of exercise in the process." As for his likely Democratic opponent, then–Massachusetts governor James Michael Curley, the youthful Republican was equally confident. "You know about him," he exclaimed. "I think I can give him some exercise too and it will be impossible for him to pin the reactionary label on me as he has on other Republicans."[19]

Securing the Republican nomination was no easy affair. In fact, Lodge entered the Republican state convention in June trailing rival Sinclair Weeks, the ultraconservative mayor of Newton, in delegates. But enlisting the help of veteran Republican operative Thomas W. White, Boston's collector of internal revenue under President Calvin Coolidge, the Beverly representative was able to overtake Weeks.

At White's urging, Lodge met individually with the seven hundred delegates, many of whom had been hurt financially in the depression and shared the Beverly lawmaker's advocacy of remedial federal action. "Stand in the lobby and shake hands," the former tax collector instructed. "Be sure to smile—then they'll think you've got it in the bag." Lodge followed this advice and cut a deal with Haigis supporters, promising them he would back their candidate's drive for the gubernatorial nomination. In return, they promised to back him over Weeks. The strategy worked. When balloting concluded, Lodge found himself the winner by thirty-seven votes.[20]

In the fall campaign, Lodge took the political high road against Governor Curley, who was known for his caustic wit and bullying tactics. He refused to mention his Democratic rival by name even when the former Boston mayor denigrated him as "Little Boy Blue." "I . . . believe that this campaign is too important for the people's time to be wasted by personal abuse and mudslinging," Lodge retorted. "I certainly shall never attack the character or the person of my Democratic opponent. . . . I believe the voters are asking the question: where do we go from here?"[21]

To this question Curley had no ready answer. His two-year term (1934–36) as governor had been a conspicuous failure; he promised "work and wages" to the state's 180,000 unemployed but could provide neither. Federal relief agencies were weary of his reputation as a corrupt machine politician and were loathe to have millions in aid entrusted to his care. Moreover, President Franklin D. Roosevelt had an abiding personal dislike of Curley and his incessant carping against the New Deal. Necessary financial help from the federal government therefore was withheld, dooming whatever hope there might have been for an improved economic situation in Massachusetts.[22]

During the campaign Lodge took Curley to task on this issue, holding him personally responsible for the state's not receiving its fair share of relief assistance from Washington. "Although we are eighth in population and ninth in our contribution to Uncle Sam's treasury, we are [forty-fifth] among the [forty-eight] states in the percentage of our relief load paid for by Washington," the Beverly representative informed voters. "Think it over. . . . If we had all that has been taken out we would not know there was a depression in Massachusetts."[23]

Further undercutting Curley's bid for Senate office was the third-party candidacy of former Suffolk County district attorney Thomas C. O'Brien, then running under the banner of the National Union for Social Justice, the political arm of reactionary Detroit radio preacher Charles E. Coughlin's growing national following. Coughlin, a widely popular figure among Irish Catholic voters in the state, had urged O'Brien to enter the race after learning of Curley's efforts to embrace Roosevelt, with whom the prelate had fallen out politically. As an instrument of political revenge, O'Brien succeeded beyond anyone's wildest expectations, siphoning off over 130,000 votes from Curley's voting base in urban centers such as Boston, Lynn, and Fall River. "Without O'Brien in the race, Curley would have been within ten thousand votes of Lodge," Curley's critical biographer Jack Beatty maintains, "a number small enough to be responsive to a presidential endorsement."[24]

Yet no presidential seal of approval was forthcoming. Viewing Curley with the same disdain he usually reserved for his bitterest political enemies, the president made it clear on a campaign swing through Boston that fall that he was not "enthusiastic" about his fellow Democrat. Indeed, he gave the "Purple Shamrock" the cold shoulder before an assembly of newspaper photographers, when the latter tried desperately to get a smiling pose with the commander in chief.[25]

In an attempt to deflect attention away from his lackluster gubernatorial record and his inability to gain Roosevelt's ear, Curley started accusing his youthful challenger of being a reactionary in the supposed mold of his late grandfather—"a young man who parts both his hair and his name in the middle."[26] This effort quickly backfired when Lodge reminded voters of the liberal record he compiled as a Beacon Hill lawmaker on labor and economic relief issues. He also earned the empathy of Republicans and Democrats statewide by vigorously defending the memory of the Old Senator.

"My opponent has charged my grandfather with having scorned the working man," he told a large campaign rally in Brockton, a blue-collar city twenty miles south of Boston. "Well, my grandfather did not fail loyally to represent the people of Massachusetts in the Senate. I suppose my opponent would rather have us involved in a European war than be spared entanglement in the League of Nations. I suppose my opponent prefers the ruinous competition of foreign sweat shops to the policies of my grandfather and protection for the American workman. I am proud of my grandfather's record."[27]

Annoyed by the lack of progress his personal attacks were having on the young challenger, Curley tried to have Lodge's name stricken from the voting ballot. Arguing that Henry Cabot Lodge Jr. was not a proper name, because "junior" is the accepted term for a son and Lodge was not the son of Henry Cabot Lodge Sr., the governor, through a political intermediary, former state auditor Alonzo B. Cook, brought legal action before the state Ballot Commission to have his opponent's name removed.[28]

The situation was further compounded by the fact that the person entrusted with reviewing the case was Charles McGlue, a Curley appointee and longtime personal retainer. "For all we knew," Boston banker and Lodge campaign treasurer Robert C. Cutler later recalled, "McGlue might rule Cabot off the ballot and we might never get him back in time for the election." Lodge avoided this worst-case scenario when he produced a birth certificate with "Jr." clearly written on it. The governor conceded defeat and promptly withdrew his legal action. "The funny thing was that Curley's birth certificate—we checked that too—was different," Cutler noted. "He didn't have the middle name, Michael, on the certificate. But we didn't attack him on it."[29]

With even this lame avenue of attack blocked off, Curley resorted to exploiting ancient Irish versus Brahmin antagonisms by claiming that Lodge belonged to an elite propertied class that lived off the labor of others. "You young Republicans have no more chance to join the Somerset Club than I have," the "Rascal King" gleefully informed one Springfield audience, "if your ancestors didn't get rich in the first two or three generations by selling opium to the Chinese, rum to the Indians or getting in the slave racket."[30]

Remaining above the fray, Lodge ignored these personal assaults and continued touting his own liberal performance as a state legislator. "My labor and legislative record," he told voters, "is presented to you as the most convincing evidence of the constructive spirit in which I will serve you as United States Senator. I have at all times advocated and fought for liberal, humane and progressive legislation, and I shall continue to advocate and fight for such laws."[31]

When the ballots were finally counted, Lodge emerged as the only victorious GOP candidate running for statewide office. His plurality over Curley was 135,409 votes in an election year that saw Franklin Roosevelt carry Massachusetts by 174,103 votes and Democrats nationwide score sweeping victories. Indeed, Lodge became the only Republican in the country to capture a Senate seat formerly held by a Democrat. He carried every section of the state except Suffolk County, which was then as now chiefly composed of the city of Boston. But even in this traditional Democratic bastion he performed well, pulling down 33.5 percent of the vote. In contrast, the Republican candidate for governor, John W. Haigis of Greenfield, lost to Democrat Charles F. Hurley by a plurality of 28,003 votes. Unlike Lodge, Suffolk County represented Haigis's downfall as Hurley bested him by almost a two-to-one margin.[32]

Most of the credit for Lodge's victory belonged to the candidate himself. At a time when GOP politicians across the country were being swept from office because of their conservatism, Lodge possessed the necessary liberal legislative record and communication skills to convince Massachusetts voters that he was a different sort of Republican, one who cared as much about the interests of labor and the poor as he did about big business and the wealthy. This statement is borne out by how well he polled in industrial centers such as Fall River, Pittsfield, and Lynn, areas that were hard hit by the depression. In these cities Lodge captured 40.3, 48.1, and 44.8 percent of the vote respectively, while Republican gubernatorial candidate John Haigis pulled down only 26.2, 44.2, and 40.4 percent of the vote.[33]

As a first-term U.S. senator, Lodge moved even further from the rigid conservatism of his grandfather as the political and economic realities of the depression forced him to question the Old Senator's advocacy of a minimalist government. He acquired a reputation for being moderate to liberal on most domestic issues. "I decide each issue on its merits," he told a reporter upon entering office. "I have no fixed prejudices or policies. I would like [to be known] as a practical progressive. That means I take up each issue as it presents itself, or perhaps as I present it, and take a stand on it then or there. But you don't have to guess where I stand. I like to make myself clear on that and, if I'm wrong, all right. I'll admit it."[34]

This pragmatic approach to legislation was evident in 1937, when Lodge became one of only two Republican senators to vote for the Fair Labor Standards Act, which established minimum wages and maximum hours for workers. In explaining his vote, the freshman lawmaker cited the need to stop the flight of industry from Massachusetts and other northern industrial states to the lower-wage, nonunionized sections of the Deep South and Far West.

"We don't allow one state to go to war with another or raise the tariff against another's goods," he argued, "so why in God's name should we allow one state to ruin another by undercutting its labor standards."[35] This stance won him few friends in the GOP congressional caucus, but it more importantly cemented his reputation as a friend to the workingman in the minds of his constituents back home.

   Though Lodge had qualms about the way federal relief was distributed ("I think" President Roosevelt "would have obtained greater results in federal relief, for example, with local control"), he nonetheless was an enthusiastic backer of such New Deal programs as the Works Progress Administration, which provided jobs for over 2.5 million skilled and semiskilled laborers nationwide. "I am opposed to any reduction in the Massachusetts relief quota,"

Senator Henry Cabot Lodge Jr. tips his hat to a South Boston crowd during the 1939 St. Patrick's Day Parade. Courtesy of the Massachusetts Historical Society, Boston.

Lodge maintained, "and will support that system which will best guarantee to Massachusetts and its cities and towns their fair share."[36]

To ensure the Bay State received its "fair share," Lodge unsuccessfully called for the establishment of a national unemployment census to determine the exact relief needs of each section of the country. "Until we have the facts we can never deal with this problem, either in the interest of the taxpayer or in the interest of the unemployed man or woman," he asserted. "As long as we are in ignorance, this question will continue to frighten us and we shall be like ships lost in the fog. I say give light and we will find our way. Let us get the facts on this problem. We can then apply the magnificent resources of the United States to its solution."[37]

Other major domestic initiatives that Lodge supported in his first term were an increase in social security benefits for the elderly and the payment of prevailing union wages to workers on housing projects insured by the Federal Housing Administration. He also voted against the Supreme Court nomination of Hugo L. Black on the grounds that the Alabama senator once claimed membership in the Ku Klux Klan. "I . . . opposed his confirmation," Lodge thundered, "because of my strong convictions that a Supreme Court judge should be tolerant, liberal and judicial in his view of the religious faiths and racial equality of his fellow citizens. Not a shred of evidence was advanced to remove the cloud of doubt concerning Senator Black's attitude on these fundamentals."[38]

On foreign policy issues, Lodge continued to toe the same isolationist line as his grandfather. He felt that the United States should not become embroiled in the affairs of countries outside the Western Hemisphere. Though he opposed the Neutrality Act of 1937, which attempted to make permanent earlier congressional bans on loans and the sale of armaments to nations at war, he did so out of the belief that such legislation did not go far enough. The act "said in substance that the nations at war could trade with us if they called for the goods in their own ships and paid cash," he explained. "This place[s] us on the side of the nation with the biggest navy or the strongest power, and public opinion might not be on that side. So I voted against it."[39]

When World War II began with Germany's invasion of Poland in September 1939, Lodge held fast to the position that the United States remain neutral. He unsuccessfully opposed efforts by the Roosevelt administration to amend the 1937 Neutrality Act, allowing arms and munitions to be exported to England and France on a "cash and carry" basis. "I believe we should be absolutely neutral in the European conflict," he contended. "To enact a 'cash and carry' law would mean that ultimately we would be drawn into the European war and be obliged to send an army over there to protect the financial interests of our traders in war goods."[40]

Lodge's hard-line isolationist stance was not uncommon for the period, as people ranging from Charles A. Lindbergh to Joseph P. Kennedy voiced similar sentiments. Indeed, public opinion polls taken in the late 1930s and early 1940s indicate that a clear majority of Americans were opposed to any type of U.S. involvement overseas. Bitter memories from World War I involving mass carnage, unpaid war debts, and revelations that greedy American financiers and munitions makers, the so-called merchants of death, may have facilitated the country's entry into the conflict no doubt accounted for this popular attitude.

In explaining his own isolationist views, Lodge revealed a surprising naiveté over the escalating conflict in Europe. "The fight in Europe is not our fight, it is theirs," he argued. "If the British and French empires cannot stand without help, then they deserve to fall. England, France and Poland and their European sympathizers far outnumber Germany and her allies in men and resourcefulness, and I see no good reason why we should be called upon to aid them, even though our sympathies are on their side."[41] Also contributing to the Republican lawmaker's intransigence was the knowledge that his position was popular among Irish Catholic voters in Massachusetts, who traditionally shed no tears over Britain's problems.

Sweeping Axis victories in France in 1940 compelled Lodge to revise his isolationist thinking, however. He voted for the Lend-Lease Act of 1941, which authorized the president to sell, lend, transfer, or lease materials of war to countries such as England whose defense was considered vital to the security of the United States. While admitting that the legislation violated the principle of American neutrality, the Brahmin Republican explained that the measure was necessary to deter foreign aggression. Britain was teetering on the edge of military defeat, and the chances of Germany gaining control of the Royal Navy and coming within striking distance of the Western Hemisphere no longer seemed remote. "The bill," Lodge wrote a political associate, "is naturally not perfect but far better than no bill at all in the present emergency, where time is of the essence."[42]

The surprise Japanese attack on Pearl Harbor on December 7, 1941, removed Lodge permanently from the isolationist camp. "The time for united action has come," he announced. "The time for words has passed." Years later he expressed embarrassment when reminded of his prewar views on foreign policy. "I was one hundred percent wrong in believing that we could stay out of the Second World War," he told a writer in 1952. "But that was my first incarnation. I'm now an older and wiser man—at least I hope I am."[43]

Lodge's prewar isolationism became a major campaign issue when he ran for reelection in 1942. His Democratic opponent, an obscure two-term congressman from central Massachusetts named Joseph E. Casey, voiced the opinion that had the Republican lawmaker's views on foreign policy prevailed, "our beloved country might now be writhing under the heel of the Axis." To counter such criticism, a now more confident Lodge took the position that his isolationism had been the product of well-founded concerns over the country's military preparedness. "I know," he told supporters, "that the same devil's potion that maimed and wrecked and blinded the heroes of World War I was being brewed in Axis laboratories for the maiming, the wrecking and the blinding of the youth of this generation, and I believed that if we threw our sons against the Axis legions before they should be properly trained and equipped, nothing could save us from preliminary defeats which could be repaired only at the cost of countless American lives."[44]

In point of fact, Lodge had been a proponent of military preparedness in the period leading up to Pearl Harbor. He vigorously supported efforts by the Roosevelt administration to increase the size of the armed forces and to institute a program of military preparedness. The Republican also had been an early backer of the Selective Training and Service Act of 1940, which authorized the first peacetime draft in the nation's history. His enthusiasm for compulsory military service stemmed in no small degree from personal experience. Since 1924 he had been active in the army reserve as a cavalry officer, taking part in maneuvers on a regular basis. "The civilian soldier," he maintained, "has brought the Army his civilian skills, a fresh viewpoint—he works hard and accepts hardships without a grumble. There is no question of his value."[45]

In the summer of 1942 Lodge was placed on active duty and assigned to a tank unit that was sent to Libya for a joint two-week training exercise with the British Eighth Army. While there, Lodge's unit inadvertently became embroiled in the first recorded tank battle between American and Nazi forces. German general Erwin Rommel's Afrika Corps had launched a surprise attack on the Allied position near Tobruk, which was held by the Eighth Army. What followed was one of the bloodiest engagements of the war. "Although it is difficult to keep an accurate score in a tank battle," Lodge wrote afterward, "the American crew[s] knocked out at least eight German machines before the Germans brought up their eighty-eight millimeter guns and the British gave the order of retreat."[46]

Lodge came away from the battle, which was a major Allied defeat, with a greater appreciation for the efficiency of the German army and for his own mortality. "It's just a piece of luck whether they get you or not," he told reporters afterward. Indeed, the senator turned tank officer had narrowly avoided becoming a casualty when the command car he was driving in came under attack by dive-bombing German Stuka planes. "We jumped out of the car," he remembered, "and dived headlong for a slit trench just about the time they dived." He later added, "I was safe, but it was certainly not due to any senatorial immunity."[47]

Lodge was praised for his "fine service" by Secretary of War Henry Stimson upon his return stateside in early July. He also was politely informed of a July 1 presidential executive order requiring all members of Congress serving in the armed forces to be taken off active duty. "I cannot but feel," Stimson wrote him, "that you will render more service to the American people by performing the important duties of a United States Senator rather than devote your energies solely to the purely military phase of the war as a junior officer."[48]

Perhaps relieved to be removed from the horrors of frontline combat, Lodge took the news without a hint of argument or complaint. "I told the War Department that I am always at their service, and if they want a tank officer at any time, they can have me," he said.[49]

The North African combat experience became politically useful to Lodge during his fall reelection campaign. When Senate challenger Joseph Casey attempted to characterize his army duty as being nothing more than "a Cook's tour of the Libyan desert," the now veteran politico was quick to counterattack. "I can assure you it wasn't a Cook's tour," he angrily protested. "I did what was expected of me, obeying orders, as did every man in the outfit. A slur directed at me, insofar as that expedition is concerned, also slurs the brave men who carried their country's flag across shell-torn sands into the smoking mouths of enemy guns, and I resent that too."[50]

Apparently Bay State voters felt the same way, as Lodge was returned to the Senate by a comfortable 80,197-vote margin. In turning back Casey's challenge, the unbeaten Republican repeated the pattern he had established against Curley in 1936. He won every county in the state except Suffolk and did well in industrial centers such as Fall River, Lynn, Lowell, and Brockton, where his pro-labor stands secured the support of the rank and file.[51]

Still, Lodge's performance was subpar in comparison to fellow incumbent Republican Leverett Saltonstall, who decisively crushed Democrat Roger L. Putnam of Springfield by 128,137 votes for the governorship. Unlike Lodge, however, the ubiquitous Saltonstall did not have to fight charges of isolationism, as he ran under the campaign slogan "Our Great War Governor."[52]

Back in Washington, Lodge devoted his energies to helping the country win the war. As an active member of the Senate Armed Services Committee, he spoke out against bureaucratic waste and inefficiency, sought improvements for the conditions of GIs, and urged the establishment of a unified command structure for all land, sea, and air forces. "Senior office[r]s of both the Army and Navy are deeply impressed with the need for unity" of the services, he lectured his fellow senators. Mindful of the economic hardships many soldiers' families endured on the home front, the Bay State lawmaker also supported legislation increasing federal subsidies to servicemen's wives and children.[53]

Frustrated by his own modest contribution to the war effort and sensing that staying out of the "big show" to come in Europe would adversely affect his political future, Lodge resigned from the Senate in February 1944 for active combat duty. "The fact that the United States is entering the period of large-scale ground fighting has, after grave thought," he explained in his letter of resignation, "brought me to the definite conclusion that, given my age [he was forty-two] and military training, I must henceforth serve my country as a combat soldier in the Army overseas."[54]

In so doing, Lodge became the first senator since the Civil War to give up his seat to fight for his country. None other than President Franklin Roosevelt praised him for his action. "I want you to know . . . that I would do just what you are doing, if I could," the commander in chief informed him. "I missed being with the guns in 1917–18. It's too late now. I envy you the opportunity that is yours and I congratulate you upon the decision you have made."[55]

A commissioned major with the American Sixth Army Group, Lodge saw his share of action as a frontline reconnaissance officer in Italy and France. Traveling by a single-motored L-15 scout plane or by jeep, he routinely braved antiaircraft gunfire and minefields to gain an accurate understanding of the enemy's strengths and weaknesses. "He was utterly without fear," remembered one fellow officer.[56] Indeed, his commanding officer, Major General Willis D. Crittenberger, thought so highly of his displayed courage under fire that he awarded him a Bronze Star medal for bravery.

"On numerous occasions," read Lodge's Bronze Star citation, "Major LODGE, without regard for personal safety, executed missions of a specific nature which required his exposure to enemy fire and the traversing of mined roads and areas. . . . His services rendered during this period were in keeping with the highest traditions of the United States Army." For his continued "meritorious service," the former Massachusetts lawmaker was promoted to lieutenant colonel and assigned to the First French Army, where he served as a senior liaison officer and translator (Lodge spoke fluent French) to General Jean de Lattre de Tassigny.[57]

From the beginning the assignment was a difficult one. A competent but arrogant field general, de Lattre resented any changes to his order of battle by senior American military personnel. As liaison officer, Lodge's main function was to smooth over these bruised feelings and to facilitate a constructive dialogue between the American and French commands. Sometimes, however, this task proved easier said than done. When Lodge was given the delicate assignment of informing de Lattre that he would have to rearrange the disposition of his troops before a major offensive in the Alsace region of France, the latter flew into a rage. "What is this politician—only a lieutenant colonel, telling us elementary tactics?" the French general fumed. "What does he know about it? We are professionals; we know our business!"[58]

Summoning all the tact and diplomacy he could, Lodge patiently yet firmly persuaded de Lattre to comply with the wishes of his American superiors. "As far as I'm concerned," recounted General Jacob L. Devers of the U.S. Seventh Army, on whose behalf the once and future senator was acting, "Lodge was more than my liaison that day. He was acting in my place."[59]

Lodge with Supreme Allied Commander Dwight D. Eisenhower and French General Jean de Lattre de Tassigny during World War II. In February 1944 Lodge had become the first U.S. senator since the Civil War to resign his seat for active combat duty. Courtesy of the Massachusetts Historical Society, Boston.

By war's end, Lodge had compiled an enviable record of service to go along with six battle stars, the aforementioned Bronze Star, and France's Legion of Honor and Croix de Guerre honors. "When you left the Senate and went into the Army," wrote an appreciative Secretary of War Henry Stimson in 1945, "you made a decision which few Americans have . . . and your work in the Army has shown that you were right in your decision."[60]

Returning home from the war, Lodge wasted little time getting back into politics. He announced that he would oppose five-term Democratic U.S. Senator David I. Walsh of Fitchburg for his seat in 1946. In deciding to run again, the decorated army veteran admitted to having a number of reservations. "It is hard," he revealed, "to be in a competitive situation with the present Senior Senator with whom my grandfather and later I, myself, have always had courteous relations. But public service is difficult and the duties imposed by our two-party system must prevail over personal feeling."[61]

At seventy-three years of age, Walsh, the first Irish Catholic in Massachusetts history to win a U.S. Senate seat, no longer commanded the kind of widespread support that had once earned him the nickname "The People's Choice." He had incurred the displeasure of returning veterans by his prewar isolationism and his opposition to military preparedness. Strong-willed and independent, the Canton Democrat had also alienated liberal elements within his own party by taking conservative stands on labor and social reform issues. "He has forfeited the friendship of all the genuine New Dealers," the *Boston Herald* reported, "and the C.I.O. will refuse to endorse him against Lodge."[62]

Adding to Walsh's political troubles was the stigma of personal scandal. In 1942 his name turned up in an FBI probe of a Brooklyn, New York, "house of degradation" that was supposedly frequented by Nazi spies. The brothel's owner, an émigré named Gustave H. Beekman, revealed in a signed affidavit that the senior Massachusetts senator had been a regular customer at the establishment, which specialized in servicing male homosexual clients. Walsh, a lifelong bachelor and closet homosexual, publicly denied Beekman's charges. "It's a diabolical lie absolutely without foundation," he claimed. "I have never in my life been to such a place."[63]

Following a hastily convened Justice Department investigation, Walsh was cleared of any wrongdoing by FBI Director J. Edgar Hoover, who ironically was later rumored to be a closet homosexual himself. "You may rest assured," Hoover wrote him, "that I was happy indeed to render every possible assistance in establishing the facts which have so thoroughly disproved the unjust allegations which were made against you."[64]

For his part, Lodge made no mention of the scandal during the fall cam-

Decorated combat veteran Henry Cabot Lodge Jr. is greeted back home by some enthusiastic Young Republican Club committee members in August 1946. Courtesy of the
Boston Public Library, Print Department.

paign. Walsh was an old family friend, and besides, it had never been the veteran Republican's style to make personal attacks on opponents. He relied instead on discussions of postwar economic issues such as price inflation, labor
strife, and the shortage of consumer goods to draw voters' attention. "More
than a year after the end of the war," he told a Springfield rally, "we confront
shortages of sugar, soap, white shirts, clothes for children, while newspapers
tell us of factories closing down for lack of raw materials and of automobile
companies scrapping their plans to expand." The problem, he asserted, was not
so much unfavorable economic conditions as it was "a low grade of [Demo-
cratic] leadership which is endangering the whole peace for which we fought
and for which our government was completely unprepared." To turn things
around, the former state legislator urged voters to support activist-minded Republicans like himself who were committed to preventing "another depression."[65]

This emphasis on economic issues, along with Lodge's comparative youth
and veteran status, which appealed to returning servicemen, proved a winning
combination. The Republican trounced Walsh by 344,253 votes, giving him
the largest plurality of his political career. He won every county in the state and
achieved a "Republican dream" by carrying the city of Boston. "No Yankee

ever forgets such a thing," he later exclaimed, "it's like Calais on Queen Elizabeth's chest." Also contributing to Lodge's landslide victory was his strength
among blue-collar workers, who remembered his legislative efforts on their
behalf in the 1930s. He captured almost half the vote in big union cities such as
Lynn, Springfield, and Worcester, an extremely good showing for a Republican. Lodge's performance even outdid that of fellow Republican Robert F.
Bradford of Cambridge, who ousted incumbent Democrat Maurice J. Tobin
from the governorship by "only" 148,409 votes. Indeed, Bradford just missed
winning Boston by 7,902 votes in what became a Republican landslide nationwide.[66]

Again, as in 1936, Lodge benefited from going against a scandal-ridden
opponent in the denouement of his political life. The situation would be far
different six years later when the Republican lawmaker squared off against
John F. Kennedy, a man entering his political prime.

The U.S. Senate Lodge returned to was bursting with activity from America's newfound status as a global superpower. Momentous bills dealing with
the sending of military aid to Greece and Turkey, the Marshall Plan for the economic reconstruction of Western Europe, and the creation of the North Atlantic Treaty Organization were debated on and passed by wide bipartisan
margins. "The Senate at that time was at its best," Lodge later wrote in his
autobiography.[67]

Indeed, as a member of the Foreign Relations Committee, Lodge had
a significant hand in shaping many of these policies and helping line up key
Democratic and Republican support. "I cannot begin to tell you," wrote fellow Republican Arthur Vandenberg of Michigan, in the late 1940s the leading proponent of bipartisan internationalism in the Senate, "how much I
appreciate your always loyal, vigorous and effective support. You're in a class
by yourself—bless you."[68]

With regards to the far-reaching Marshall Plan, Lodge gave "no fewer"
than 335 speeches in support of the measure, all the while asserting that a recovery program abroad "would benefit Americans as well as Europeans."
Equally important, he made substantive improvements to the final draft version of the legislation, including the provision that reciprocal agreements regarding the stockpiling of strategic materials be mandated. He also insisted
that the beneficiaries of Marshall Plan aid be obliged to adopt economic policies encouraging the long-term social and political integration of each country
into a future "United States of Europe."[69]

"We want," he told his constituents, "a world in which two giants [the
United States and Soviet Union] aren't standing toe to toe going at each other

all the time. Anything like the Marshall Plan that helps build up a strong third force in Western Europe is a good thing for civilization and in the long run, for us."[70]

Lodge's former pronouncements about the virtues of isolationism had thus fallen away, to be replaced with new ones celebrating the merits of internationalism and cooperation. He became an outspoken advocate of the United Nations Organization and the concept of collective security. World War II had convinced him that true national security could not be achieved if the United States operated an independent foreign policy outside the family of nations. "Above all," he emphasized, "let us realize that our foreign policy exists—and our effective support of the United Nations is possible—only in proportion to the national strength behind it."[71]

Lodge was also active in the domestic sphere. In 1947 he and Congressman Clarence Brown of Ohio proposed the creation of a bipartisan commission to reorganize the executive branch of the federal government. "I was impressed then—and still am—with the ineffectiveness of government," Lodge later wrote. "Very often, after legislation has been enacted, funds appropriated, and personnel appointed, nothing much happens. It was a little known fact . . . that there had been no effort to organize the government in the interest of economy and efficiency since the founding of the United States in 1789. I therefore sponsored the Senate bill creating [the Commission on Organization of the Executive Branch of Government]—the first effort to organize the government since the founding of the Republic."[72]

Chaired by former Republican president Herbert Hoover, the commission made 273 recommendations to make the federal government more efficient. Seventy-two percent of the commission's recommendations were eventually passed by Congress, bringing an overall savings of three billion dollars to taxpayers.[73]

Structural reform was again at the top of Lodge's legislative agenda in the late 1940s when he cosponsored a constitutional amendment abolishing the electoral college and providing for the direct election of the president and vice president. "The Lodge amendment," reported the *New York Times,* "would provide that each state's electoral vote for President and Vice President directly reflect the popular vote. Thus the present 'unit rule' would be abolished, whereby the state's entire bloc of electoral votes now goes wholly to the candidate who receives the most popular votes." While the bill sailed through the Senate, it failed to receive the requisite two-thirds majority in the House amid Republican fears that the proposed amendment would strengthen Democratic control over the already "Solid South."[74]

On "bread and butter" issues affecting the lives of ordinary citizens, Lodge maintained his prewar liberalism. He supported better housing, a higher minimum wage, expanded social security coverage, and federal aid for education. He also opposed provisions in the National Labor Relations Act of 1947, better known as Taft-Hartley, that outlawed union shops.[75]

Such liberal stands won him few friends among the "Old Guard" leadership of the Republican Party, men such as Robert A. Taft of Ohio, Kenneth Wherry of Nebraska, and William Jenner of Indiana. They saw in these positions examples of the creeping "state socialism" that had allegedly characterized the New Deal under President Franklin Roosevelt. To such critics Lodge offered the following rejoinder in 1950: "I don't see why we must choose between state socialism and no social progress at all. I don't see why we shouldn't use the power of the government to fill in the chinks that private enterprise can't fill for us."[76]

As chairman of the Resolutions Committee at the 1948 Republican National Convention in Philadelphia, Lodge successfully lobbied to have these liberal sentiments embedded in the party platform. Promising a newer, progressive, and forward-looking approach to governing, the platform called on the federal government to improve labor-management relations, provide better health care, promote slum clearance, end racial discrimination, and upgrade existing old-age benefit programs.

When the party suffered shattering election losses in November, Lodge blamed the setback on the unwillingness of party conservatives to get behind the convention platform. "The G.O.P.," he warned in a *Saturday Evening Post* article in 1949, "has been presented to the public as a rich man's club and as a haven for reactionaries. . . . To say that [the Old Guard conservatives] represent the rank and file of the Party is, in my view, a gross untruth. Certain it is, however, that the Republican Party must broaden the scope of its appeal so that there can be no doubt that it is a party for all elements of the people. . . . I have faith that we will make a liberal record, that we will try again and that the people will again use us as their servants. But we must make the decision that we want to be a popular party."[77]

Lodge thus fired the first shot in an ideological war that would determine not only the future direction of the Republican Party but also his own political fate in 1952.

Chapter **THREE**

★ ★ ★

Laying the Groundwork

JOHN F. KENNEDY began laying the political groundwork for a
statewide run in the spring of 1951 by scheduling speaking engagements
at various Rotary Club meetings, church picnics, chamber of commerce
luncheons, and Veterans of Foreign Wars gatherings throughout Massachusetts. Flying to Boston from Washington, D.C., every Thursday night, the
Democrat used the long three-day weekends for campaigning. "No town was
too small or too Republican for him," remembered Dave Powers, a 1946 congressional race holdover who was in charge of arranging many of the young
Democrat's appearances. "He was willing to go anywhere and every group was
glad to have him, not only because he was an interesting political figure, but
because he never charged a dime for expenses."[1]

A review of Kennedy's public appearances in 1951 reveals that the Democrat crisscrossed the state, appearing at such diverse venues as the B'nai B'rith
Jewish Community Center in Haverhill, the Franklin County Selectmen Association in Springfield, the League of Women Voters in Newburyport, the
Berkshire Hill Conference in Pittsfield, the Catholic Women's Club in Framingham, and the Jefferson-Jackson Day dinner in Boston.[2]

His speech topics usually touched on two main themes: the decline of
the Massachusetts economy and the need to meet the Soviet challenge from
abroad. Of the two, Kennedy spent an inordinate amount of time stressing the
latter. Indeed, he felt that the threat of World War III remained a distinct possibility, given what he thought was the military unpreparedness of the West.
"Most Europeans," he warned a Red Cross drive audience in Fall River,

Congressman John F. Kennedy waves to the crowd in North Adams, Massachusetts, in 1951. "He was willing to go anywhere and every group was glad to have him, not only because he was an interesting political figure, but because he never charged a dime for expenses," remembered close aide Dave Powers. Courtesy of the Boston Public Library, Print Department.

"believe that there will not be an open war with the Soviet Union, but every month of weakness that goes by is an invitation to war."[3]

As for the sluggish performance of the Bay State economy, he told a Congress on Industrial Organization gathering in Boston that blame could be placed directly on out-of-state competition from the South, where lack of unionization and low wages lured many businesses away from Massachusetts. He added that this problem could be "wiped out" by strong federal laws encouraging unionization and higher wages.[4]

Overall, these appearances afforded Kennedy the opportunity to increase his name recognition among voters outside his district. However, they failed to provide him the kind of detailed political information about a community he needed to build an effective campaign organization. To this end, he commissioned the talents of two advance men, Anthony Gallucio, a Harvard classmate who worked on the 1946 congressional campaign, and Joseph DeGuglielmo, a popular Cambridge city councilman with political connections throughout the region. Their assigned task consisted of collecting political data on every city and large town in the state. They were especially interested in learning how their candidate might fare against Paul Dever or Henry Cabot Lodge Jr. in head-to-head competition. Indeed, their findings, confirmed by several other private poll samplings, would go a long way in determining who Kennedy would face in the upcoming election year.

As Joseph DeGuglielmo observed:

> "Well, this was about a year before '52; it was in the summer of '51. . . . If I remember right, we took about two weeks off. We had made appointments in advance of people we were going to see. Besides that at my suggestion, Tony and I adopted a procedure that we would divide when we'd get into a town and we'd go get a haircut, go in a restaurant, talk to waitresses and the rest. And what we were trying to do was evaluate the various strengths of Kennedy, Lodge and Dever. And after we got through, Tony and I evolved the theory that Dever could not be re-elected and Jack Kennedy would be a lead pipe cinch to knock him off as governor, that probably he could defeat Lodge but it would be a much closer fight than the other fight.[5]

In the process of reaching these conclusions, DeGuglielmo and Gallucio compiled a list of community leaders whom they identified as being the most likely to support a Kennedy bid for statewide office. The latter's names, addresses, and phone numbers were duly recorded on index cards along with any personal data considered politically relevant. A typical example was the description of a former Boston-area football star turned insurance adjuster: "young, very active, extremely sharp and well-liked. Should be key Irish fellow."[6]

Having thus completed their assignment, the two now weary advance men gathered up their data and reported to Kennedy at his family's summer home in Hyannis Port. Joseph P. Kennedy, who expressed a keen interest in the Gallucio-DeGuglielmo findings, also made a point of attending the meeting. Recalled DeGuglielmo:

> The father was of the impression that Jack would murder Lodge; no question, "Would murder him" were the words he used. He didn't quite agree with me on Dever. He thought Dever could win. And he asked me on what I based it. And I said, "Well, the only thing I can base it on is this: you ask people in eastern Massachusetts around Boston,

how's Dever? Well, he's weak here but western Massachusetts is going to carry him and he can't be beat. You go into western Massachusetts and you ask people, and by people I mean ordinary people in the street and I also mean professional pols. The professional pol will tell you that Dever is in real bad shape here but Boston will carry him."

Well, if each section . . . is expecting the other section to carry him and admits his section is weak, then the man is weak and can't win. So I persuaded the father, when we got through, with that theory but [the Kennedys] eventually decided that the decisions of America and the decisions of the world were going to be made in Washington and they preferred to take a crack at Washington rather than the State House in Boston.[7]

That John Kennedy would find the U.S. Senate preferable to the governorship of Massachusetts is not surprising. In his view, the latter offered less prestige and more potential for political difficulties than the former. "The trouble is," he told journalist Ralph Martin in 1959, "the Mayor of Boston has all that patronage that the Governor should have. That is the richest patronage in the state but the Governor is deprived of all that patronage and it weakens him considerably." Also accounting for Kennedy's predilection for the Senate was the appeal of being involved in pressing national and international issues rather than mundane local ones. He once told a friend while in the vicinity of the State House that he did not "look forward to sitting over there in the governor's office dealing out sewer contracts."[8]

Although Kennedy waited until April 6, 1952, to formally announce his Senate candidacy, the decision to run had been, as the testimony of De-Guglielmo makes clear, a fait accompli for several months. What prevented the young Democrat from revealing his plans any sooner was consideration of the Massachusetts political situation. In the spring of 1952 Democratic Governor Paul Dever was debating whether to seek reelection or run against Lodge. Kennedy, who faced the option of either challenging Dever in a party primary for the Senate seat (a prospect he did not particularly relish) or running for the vacated governor's chair, decided patiently to wait out the governor's decision in deference to party loyalty.

"Well, it was really up to Dever to decide," Kennedy later confided to biographer James MacGregor Burns, "and he fiddled around, didn't decide until April whether he was going to run for Governor or Senator, then he decided he couldn't beat Lodge and the night he told me that . . . I announced my candidacy against Lodge."[9]

Dever's sense of electoral vulnerability was understandable. Though he had won reelection handily in 1950, there was, by the beginning of 1952, a growing disaffection with his administration. Charges of mismanagement were being made, in particular about the much publicized state road-building program. Add to this high unemployment in the state's manufacturing centers along with a lack of public enthusiasm for his other major legislative initiatives in mental health and reformed workman's compensation law, and it became clear to Dever that taking on Lodge would be unwise, especially since the latter had demonstrated he could beat tough Democratic challengers such as James Michael Curley.[10]

Better, the Cambridge Democrat reasoned, to run again for governor and face a less formidable Republican opponent such as U.S. Congressman Christian A. Herter of Boston, than risk almost certain defeat at the hands of Lodge. As it turned out, Dever lost out in his reelection bid by fourteen thousand votes.[11]

With Dever removed as a Senate contender, John Kennedy was free to

Massachusetts governor Paul Dever (left) and Kennedy listen to President Harry S. Truman deliver a speech in 1952. Dever's decision in April not to run against Lodge for the Senate paved the way for Kennedy's candidacy. Courtesy of the *New Bedford Standard-Times.*

concentrate his efforts on building a statewide political organization. To oversee this important task, Kennedy appointed Mark Dalton, the Cambridge attorney who had managed his 1946 congressional campaign. It was an unfortunate choice. A shy and timid man by nature, the Harvard-educated Dalton lacked the requisite personal drive and imagination to head such a large-scale operation. Under his leadership, the Senate campaign got off to an unceremoniously sluggish start.

Much of the blame could be traced directly to the candidate himself. "Although [Kennedy] had done a splendid job of making himself known throughout the state over the previous four years," remembered campaign staffer Ken O'Donnell, a Harvard football captain who hailed from a socially prominent family in Worcester, Massachusetts, "he had done nothing about forming a statewide Kennedy organization at the time when he announced his candidacy. Nobody had gone to his card index file to pick and appoint local Kennedy-for-Senator organizers in various cities and towns. Jack himself was busy with other things, apparently either reluctant to give anybody else, such as Mark Dalton, the authority to select local Kennedy managers . . . or casually assuming that the rather delicate work of putting together a statewide organization was being done without his supervision."[12]

Indeed, Dalton was even "hesitant" about appointing a campaign director in western Massachusetts because it was unclear whether the candidate would approve of any of the half-dozen "prospects" then under consideration.[13] Adding to the campaign manager's woes was Kennedy's cavalier treatment of him. Once, while departing from a campaign function in Fall River, Kennedy launched into a personal tirade against Dalton for the latter's supposed inability to shield him from three inebriated supporters at the door. Thrusting his finger into Dalton's stomach, Kennedy barked, "Don't you ever let that happen to me again!" Four decades later, the details of this unpleasant encounter still remained vivid in Dalton's memory. "I was to take care of him with drunks," he recalled angrily. "I was his caretaker, his bodyguard."[14] Not surprisingly, relations between the two men began to sour.

Tensions reached a breaking point later that spring. In the presence of the candidate and assembled staff, Joseph P. Kennedy lit into Dalton for his supposed mishandling of campaign finances. "Dalton, you've spent ten thousand dollars of my money and you haven't accomplished a damn thing!" the ambassador screamed. One witness to the incident—Larry O'Brien, a seasoned political operative from Springfield, Massachusetts, brought aboard to assist in the formulation of campaign strategy—recounted afterward that the beleaguered campaign manager "rushed" from the room in a "distraught" state of mind. When finally tracked down in the reading room of the Boston Athenaeum, a private library on Beacon Hill, Dalton curtly informed campaign aide Ken O'Donnell that he was finished as campaign manager. "What's he getting so hot and bothered about?" the elder Kennedy fumed. "We were only having a conversation. I didn't mean to offend him."[15]

Dalton's untimely exit put into sharp focus the kind of influence Joseph P. Kennedy wielded over the campaign. Though John Kennedy in later years downplayed the notion that his father had any significant role in the Senate race, existing evidence suggests otherwise. Working "around the clock" from his private suite at the Ritz-Carlton Hotel in Boston, the elder Kennedy kept close tabs on all campaign activities. He was always "consulting people, getting reports, looking into problems," reported campaign speech writer John Spiegel. "Should Jack go on TV with this issue? What kind of an ad should he run on something else? He'd call in experts, get opinions, have ideas worked up."[16] All told, he spent hundreds of thousands of dollars of his own money in a no-holds-barred attempt to see his son get elected.

Journalist Ralph Coghlan of the *St. Louis Post-Dispatch* became one of the "experts" the ambassador brought into the Senate fight. Entrusted with generating favorable publicity for the Democratic challenger, Coghlan made arrangements with various media outlets during the Democratic National Convention in July to "have the spotlight fall on Jack," even though the latter was attending the convention as a nondelegate. Hence, John Kennedy was seen being interviewed on television "in such places as hotel lobbies, the lobby of the convention hall and the actual floor, with noteworthy frequency." As the *Dorchester Citizen* observed, "At the convention Kennedy became one of the recognized leaders in the Democratic party. He made several television appearances and also was interviewed on nationwide hook-ups."[17]

"The old man wants performance," Mark Dalton once exclaimed. "He's a taskmaster."[18]

To be certain, if the candidate misspoke or made an embarrassing public gaffe, his father wanted to hear about it right away. Mistakes, at least those made by campaign subordinates, were not to be tolerated. "I remember one night eight of us were in Mr. Kennedy's apartment watching Jack make a TV speech," recalled R. Sargent Shriver, a *Newsweek* assistant editor the ambassador recruited to write speeches for the campaign.

> There was a guy that wrote the speech and the guy from the advertising agency and all the yes men sitting there with Mr. Kennedy smack in front of the tube. After it was all over, Mr. Kennedy asked what they

thought about it. They gave these mealy mouthed answers and all of a sudden Mr. Kennedy got ferocious, just ferocious. He told them it was the worst speech he'd ever heard and they were destroying Jack and he never wanted to see his son have to get up on TV and make such a fool of himself again. The guy who wrote the speech said he couldn't talk to him like that and Mr. Kennedy got red and furious and told him if he didn't like it to get out. He told them they would have a meeting in the morning and come up with a whole new concept because they were ruining this precious commodity they had and he gave a long speech about how wonderful Jack was.

When John Kennedy finally called to ask how his television appearance had gone, the former ambassador immediately composed himself in a move designed to boost his son's confidence. "Boy, Jack, you were great," he replied.[19]

While Joseph Kennedy exercised enormous authority, it was the candidate himself who ultimately determined how the Senate contest was to be run. His father "anticipated problems, imported talent to handle them," John Spiegel later admitted. "But Jack is the one who made the final decisions." Indeed, John Kennedy kept abreast of all details pertaining to his campaign, including the operational expenses incurred from office staffing and telephone use. "I am warning everyone that no bills will be paid unless you have approved the matter in advance and I do not care how hard boiled you are with everyone on this," he bluntly informed one aide in a campaign memo.[20]

This hands-on approach even extended to issues dealing with publicity. "During the campaign," he wrote speechwriters Timothy Reardon Jr. and R. Sargent Shriver, "we should have a different thought each day. Each must be a noteworthy idea. Whip them into shape so [campaign press aide] Ed Wagner can write the news releases along with the schedule, i.e. Congressman Kennedy said at a meeting in North Attleboro last night, etc., etc."[21]

"People think that because [Joseph Kennedy is] a vigorous and dominating man that he's going to tell me what to do or that he's doing everything for me," John Kennedy later complained. "But I make up my own mind and my own decisions."[22]

With Mark Dalton's departure, the responsibility of running the day-to-day operation of the campaign fell to Robert F. Kennedy, the candidate's younger brother. Only twenty-six years old and a recent graduate of the University of Virginia Law School, Robert had little in the way of a political background to prepare him for his new job. In 1946 he had played a minor role in his brother's congressional campaign by helping organize three "unfriendly" wards in East Cambridge. "My job was to meet as many people as possible, hoping to reduce the vote against us from five to one to four to one," he later recalled. "Actually, that's what the campaign consisted of: contacting people."[23]

Other than this brief foray, however, Robert had no political experience. When he was initially contacted by his old Harvard football teammate and campaign aide Ken O'Donnell about assuming the controls of his brother's faltering statewide organization, he voiced trepidation. "I'll screw it up," he said. But upon further reflection and some persuasive arm twisting by Joseph P. Kennedy Sr., he resigned from his post as an attorney for the Justice Department's Internal Affairs Division to head the campaign. "I owe it to my brother Jack to return to Massachusetts and do my part before the Democratic primary in September," Robert explained.[24]

Such loyalty was not out of character. As the seventh of nine children, Robert was forever trying to earn the respect, love, and attention of his parents and older siblings. When you came from that far down the family pecking order, he liked to say, "you have to struggle to survive."[25]

"He was," prep school friend David Hackett once observed, "neither a natural athlete nor a natural student nor a natural success with girls, and had no natural gift for popularity. Nothing came easily for him. What he had was a set of handicaps and a fantastic determination to overcome them."[26] At Harvard he accomplished something his older brothers only dreamed of achieving: a varsity letter in football.

"I can't think of anyone who had less right to make the varsity than Bobby when he first came out of practice," teammate and lifelong friend Ken O'Donnell later remarked. "The war was over, and we had plenty of manpower, all of it bigger, faster and more experienced than he was. But every afternoon he would be down on their field an hour early, and he always stayed an hour later. He just made himself better."[27] This ability to put in long hours of sacrifice for the greater good no doubt endeared him to John Kennedy. Though separated by nearly a decade in age, the two brothers had nevertheless enjoyed a close relationship over the years that was made closer by Robert's participation in the 1946 congressional race. Now the 1952 Senate campaign beckoned, and with it came a newer and greater set of challenges.

Dismissed by some campaign staffers as a "front man" for his father, Robert had to labor extra long and hard to prove his detractors wrong. "Bob was all business," remembered Larry O'Brien. "He would explain what he wanted done, and no one could deny that he was setting an example with the fifteen and twenty-four [hour] days he was working on Jack's behalf." Not even the tiniest detail escaped his attention. When a workman refused to hang a Kennedy poster on a Charlestown drawbridge from a forty-foot ladder, he performed the task. "While I was holding the ladder," Dave Powers recalled, "I was wondering how I could explain it to the Ambassador and Jack when Bobby fell and broke his neck. I also said to myself, if I had his money I would be sitting at home in a rocking chair instead of being up there on the top of that ladder."[28]

Nor was he shy about stepping on other people's toes. When a prominent state labor leader dropped by the Boston headquarters to exchange pleasantries with the campaign staff, Robert flew into a rage. "If you're not going to work, don't hang out here," he curtly informed the visitor. On another occasion he had to be restrained from physically assaulting a state representative after the latter had made some derogatory statements about his brother. "Bobby didn't like hangers-on in politics," explained campaign worker Helen Keyes. "He liked doers. He had very good judgment and yet, because he was so young he blew up at a lot of things. Bobby was very abrasive, as he always was with certain people."[29]

To be sure, veteran Democratic politicians in Massachusetts found personal dealings with the new campaign manager particularly difficult. "To me he was a self-important upstart and know-it-all," remarked Thomas P. "Tip" O'Neill. "To him, I was simply a street-corner pol." At the same time, Robert also provided a needed buffer between campaign staffers and the interfering Joseph P. Kennedy. "Outsiders," explained historian James W. Hilty, "lacked sufficient cachet and could not effectively comprehend the peculiar mannerisms of this close-knit family." "Bobby has always had a lot of moxie and guts," Joseph Kennedy later bragged. "I doubt if Jack ever makes any enemies. But Bobby might make some. Not that Jack isn't just as courageous, but Bobby feels more strongly for or against people than Jack does—just as I do."[30]

In his own defense, the man who would later be dubbed "Ruthless Bobby" by his enemies let it be known that he was not out to make friends, only to win votes for his older brother. "They don't have to like me," he told Dave Powers. "I only want them to like Jack."[31] To achieve that goal Robert went about putting together a statewide political organization from the data DeGuglielmo and Gallucio had earlier compiled.

Working closely with Larry O'Brien, the younger Kennedy set up a network of some 286 campaign directors, or "Kennedy secretaries" as they were called in communities across the state. The title "secretary" was not without significance. "We could have called them Kennedy chairmen," O'Brien related, "but that might have offended the local party chairmen, who in theory were still chairmen of everything—our campaign included—so we settled on the more modest title of secretary."[32]

Though many of the secretaries had no prior political experience, nearly all of them had a solid record of community involvement. This was of extreme importance because the Kennedy campaign was trying to appeal to a new and younger generation of Democratic voters who had grown disillusioned with the "boisterous rhetoric and outmoded antics" of old-time political bosses such as James Michael Curley, from whom Kennedy had made a conspicuous point of distancing himself as a congressman. These voters, many of them veterans of World War II and college-educated, felt strongly that "public service" was a serious endeavor where "practical jokes and dirty tricks" had no place.[33]

As Ken O'Donnell recalled:

> What we did was to find the right people in each town, the one guy who would work and do it. That was the most important thing of all.

John F. Kennedy is welcomed at his Fall River campaign headquarters. Under the direction of Robert F. Kennedy and Larry O'Brien, a vast network of campaign "secretaries" was set up throughout the state. Courtesy of the John F. Kennedy Library.

And once we picked the guy we had to keep him. After all, you can't fire a guy who's working for nothing. What you could do is to give him an executive assistant later on who takes over or tries to. But we found wonderful people. The thing was that we went into towns where Democrat was a dirty word and nobody ever had tried to start an organization of any kind. And we found people with enthusiasm, who liked Kennedy, who worked their heads off for free.[34]

Special emphasis was placed on communities outside Boston that had a voter registration in excess of thirty thousand, a practice never heretofore seen in a statewide campaign in Massachusetts. Cities thus targeted included Brockton, Cambridge, Fall River, Holyoke, Lawrence, Lowell, Lynn, Malden, Medford, New Bedford, Pittsfield, Quincy, Somerville, Springfield, and Worcester. The campaign's pitch to these declining industrial communities was that Kennedy would "DO MORE" than Lodge in protecting "our great textile, shoe and fishing industries from unfair labor competition both at home and abroad." As one glossy, eight-page Kennedy campaign pamphlet put it, the Democrat could be counted on to "wage a better fight" for the "preservation and expansion" of Massachusetts industry.[35]

Supervising the distribution of such campaign literature was Robert F. Kennedy. Though he played a significant role in the daily administrative workings of the campaign, existing newspaper accounts and archival records indicate he had no input on broader issues of substance such as determining the content of his brother's speeches. That responsibility rested solely on the shoulders of John Kennedy. Indeed, for all his outward bluster and volatile attitude, Robert Kennedy was still in the process of learning the political ropes. "I was more concerned with organization," he later confessed. "I didn't become involved in what should go in a speech, what should be said on a poster or billboard, what should be done on television."[36]

James W. Hilty, the most thorough and fair-minded of Robert Kennedy's biographers, concurs with this assessment. Robert, writes Hilty, "handled the administrative details and left the strategizing to his brother, his father and Larry O'Brien." More an office manager at this stage of his career than the grand political strategist he was to become during the 1960 presidential campaign, Robert occupied himself with mundane administrative tasks such as making sure envelopes were stuffed, campaign bills were paid, and volunteers kept busy. "Politicians," he later complained, "do nothing but hold meetings and decide what work should be done and never do any work. The main difference between our campaign and others was that we did work."[37]

A secretary's regular responsibilities included directing all local campaign efforts, whether it was checking and updating community voting lists, recruiting volunteers, sending out mass mailings, conducting door-to-door canvassing, or holding a rally. In the meantime, they were to keep in close daily contact with the main Boston headquarters on 44 Kilby Street. "We had meetings every night in some city or town in the country," recalled John J. Droney, a campaign secretary in suburban Middlesex County. "And this is how [the Kennedy camp] organized. They had meetings, follow up, [and] made sure that the work was being done and the stickers were being given out and that we had house parties." "It was," as Larry O'Brien would later reveal, the most "nearly perfect" campaign organization he had ever been associated with. Nothing was left to chance. When Kennedy-for-Senator buttons and placards were being distributed, for instance, volunteers were instructed to get the name and address of every person who accepted one. Later these same people would receive in the mail a personalized note thanking them for their support.[38]

"We organized each precinct," Robert Kennedy boasted to an interviewer a decade afterward. "The philosophy was to see if we could get as many groups as possible going and active. Perhaps there would be overlapping. A woman might be an Italian and she might be twenty-one, so she'd be in a young person's club for John Kennedy, she'd be in the Italian Club for John Kennedy and she'd be in the Women's Club for John Kennedy. [Campaign workers] would leave things at the hairdressers, and on buses, so that there'd be material and information about John Kennedy. There was a great spirit in the campaign that I don't think existed to that time in the state of Massachusetts."[39]

This "great spirit" did not extend to the candidate's hometown, however. Outside the friendly confines of the Eleventh Congressional District, Kennedy's Boston organization was weak owing to the young Democrat's political independence over the years. Kennedy "did not do things that a pol's pol would do," explained longtime South Boston political leader John E. Powers. "He wasn't susceptible to doing favors or dispensing patronage, and that was what built a city organization in those years."[40]

To correct the situation, a deal was struck between the Kennedy camp and Governor Paul Dever, who enjoyed immense popularity among Democratic operatives in the city. In exchange for a joint Kennedy-Dever operation in Boston headed by John Powers, the Kennedy organization agreed to pick up a sizable portion of the tab for operational expenses such as staffing and advertising, which conservative estimates placed in the tens of thousands of dollars.

Kennedy received a further political boost in late June when twice-elected

Boston mayor John B. Hynes publicly endorsed his candidacy. Hynes expressed the hope that his former campaign supporters would support Kennedy "as devotedly as they did me." Thus at the price of some "independence," John Kennedy gained invaluable access to political machinery that helped him, come November, secure the same percentage of votes citywide as Dever.[41]

Such access proved useful in late July as the filing deadline for nomination papers descended upon the two senatorial candidates. While only 2,500 names were needed to secure a spot on the state ballot, Kennedy's camp submitted a record 262,324 signatures. On hand to witness the historic occasion was none other than George Cabot Lodge, Lodge's eldest son, covering the event for the *Boston Herald*. "I could see from the expression on George's face what he was thinking," Dave Powers later recalled. "Here it is, only the twenty-eighth of July. They've done all this work and my father hasn't even started yet."[42]

Though an exaggeration, Powers's trenchant observation was not without some basis in fact. Outside of a rudimentary field organization headed by former Lynn mayor and state senator Albert Cole, an old friend from his state legislature days, Henry Cabot Lodge Jr. had heretofore devoted little time or energy to his reelection effort. He "neglected his campaign outrageously," acknowledged fellow Republican Camman Newberry, a North Shore neighbor and Little, Brown editor who had assisted Lodge in various political contests, "because that was the year Eisenhower was running [for president] and Cabot was Eisenhower's campaign manager and he just paid no attention to his race up here at all."[43]

Indeed, while the Kennedys were busy appointing secretaries, scouring the state for volunteers, and opening local campaign headquarters in such locales as Lynn, Worcester, and Pittsfield, Lodge had been noticeably inactive. The Republican lawmaker could instead be found far outside the borders of Massachusetts making speeches, issuing press releases, attending fund-raisers, and lining up delegates on behalf of Eisenhower. "Cabot had been solidly in the Ike business for about a year," lamented Mason Sears, a close political advisor and a second cousin of Lodge's wife. "He was very tired and this took a great deal of spark out of him."[44]

So out of touch was Lodge with his political base back home that he failed to grasp the extent to which the Kennedys were mobilizing their supporters, particularly when it came to circulating nomination papers. "It is rather surprising that there should be no Kennedy papers in circulation," the befuddled candidate wrote Albert Cole on June 13, six weeks before his opponent filed a record tally of signatures.[45]

John F. Kennedy files nomination papers for the U.S. Senate
against Lodge in late July 1952. The Democrat submitted a
record 262,324 signatures. Courtesy of the Boston Public Library, Print
Department.

"I cannot take it away from [the Kennedys]," recounted Maxwell Rabb, a
talented Brookline attorney who had been Lodge's administrative assistant
since the late 1930s. "They did a first-class job [of organizing], but this was not
Lodge. He would have done much better [if he had concentrated exclusively
on his Senate race]. He had taken on this baby, the Eisenhower [presidential
campaign], and it left him in a sense with, I won't say divided loyalties, but
with divided attention. Oh, it took up his full time."[46]

Lodge's self-sacrifice sprang from his own misgivings concerning the direction the GOP had taken over the previous two decades. Unlike the doctri-

naire conservatives who composed the bulk of the Republican membership in Congress, Lodge did not view the New Deal or its successor, the Fair Deal, as pernicious attempts to impose a form of state socialism. He saw them instead as needed reform measures, imperfect though they were, to provide a "safety net" for the people suffering from the jarring effects of economic dislocation, illness, or old age. He described efforts by conservative Republicans to repeal the New Deal–Fair Deal programs as "anchored in the dead past." "We were not put in office to set back the clock," Lodge admonished after the GOP had regained control of Congress in 1946 thanks to public weariness over two decades of Democratic rule. "We Republicans are on probation."[47]

The probationary period for the Republican Party among American voters ended in 1948 as the Democrats reclaimed majorities in both houses of Congress and, in the political upset of the century, retained control of the White House when incumbent President Harry S. Truman successfully beat back the challenge of Republican Governor Thomas E. Dewey of New York. The losses, coming as they did in the wake of high expectations within the GOP, were particularly bitter pills for party moderates such as Lodge to swallow. The moderates blamed party conservatives for scaring potential voters away from the GOP banner with their talk of rolling back New Deal social programs and supporting a more isolationist, anticommunist foreign policy. "We've been told we had the heavier and more powerful crew," Lodge said afterward. "But they didn't win us any races. I'm sick of that. I want to see the Republicans serve the people, not lecture them. When a man comes into a gasoline station for gas, you just don't argue with him. You give him gas."[48]

What Lodge wanted was for the GOP to "modernize" itself with a new progressive reform agenda that was not a "me too" copy of the Democrats' but something that would put Republicans on a long-term competitive basis with the party of Roosevelt and Truman. As Lodge told one would-be supporter on a 1952 campaign stop in western Massachusetts, "I'm a different sort of Republican." He was different in that he publicly professed to have no overarching ideology or adherence to any "ism." "If there's a good proposition and a Democrat offers it, I'm for it; if it's lousy and a Republican offers it, I'm against it," he said.[49]

There were expedient political reasons for taking this nonpartisan route. "In fact the only hope for the Republican Party lies in attracting Democrats and Independents," Lodge argued. "This fact becomes apparent when you realize that all the Republicans in the nation today add up to only thirty-one percent of the total vote." From a personal self-interest standpoint, it also made good political sense because Massachusetts in the post–World War II period was becoming more Democratic in voter makeup. "It is the margin of supremacy of the Democrats that perhaps dictates the casting of some of the votes of Lodge that arouse resentment of stand pat Republicans," *Boston Herald* columnist W. E. Mullins observed in 1952. "Men like Senators [Robert] Taft [of Ohio], [John] Bricker [of Ohio] or [Eugene] Millikin [of Colorado] could not be elected here in all probability."[50]

Lodge was not alone among Senate Republican moderates in urging his party to refashion its sense of political direction. Irving Ives of New York, Owen Brewster of Maine, George Aiken and Ralph Flanders of Vermont, Wayne Morse of Oregon, and fellow Bay Stater Leverett Saltonstall all joined him in demanding party reform. These moderates supported Lodge's bid in 1949 to unseat the leader of the conservative wing of the party, Taft, as chairman of the Senate Republican Policy Committee.[51]

The decision to take on Taft stemmed from Lodge's own sincere desire to reform the Republican Party. He felt that if conservatives continued to hold sway in party policymaking councils, the GOP was doomed to more humiliating defeats at the polls. "There are millions of Republicans in this country who want the party to engage in more than a rearguard reaction," he claimed.[52] Taft, however, was no political pushover. "Mr. Republican" was an excellent debater and a skilled political in-fighter that belied the laid-back image of his father, William Howard Taft, who had been both president of the United States and chief justice of the Supreme Court. Over his long public career Robert Taft had vigorously opposed most social reform programs and had taken a stubbornly isolationist stance on foreign policy. "We have quietly adopted a tendency," he complained in the late 1940s, "to interfere in the affairs of nations, to assume that we are a kind of demigod and Santa Claus to solve the problems of the world . . . it is easy to slip into an attitude of imperialism where war becomes an instrument of public policy rather than its last resort."[53]

In defending his conservative positions, the Ohio lawmaker sometimes got carried away with his rhetoric, as was the case in 1936 when he publicly questioned the patriotism of President Roosevelt. "If Mr. Roosevelt is not a communist today," he charged, "he is bound to become one."[54] Indeed, Taft was not the type to take a challenge to his authority lightly, and Lodge's was no exception.

Skillfully lobbying support among conservatives and uncommitted moderates such as Arthur Vandenberg of Michigan, Taft easily defeated Lodge's bid to unseat him as chairman of the Republican Policy Committee by a 28–14 vote. Lodge had formally based his challenge on narrow procedural grounds.

Policy Committee rules stipulated that chairmen could not succeed themselves, but Taft, a master parliamentarian, outflanked his younger Massachusetts rival by amending the rules to permit his reelection.[55]

"I deeply regretted that I could not vote for Lodge in this instance," Vandenberg lamented in his diary afterward. But the prospect of unceremoniously dumping Taft, an old and valued political ally, had no appeal to the veteran Michigan politician, no matter how much he may have been in sympathy with the views of Lodge and his fellow moderates. Wrote Vandenberg, "I deeply felt that [Taft] had rendered great Republican service; that [Taft] had been given a 'moss-back' reputation which he does not deserve; that we shall need his aggressive wisdom in the [Eighty-first] Congress; yet that it would be best for the Party, and for him, if he would voluntarily step aside, but not otherwise."[56]

Embittered by the result, Lodge was defiant in his answers to reporters' questions following the party balloting. "Every time they [Republican conservatives] throw the ball, I'll step to bat," he vowed. "It's not over."[57] And it wasn't over. The fight for the 1952 GOP presidential nomination still beckoned, and Lodge was determined to stop Taft or anyone else of his ideological persuasion from attaining this coveted prize.

Ultimately Lodge's hopes for modernizing the GOP and turning back the conservative tide came to rest on the shoulders of Dwight D. Eisenhower. In his view, Lodge felt he had the ideal candidate to defeat Taft and regain the presidency for the Republican Party for the first time in twenty years. Outwardly warm, friendly, and charming, "Ike," as he was known to millions of Americans, was the most popular war leader since Ulysses S. Grant. A West Point graduate, Eisenhower had served as Supreme Allied Commander when Western Europe was liberated from Nazi occupation. At war's end President Harry S. Truman named him army chief of staff, a post he held with distinction until 1948, when he resigned to become president of Columbia University. In 1951 he took a leave of absence to head the North Atlantic Treaty Organization in Paris.

The problem facing Lodge was whether he could convince Eisenhower, a closet Republican, to commit to a presidential run. The task was daunting. Since 1946 several Republican as well as Democratic leaders had unsuccessfully tried to recruit the general as a standard-bearer for their parties. Each time the war hero waved them off by insisting he had no interest in the presidency.

This attitude abruptly changed on September 4, 1951, when Lodge paid Eisenhower a personal visit to his Paris headquarters. Stating that his business was to convince the general to seek the 1952 Republican nomination for the presidency, the Massachusetts lawmaker presented his case. If Eisenhower did not run, Lodge argued, Taft would almost certainly become the Republican nominee and lead the GOP to another ignominious defeat in the following year's general election. "You must permit the use of your name in the upcoming primaries."[58]

Eisenhower was deeply impressed by Lodge's line of reasoning. Three years earlier, he had confided to a writer friend that Taft's nomination, given his strongly held isolationist views, "would nullify all the things I have fought for and worked for" in Europe. Now it appeared that his worst fear stood a chance of becoming a reality. He thanked Lodge for his time and told him he would "think it over." Years later he revealed in his memoirs that his conversation with the Bay State Republican was a "turning point" in his decision to seek the White House.[59]

In his 1973 autobiography, *The Storm Has Many Eyes,* Lodge claimed that his actions during this period were guided by an unselfish desire to maintain the political viability of the GOP and to preserve the two-party system. "If Senator Taft were nominated for president and defeated in 1952," he wrote, "the Republican party would either disintegrate completely or shrink into a small minority of extreme reactionaries and, in the South, a crew of patronage-hungry professionals. The great mass of rank and file Republican voters would desert it. This would destroy the two-party system and thus our ability to bring about orderly change in America, shaking the very foundations of our government."[60]

Political self-interest may have also come into play. Given the large number of registered independents in Massachusetts (about a third of the electorate in 1952) and the potential for crossover votes to the universally popular Eisenhower, Lodge could have reasonably expected to siphon off some of this support for his own Senate reelection campaign and ride to victory on the general's coattails. Indeed, one local paper later conjectured that "heavy publicity" and the "immense prestige" of leading a winning presidential nomination fight were worth "endless hours of stumping in Massachusetts."[61]

Whatever the underlying motive, Lodge's intervention proved timely and decisive. On January 7, 1952, Eisenhower announced that he would allow his name to be placed on the ballot of the New Hampshire Republican primary, thus formally kicking off his presidential campaign. The person he tapped to manage his campaign was none other than Lodge. The choice was a shrewd one. The junior Massachusetts senator was a prominent Republican of national stature who supported Vandenberg for president in 1948, thereby making him acceptable to factions within the Eisenhower camp hostile to former GOP nominee Thomas Dewey.[62]

In the ensuing race for the Republican presidential nomination, Lodge won few friends among the conservative party faithful, who supported Taft without reservation and who dismissed Eisenhower's candidacy as a misguided attempt to place a moderate at the head of the ticket. Given this inclination, conservatives were understandably outraged when Lodge publicly accused the Taft forces in Texas of "stealing" delegates prior to the opening of the Republican National Convention in July. The charge stemmed from the pro-Taft Texas Republican State Executive Committee's decision not to recognize a disputed slate of Eisenhower delegates.[63]

Sensing a political opportunity, Lodge and the rest of the Eisenhower campaign brain trust made an issue of the "Texas Steal" during the July convention. At the insistence of Lodge, an amendment to the convention rules was drawn up forbidding contested delegates from voting to seat themselves. On a suggestion made by Representative Hugh Scott of Pennsylvania, the name "Fair Play Amendment" was adopted to give the measure a sense of moral urgency. The hope was that a successful introduction of such an amendment at the outset of the proceedings would establish a "winning psychology" for the Eisenhower forces, who entered the convention trailing Taft in delegates.[64]

The danger existed, however, that Taft would surrender every contested delegate to Eisenhower, thereby nipping in the bud the entire Fair Play Amendment strategy. "If they do that we are sunk," Lodge aide Maxwell Rabb told a journalist at the time. "The worst thing that could happen to us would be for them to concede us everything." Luckily for the Eisenhower camp, no such scenario developed. Taft stubbornly maintained he had won the disputed Texas delegation fairly and squarely. Nonetheless, the Ohio Republican did send out private feelers to Lodge requesting that a public vote on the issue be delayed or removed entirely from the convention schedule. In return, an assurance was given that contested delegates would get the opportunity to vote either in committee or on the floor once their own seats had been established. Lodge balked at such a deal. "I will not consort with evil," he loftily declared.[65]

The vote on the Fair Play Amendment went ahead as planned. The measure carried, 658–548, thus setting into motion Eisenhower's convention bandwagon. "As a result of that first victory on the floor," wrote *Boston Herald* reporter George Cabot Lodge in an unpublished account of the convention, "the Eisenhower organization won a number of wavering delegates; identified itself with a good moral cause; established the fact that they had the votes; dominated the next day's headlines; and seized the initiative."[66]

Indeed, Eisenhower went on to win the GOP nomination on the first ballot. In later years, Lodge argued that any compromise on the Fair Play Amendment would have resulted in the nomination's going to Taft. "The Eisenhower candidacy standing alone, could never have drawn 658 votes," he related. "Some other way had to be found to get the delegates to stand together. The 'fair play' amendment was it."[67]

Eisenhower's nomination was tremendously satisfying for Lodge. Not only had he played a prominent role in orchestrating the victory, but he had more importantly secured a place of influence for moderates like himself in top GOP policy-making circles, at least for the immediate future.

"Lodge pursued his dream with dogged determination," reported W. E. Mullins of the *Boston Herald* at the close of the convention. He "long since concluded that Taft's nomination would be disastrous to the party. He had no confidence in his colleague's capacity to be elected in November. He foresaw the spectacle of other Republican candidates being liquidated in the close states. He feared Taft's nomination would prolong the party's agony and even menace it with destruction as a national institution."[68]

Yet storm clouds were gathering over Lodge's own political horizon. One Massachusetts delegate, influential newspaper publisher Basil Brewer of New Bedford, an avid Taft supporter, became so enraged by the convention's proceedings and Lodge's part in them that he cast the sole dissenting vote against a motion that would have made the nomination unanimous for Eisenhower. "It was," noted Lodge biographer William J. Miller, "an act symbolic of further bitterness to come."[69]

Of more immediate concern was Lodge's tardiness in launching his own Senate reelection campaign. Drained by his exertions on behalf of Eisenhower, he simply failed to do the necessary organizational spadework required of an incumbent. A "senatorial contest in Massachusetts," political strategist Mason Sears once noted, "normally requires at least twelve months of campaigning. In this respect I would observe that Senator Lodge was so deeply involved in promoting General Eisenhower's candidacy for President that it was physically impossible for him to devote any time to his own candidacy until the last three months."[70]

Indeed, time did not appear to be on Lodge's side in 1952.

Chapter **FOUR**

★ ★ ★ ★

Kennedys on the Move

W HILE GOP presidential politics prevented Henry Cabot Lodge Jr. from spending much time in Massachusetts during the first eight months of 1952, no comparable limitations were placed on his challenger. Sensing an advantage, John F. Kennedy embarked on a whirlwind tour of the state, shaking as many hands, visiting as many factories, and attending as many rallies as he could. During one particularly hectic stretch in early May, he appeared at a "Ladies Night" in Peabody, spoke at a Baptist Church Council meeting in Taunton, attended a luncheon and reception for the Gold Star Mothers of Suffolk County in South Boston, posed for photographers at a Little League game in Milton, and dined at a Knights of Columbus gathering in Fitchburg.

Apart from a brief and uneventful sojourn to the Democratic National Convention in the third week of July, Kennedy devoted his every waking hour to campaigning in the Bay State. "Anybody who wants to know how I beat Lodge can look into it and he'd find I beat Lodge because I hustled," Kennedy later boasted.[1] That the Democratic hopeful labored tirelessly, there can be no doubt.

Subsisting on a steady diet of cheeseburgers and milkshakes that he procured from various roadside establishments, the candidate maintained a grueling campaign schedule that saw him make appearances in all 351 communities of the state. "He was on the move constantly for eight months," confirmed early Kennedy biographer Joe McCarthy, "visiting the larger cities [in the state] eight or nine times and each of the small towns at least once . . . and talking at meetings from early morning until late at night for seven days a week."[2]

Not even a serious back injury slowed him down. While on a campaign stopover at a Springfield fire station in May, Kennedy decided to mug for the cameras by sliding down a fire pole. "He landed with a jolt and doubled up with pain," recalled campaign staffer Larry O'Brien. "We hurried him to his hotel and called a doctor, who confirmed that Kennedy had aggravated his old back injury and would use crutches."[3]

Worried that the sight of such props would belie his image as a vigorous young candidate, Kennedy henceforward settled on the following routine before making a public appearance. "When he came to the door of a hall where he was scheduled to make a speech," remembered an aide, "he'd hand the crutches to one of us and throw his shoulders back and march down the aisle as straight as a West Point cadet. How he did it, I'll never know."[4]

Equally impressive was the diverse array of people that Kennedy attracted to his campaign. They ranged from graduates of elite colleges to blue-collar workers to suburban housewives, all sharing in the belief that the candidate brought something new and exciting to everyday political life. One such "true believer" was Robert P. Cramer of Williamstown, a sleepy academic community located in the northwestern corner of the state. A 1940 graduate of Williams College, Cramer had struck up a casual friendship with Kennedy in the late 1940s through mutual prep school acquaintances. "We seemed to hit it off from the very beginning," remembered Cramer, who worked at a paper company in Adams during this period.

> He was in the Congress at that time. And I went to visit with him both on the Cape and in Washington. Again, in 1952, when he was running for the U.S. Senate against Senator Lodge, he called and told me he didn't have anyone up in my area [western Massachusetts], and would I be willing to be his coordinator in the Berkshires [a region of western Massachusetts]. I told him, naturally, that I was very flattered and didn't have much experience in politics, but would be delighted to do anything I could to help out. I really felt that he was the kind of person that Massachusetts needed in government. . . . Here was a Harvard graduate, top scholar . . . independently wealthy, who wasn't afraid to speak his mind. No reflection meant on any previous candidates out of Boston, but you understand. They just hadn't projected a good image in western Massachusetts. So, the first thing I did was go down to the town hall and register as a Democrat.[5]

Not long afterward, Cramer began to contact friends in and around the Williamstown area that he knew had some connection with politics. From them he received names of local Democrats such as Robert Capeless of Pittsfield and Julius Calvi of North Adams, who potentially might be interested in building a Kennedy campaign organization in western Massachusetts. "So I got all these people together at a party at my house in Williamstown," Cramer later recalled, "and we all sat down with Jack, and of course we asked them if they would support Jack. I don't think we ever had a refusal. He was really well liked. I don't know how exactly his name got so well known up in the Berkshires, but even then he was very popular, and everybody seemed to get on the bandwagon."[6]

Kennedy had helped his own cause by making himself accessible to voters in western Massachusetts over the previous twelve months through a series of speaking engagements and public appearances. "I can remember Jack coming up to Pittsfield, and that area, and we went door to door in some of the towns," Cramer said. "Some of the little towns like Washington and Florida and Egremont, and a few places like that. I don't think they'd ever seen a Democrat campaigning up there before. . . . [Kennedy] was pretty good. He was clean, and he had a lot of literature. He'd go [up] to doors and he'd talk to, you know, knock and talk to people. . . . He was very personable, very presentable, and left a lot of literature at every doorstep."[7]

According to Robert Capeless, the former mayor of Pittsfield, it wasn't the organization of campaign secretaries in western Massachusetts that engendered public interest in Kennedy, but rather the attractive personality of the candidate himself. The secretaries "didn't make any difference in his campaign," Capeless maintained. "They would hire the hall for him when they were instructed or buy radio time. They would take care of things when he was coming to town like putting ads in the papers or providing a little platform for him to stand on. [Some secretaries] would boast, 'I brought about seven hundred people for Kennedy.' They didn't bring out seven hundred people. Give them a dull candidate and see if they would bring out seven hundred people."[8]

The same held true in other parts of the state. In Fall River, an industrial city located on the southeastern tip of Massachusetts, a bus driver by the name of Edward C. Berube became a committed Kennedy supporter when he witnessed the candidate give a campaign speech in French to a gathering of French Canadian voters. "I didn't know he was going to speak French, see," Berube reminisced years later. "He said a few words in French, how nice it was for him to be there, and he was looking forward to meeting everybody before he left. It was just maybe two or three sentences, but it went over terrific. And I looked at him, you know, and the French was very good. Of course, I'm French, but my mother was English, and I don't speak French too good. I don't understand very well, but I can make out. So I was very impressed with how he did, and this is how he won over the people."[9]

Another person "won over" by Kennedy was Stoneham resident Anna Mae Arsenault, a former telephone operator turned housewife in the early 1950s. "I was in my late thirties and not working," she later recalled. "I was actually not very interested in politics at the time, but [as a Kennedy volunteer] I spent many hours folding leaflets, sealing envelopes, and sorting mail. If the Kennedys were to be appearing in town or somewhere, a call would go out and some of us younger people would just gather there and be part of their entourage—that is, the people around them. That's how the Kennedys did it. They always had a lot of people around them. In those days the Kennedy name wasn't like it is today. They couldn't draw a crowd just by being there. They were very well organized."[10]

Arsenault had initially been drawn in to the campaign through the persuasive entreaties of her mother, Catherine Salvage, an active member of the Stoneham Democratic Town Committee. But it was only through meeting with the candidate herself during a local reception at Stoneham Town Hall that Arsenault became an unabashed Kennedy supporter.

"The first thing I remember was his piercing eyes," she said. "He looked right at you, and it seemed like he had a capacity to look at a lot of people but make it seem like he was looking right at you. He was very personable. I don't remember him discussing any political issues or issues of the day or anything like that. It was always, 'Thank you for coming,' or, 'My family is grateful to you.' Things like that. He wanted to say hello to everybody. We were just swept up into it."[11]

In such a context, it made little difference to voters such as Arsenault and Berube at what end of the ideological spectrum Kennedy stood; what counted was how favorably he came across personally. "If you talk with a thousand people evenly divided between liberals and conservatives," mused Kennedy supporter Robert Cramer, "you find that five hundred conservatives think that Jack is a conservative. It's because they want to think it. They want to think they belong with him."[12]

Kennedy's Boston campaign secretary, John E. Powers, observed: "Jack is the man who put a Brooks Brothers suit on the Democratic Party. You've heard the line that he's the kind of man that every elderly woman wants to mother and every young woman wants to marry. Well, he's also the kind [of] man that

Robert F. Kennedy reluctantly served as his brother's campaign
manager in 1952. "The main difference between our campaign
and others was that we did work," he later claimed. Courtesy of the
John F. Kennedy Library.

another man would like to go on a lion [hunt] with. When you have natural
attributes like that, you go sell them. You don't hide them."[13]

Adding to the candidate's charismatic appeal was the active and visible role
his family played in the campaign. As one Lodge supporter lamented, "I don't
worry about Jack Kennedy . . . it's that family of his . . . they're all over the
state."[14] While Joseph P. Kennedy preferred keeping out of the public eye to

avoid charges that he was manipulating his son's campaign, the rest of his family, without Edward M. Kennedy, who was serving a two-year hitch for the U.S. Army in France and Germany, eagerly threw themselves into the political fight. As previously noted, Robert Kennedy worked behind the scenes as campaign manager, but once, when his brother and other family members were unavailable for a scheduled campaign speaking engagement, the then-publicity-shy "Bobby" reluctantly filled in. His brief comments went as follows: "My brother Jack couldn't be here. . . . But if my brother Jack were here, he'd tell you Lodge has a very bad voting record. Thank you."[15]

Maintaining an appreciably higher profile than Robert Kennedy in the campaign were the candidate's three younger sisters, Eunice, Patricia, and Jean. "They were exactly like old-fashioned, burlesque pony ballet, wonderfully good looking girls, with their long legs and great manes of hair, attacking the voters sort of en masse," recalled Joseph Alsop, a nationally syndicated newspaper columnist assigned to cover the race.[16]

Indeed, when they were not traversing the main streets and back roads of Massachusetts on their brother's behalf, the "Kennedy women" could be found delivering stump speeches, supervising the distribution of campaign literature, ringing doorbells, and generally ingratiating themselves with the electorate. In one fourteen-hour period the sisters barnstormed the entire length of Cape Cod, making campaign stops at Falmouth, Bourne, Sandwich, Hyannis, South Yarmouth, Harwich, Orleans, Wellfleet, and Provincetown. "Those girls worked like peons," marveled Dave Powers. "When they campaigned in Framingham, they knocked on every door in town. If someone was out when they knocked on the door, they'd go back the next morning."[17]

Eunice Kennedy, in particular, became adept at engaging in this kind of retail politics. Campaigning at a furious pace several hours a day, she urged Democratic Party regulars "to get out the vote" for her brother. "John F. Kennedy has dedicated his life for the benefit of the people," she said. To many relatives and friends this sort of dedication was not surprising. "Eunice is a lot like me," John Kennedy once confided. "She's full of nervous energy. She's always calling me up asking if she can go here or there for me. She's just as competitive as the boys."[18]

Another family member who showed an aptitude for the rigors of political life was Ethel Skakel Kennedy, the wife of Robert F. Kennedy. Though several months pregnant with their second child, Ethel took it upon herself to be available for speaking engagements and political rallies throughout the campaign. In fact, the September night she gave birth to Joseph P. Kennedy II in a Boston delivery room, she found time to squeeze in a speech at Fall River,

A common sight: Kennedy sisters Jean and Eunice distributing campaign literature door to door. "Eunice is a lot like me," John Kennedy later confessed. "She's full of nervous energy. . . . She's just as competitive as the boys." Courtesy of the John F. Kennedy Library.

some forty miles away. "I'm just crazy about Jack, and I'm only an in-law," she told campaign audiences.[19]

As impressive as these efforts were, none could equal, in terms of sheer popular enthusiasm generated, the contribution made by Rose Fitzgerald Kennedy. Simply put, she was her son's most effective goodwill ambassador, as her eloquent speech, indefatigable charm, and understated feminine beauty captured the imagination of voters statewide. As one local newspaper put it, "Devoted to her family and its interests, Mrs. Kennedy has made the Congressman's campaign her campaign and has eagerly joined with him in his spirited fight for office. Anxious to tell the voting public about her son's qualifications for the Senate, she is personally contacting as many voters as possible."[20]

"Rose wowed them everywhere," acknowledged Dave Powers. "She greeted the Italians in the North End [of Boston] with a few words of Italian and told them how she grew up in their neighborhood. In Dorchester, she talked about her days at Dorchester High School. She showed them the card index file she kept when her kids were little to keep track of vaccinations and medical treatment, and dental work. At a high-toned gathering of women, she'd talk for a few minutes about Jack, and then she'd say, 'Now let me tell you about the new dresses I saw in Paris last month.' They loved her."[21]

Rose Kennedy was no amateur when it came to politics. As the daughter of former Boston mayor and U.S. congressman John "Honey Fitz" Fitzgerald, she had been taught at a young age how to be at ease in public and how to connect with voters; 1952 proved no exception. "She'd tell those people that she knew her son better than anyone, and she knew what kind of Senator he'd be," remembered campaign aide John E. Powers. "There would be a lot of Gold Star mothers in her audiences, and mothers who were in anguish about the Korean War; and she'd tell them that she knew what it was to lose a son in war. She was tremendous."[22]

Indeed, Rose "faltered" in a speech in Boston late in the campaign when she brought up the subject of Joseph P. Kennedy Jr. In a rare display of public emotion she "broke down and wept" after she told a Democratic forum audience that her son John "does not need to be told what war does to a family. He knows the sorrow and the grief that comes to the lonely mother, the grief-stricken bride and the heartbroken sister."[23]

Rose would also be crucial to the success of a series of public tea receptions held around the state in such locales as Worcester, Springfield, Holyoke, and Fall River that lent a much-welcomed air of refinement to the otherwise coldly efficient Kennedy political operation.

The "Kennedy teas" were a holdover from the 1946 congressional campaign. During that race, John Kennedy had made a concerted effort to court women voters by attending a number of house parties and neighborhood tea receptions throughout the Eleventh Congressional District. "The people would gather, and when Jack would come in, it was like a movie star making an entrance," recalled one campaign worker. "You could hear the women sigh."[24]

More along the lines of a social gathering than a traditional political rally, these campaign-organized events permitted the candidate to meet with members of the opposite sex in an intimate yet informal setting. Issues such as price inflation and the lack of affordable housing were discussed over generous helpings of tea and cookies. But mostly these affairs acted as a showcase for Kennedy's attractive personality, which proved disarming to many he came in contact with. "He had what we called a warm hand," remembered Thomas P. "Tip" O'Neill, "and the women would melt when he looked into their eyes."[25]

So popular did these teas become that when the candidate staged an open invitation reception at the Hotel Commander in Cambridge on the weekend before the election, over two thousand people showed up. "Before that tea the hair stylists were working twenty-four hours a day," noted campaign volunteer John Droney. "Every unmarried woman had that hope and dream that lightning would strike." Aside from the desire to be the next Mrs. Kennedy, another important factor was at work. Many of the attendees were working-class women of Irish immigrant descent who sought the social prestige of hobnobbing with a representative of arguably the most prestigious Irish American family in the country. "The mere association made them feel better about themselves," observed Kennedy family historian Doris Kearns Goodwin.[26]

In 1952 the teas continued to convey a convivial aura. Carefully planned by Pauline "Polly" Fitzgerald, a first cousin of Rose Kennedy, and Helen Keyes, a popular gym teacher from Dorchester, the affairs were a "frank play" for the women's vote, which one publication estimated was over 52 percent of the electorate in Massachusetts. "I know a lot of men thought we were wasting our time and just entertaining women who were going to vote for Jack anyway," recalled Fitzgerald. "I don't believe everyone was going to vote for him before they went. He was just a little Congressman and Lodge was a very attractive fellow. I think when they met [Kennedy] and heard him speak, they were impressed by him."[27]

To be sure, the Democratic challenger endeared himself to many prospective female voters by making a direct but simple appeal for their support. "In the first place," he told them, "for some strange reason, there are more women than men in Massachusetts, and they live longer. Secondly, my grandfather, the late John F. Fitzgerald, ran for the U.S. Senate [thirty-six] years ago against my opponent's grandfather, Henry Cabot Lodge, and lost by only thirty thousand votes in an election where women were not allowed to vote. I hope by impressing the feminine electorate that I can more than take up the slack."[28]

The procedure used for setting up the tea parties became equally straightforward. In every city or town where a reception was scheduled, Fitzgerald and Keyes recruited a locally popular Kennedy supporter, usually a male professional, to help organize the event. Commented Polly Fitzgerald: "It was difficult at that time to get a woman to work for you because housewives and other ladies, well, they didn't do this kind of thing; it was very unusual for women to

Rose Fitzgerald Kennedy (above right) and her son at one of the popular tea party receptions of the campaign. Remembered one campaign aide, "There would be a lot of
Gold Star mothers in her audiences, and mothers who were in anguish about the Korean War; and she'd tell them that she knew what it was to lose a son in war. She was
tremendous." Courtesy of the John F. Kennedy Library.

participate in politics at that time. The man we'd get from each community
would form a committee of fifty women who were prominent for one reason
or another, and we'd ask each of the fifty women to get in touch with ten people
to see if they would come to the tea and then ask each of those ten people if they
could think of ten more; in the end, you'd have five thousand people."[29]

Engraved announcements were mailed out but they called them invita-
tions "because [they] wanted to get it across that everyone was invited who
wanted to come." "When you think of some people," explained Dave Powers,
"who the only thing they ever find in the mail box is a bill and they find this invitation to go to a reception at a hotel and meet Rose Kennedy and the rest of
them—they'd put on their best hat and coat and be there."[30]

Even registered Republicans were encouraged to attend. When Remigia

Brooke, the wife of prominent GOP state operative and future U.S. senator Edward M. Brooke, learned about a tea being held near her home in Boston, she made a special point of going. "A friend came by and asked me to come to a tea for John Kennedy, who that year was running for the Senate against Mr. Lodge," she later told writer John Henry Cutler. "I like Mr. Kennedy very much, so why not go to his tea? When Mr. Lodge heard about it, Mr. Brooke said: 'That Remigia! She went to count Democrats for us Republicans!' Later, we saw Mr. Lodge and he laughed and asked me if I was still counting Democrats."[31]

Such an affirmative response, coming as it did from an unlikely source, was not uncommon. An estimated seventy-five thousand women, many from diverse socioeconomic and cultural backgrounds, went to these affairs, confirming the notion that a high level of interest existed.[32] Though most of the teas were concentrated in the Boston metropolitan area—not surprisingly, given the traditionally strong Democratic Party base there—a significant number were staged in populous outlying communities such as Lowell, New Bedford, Worcester, and Springfield. As always, their primary function lay in attracting as many potential female voters as possible.

"These tea parties that Kennedy is holding the length and breadth of the state appear to have many women, of all ages, quite excited about the young candidate," reported the *Haverhill Gazette,* a conservative daily located thirty miles north of Boston. "They ooh and they aah when you mention him, they tell you they think he is wonderful, they give every indication of yearning to run their fingers through his tousled hair. They never mention any qualifications that he may have or may lack for service in the Senate, but this would be too much to expect. All they seem to know or care about him is the fact that he's a handsome young male."[33]

At a reception in Lenox attended by over two thousand women, the local *Berkshire Eagle* noted that, in terms of sheer numbers, the event "was the greatest women's political rally ever staged in the area since women were given the voting franchise more than thirty years ago." In every sense, the paper concluded, the tea party was a success. "The Kennedys, who footed the bill, were satisfied; the women, most of whom were bedecked in Sunday's finest, enjoyed themselves; and several milliners and dress shop operators of the county, who were in attendance, were more than satisfied because [the tea] was responsible for an unusual end-of-the-summer run on hats, frocks, and shoes."[34]

A similar outpouring of enthusiasm greeted John Kennedy when he attended a scheduled tea in Swampscott later that month. Over six thousand women turned out to meet the candidate at the New Ocean House, a hotel along the rocky coastline of Boston's North Shore. "It was a beautiful day and a thoroughly successful one politically," the *Lynn Telegram-News* noted, "as the tremendous numbers of women demonstrated the political strength of 'Jack' Kennedy, whose family roots are imbedded in the governmental growth of the Bay State. . . . There were women of all ages, many who told the young aspirant to the Senate that they had voted for his grandfather, the late John F. Fitzgerald. There were bright young faces of pretty young women eager to help elect a young man with a brilliant mind and firm purpose."[35]

Most of the teas were held in large rented halls or "elegant" hotel ballrooms such as the Hotel Sheraton in Worcester and the Hotel Kimball in Springfield for the purpose of maximizing the number of people who could attend. "I always chose the halls," recalled tea party organizer Polly Fitzgerald. "It had to be not too big, but big enough. I got so I could assess the size we'd need. We always set it up the same way. A lot of people, mostly the men, thought we didn't need to rope off the areas, but we knew. They just channeled the reception line. If it was in a hotel, we'd use the hotel's coffee and tea and simple cookies. If it was in a hall, we'd discuss with the local people who might cater it. We'd try to find out if there was one firm who was especially friendly to the candidate and then use him."[36]

With his charismatic mother and sisters at his side, Kennedy usually began the affairs by thanking everyone in the room for coming, while expressing the hope that they would support his candidacy in November. Following these remarks, which on average lasted under ten minutes, the young Democrat and his family would work their way to the front of the reception line, where they would warmly greet every person in attendance. "A few women," a veteran journalist later wrote, "got so carried away with the graciousness of the Kennedy receiving line that they concluded it by bussing the candidate on the cheek."[37]

Afterward, each guest would receive in the mail a personalized note from John Kennedy thanking them for their support along with a reminder that they could render even greater service to the campaign by helping out on a local Kennedy-for-Senator committee. "Helping out" could involve answering phones, licking envelopes, handing out campaign fliers, or organizing house parties. Hundreds of volunteers were thus recruited at these events, prompting Robert Kennedy to comment, "We concentrated on the women because they do all the work in campaigns. Men just talk."[38]

Though issues such as domestic communist subversion, Soviet expansionism, and the high cost of living were touched upon, the primary focus of the teas centered on the candidate himself. As Cabell Phillips of the *New York Times* observed: "Unmarried, wealthy, Harvardishly casual in his dress, and with a distinguished war record in addition to his other attainments, he just about bracketed the full range of emotional interests of such an all-feminine group—maternal at one end and romantic at the other—irrespective of what it may have thought of his politics."[39]

As a result, Kennedy had no shortage of impassioned women supporters. "John Kennedy is the type of man who should be promoted in government life," gushed one woman attendee at a Swampscott reception in late September. "He is true and honest and aboveboard. He is a man with a purpose. I couldn't help but devote myself to his cause." Another admirer, Mrs. Mary Riley of Lynn, voiced the opinion that the Democrat was a sure bet for the U.S. Senate. "I know he is going to win this November," she said. "He's wonderful."[40]

This displayed enthusiasm for Kennedy's candidacy by women voters continued with the airing of two "Coffee with the Kennedys" morning television programs in the final weeks of the campaign. Designed to complement the existing tea party strategy, these half-hour shows accentuated Kennedy's appeal to voters of the opposite sex. Sitting on a plain living room sofa, Rose Kennedy began each telecast with a compelling personal account of why she felt her son deserved to be the next U.S. senator from Massachusetts. She mentioned his childhood accomplishments, his early interest in politics, and his extensive travels across Europe when his father served as the ambassador to the Court of St. James. "At the close of Mrs. Kennedy's intimate and interesting talk," wrote *Boston Globe* political columnist M. E. Hennessy, "the scene changed to the Congressman's private office on 44 Kilby St., where his sister [Hennessy did not specify which one] was busy answering phone calls at her brother's desk and transferring the calls to the Congressman," who thanked the callers for their interest in his campaign and promptly answered their inquiries about the prospects for world peace and his youthful appearance. Following this question-and-answer period, Kennedy "thanked the listeners for their courtesy in listening and asked those who had automobiles to volunteer their cars on election day for the transportation of voters to the polling place."[41]

To ensure the largest possible viewing audience, the Kennedy camp secured the cooperation of five thousand women volunteers in hosting "Coffee with the Kennedys" house parties when the program aired.[42] Hence, this was clearly a boon to his candidacy.

For his part, Henry Cabot Lodge Jr. publicly ridiculed the notion that the Kennedy teas and coffees were an effective campaign tactic. "I am told they are quite pleasant little affairs," he informed one audience, "and I'm sure they are non-fattening." Privately, he was less flippant. Fearing the women's vote was slipping away from him, the Republican lawmaker agreed late in the campaign to accompany his publicity-shy wife, Emily Sears, to a series of house parties organized by his supporters across the state. Cabell Phillips wrote, "At one I went to the introductions were a trifle stiff. There seemed to be some awe both of the Lodge name and the presence of a United States Senator. But the Senator wandered informally into the kitchen for a brief chat with the husbands gathered around the ice bucket, and then into the living room to meet their wives. In a few minutes, he was seated comfortably on the arm of a chair and talking casually about Korea, the Taft-Hartley Act and the prospect of developing New England water resources."[43]

In a further attempt to attract female voters, Lodge prevailed upon his sister-in-law, the glamorous Francesca Braggiotti, to come to Massachusetts to campaign on his behalf. The wife of Connecticut governor John Davis Lodge, Lodge's younger brother, Francesca Braggiotti had been born and raised in Italy, where she achieved a small measure of fame as a dancer and movie actress. Making campaign speeches and personal appearances around the state in 1952, she impressed observers with her quick wit, self-deprecating charm, and good looks. At a Columbus Day parade in East Boston, for example, a local reporter described her as being a "striking blonde" who drew "a warm round of applause from the crowd."[44] Whether her brother-in-law could achieve a similar level of enthusiasm among women voters on election day remained to be seen.

Of greater certainty was the response Kennedy could expect from Catholic voters statewide, in particular Irish Catholics. "After years of dutiful hat tipping to well-born Protestants," biographer Chris Matthews has concluded, "the Irish of Massachusetts were ready to elect an aristocrat of their own."[45] Indeed, Kennedy was a beneficiary of the ever-volatile Irish versus Brahmin issue that had dominated Bay State politics for over a century.

The origin of this ill will between the Irish Catholic community and the upper-class scions of Back Bay and Beacon Hill society dates back to the late 1840s, when the first wave of Irish immigrants arrived on these shores to escape the famine, disease, and poverty that was then afflicting their homeland. Clustered in big cities such as Boston, these Potato Famine Irish, who included in their ranks the maternal and paternal grandparents of John Kennedy, were greeted with hostility by the native Protestant inhabitants, or Yankees, as they were called. The latter saw the newcomers as threats to their jobs, religion, and established culture. Especially wary were the Brahmins, an elite propertied class whose name derived from the Indian term designating the highest priest order in Hindu culture. Brahmin families had a "distinguished past," some stretching all the way back to the original Massachusetts Bay Colony, and they were "fiercely determined" to defend their tradition-bound community from the supposed contaminating influence of the "immigrant tide."[46]

The high incidence of crime, unemployment, illiteracy, and public drunkenness among Irish Catholics seemed only to confirm Brahmin reservations. "The possibility that Irish-Catholics, with their alien culture and their detested religion, would ever be welcome or even admitted into the exclusive ranks of such a long-established social system was extremely unlikely," Boston historian Thomas H. O'Connor has remarked of the period.[47]

This social exclusion stirred up lasting animosity against the Brahmin class within the Irish Catholic community. Politically, this animosity found expression in the rhetoric of such Irish Catholic politicians as James Michael Curley, who declared that the Brahmin aristocracy was made up of "clubs of female faddists, old gentlemen with disordered livers, or pessimists croaking over imaginary good old days and ignoring the sunlit present." The son of Irish-born immigrants, Curley represented a militant second generation of Massachusetts-born citizens that grew up in the post–Civil War period and came of age politically at the turn of the century, a group that "had been reared in the combative environment of ward politics, and bred in the defiant atmosphere of clannish nationalism."[48]

Unlike the first generation, which had been taught to accept an inferior status under British colonial rule, this second generation had no such predilection and demanded greater social equality with the Brahmins. The latter proved unattainable; Brahmin bastions such as the Somerset and Algonquin clubs and the Harvard Corporation maintained a closed-door policy toward persons of Irish descent. Left with little means of recourse, these immigrant sons turned to politics to vent their anger and frustration. For politics required no advanced social standing, only numbers.

And the Irish Catholic community had the numbers by the turn of the century. Constituting over 40 percent of the population in Boston alone, the Massachusetts Irish represented an electoral force to be reckoned with and one that would dominate the local political scene for decades to come. "To a Yankee like Henry Adams," political historian Alec Barbrook later observed, it "must have seemed that the dangers of the collapse of the old civilization were very real and unavoidable."[49]

By 1952 a third generation of better-educated and more sophisticated Irish Catholic voters had emerged, yet the old animosities still persisted. When Irish Democratic Governor Paul A. Dever ran for reelection that year against Republican Christian A. Herter of Boston, he repeated an old refrain that John F. Fitzgerald had used against James Jackson Storrow in 1910. He publicly accused Herter of belonging to "an upper-crust political clique that through deliberate neglect had stifled the development of Boston."[50] That Herter was not a member of the Brahmin class made little difference. The mere inference that he might be was enough to cost the five-term U.S. congressman votes in the Irish Catholic community.

John F. Kennedy never resorted to such mudslinging in his Senate campaign, but then he didn't have to. His appeal lay in his being an "Irish Brahmin," someone who displayed the same outward characteristics of wealth and privilege that a real Brahmin possessed minus the Protestant heritage. By casting a ballot for Kennedy, third-generation Irish Catholic voters were, in the words of historian Richard J. Whalen, purging themselves of "lingering feelings of inferiority" brought about by a century of social ostracism.[51]

Henry Cabot Lodge Jr., who had in the past defeated such older, more seasoned Irish Catholic politicians as James Michael Curley, Joseph E. Casey, and David I. Walsh, was not unaware of his opponent's appeal in this regard. "Kennedy, on the other hand, has no record which would cause widespread dissatisfaction," a Lodge campaign memo reported. "He, therefore, reflects the true Democratic strength in Massachusetts much more than Curley and David I. Walsh did."[52]

Kennedy had already earned the praise of many Catholics statewide in 1950 for his well-publicized stand on the Barden Bill for federal aid to education. He insisted that the bill include a provision for transportation aid to parochial schools. When the provision was not included in the final bill, Kennedy joined the majority of the House Labor and Education Subcommittee in voting down the bill.

He later explained his vote as follows: "The issue of the church and state was never really present here. It was purely a question of providing funds to aid all children, no matter what school they went to. Direct aid to the parochial schools themselves, of course, would have been unconstitutional." Applauding his stand on the bill, *The Pilot,* the official newspaper of the Boston archdiocese, described Kennedy as a "White Knight."[53]

Though a prominent member of the "enemy" Yankee establishment, Lodge had also developed good relations with the Catholic community. His popular standing was due in no small part to his ability to take positions that were sensitive to the specialized needs and concerns of Catholic voters. In the Senate version of the federal aid bill, for example, the Republican lawmaker said he would support it only if funds were made available for parochial schools. This sensitivity to Catholic interests held true in matters dealing with immigration as well. Unlike his grandfather, Senator Henry Cabot Lodge Sr. of Massachusetts, who championed exclusionary literacy tests for immigrants, Lodge opposed legislation that restricted the number of foreign nationals, that is, non-Protestants, coming into the United States. Indeed, he took pains during the 1952 Senate race to let his Catholic constituents know that he did not support provisions in the McCarran-Walter Act that established strict quota limits on would-be immigrants from eastern and southern Europe, regions that were heavily Catholic in makeup.[54]

Also contributing to Lodge's favorable image among Catholics were the numerous acts of philanthropy he and his Episcopalian family had performed over the years for members of the Boston archdiocese. Whenever funds were needed for a charitable purpose such as the refurbishment of a local church like the Gate of Heaven in South Boston, the Lodges could be counted on to make a generous donation. The memories of such deeds stayed with Bay State Catholics a long time and prompted Joseph P. Kennedy Sr. to complain bitterly to a reporter in 1952 that all he ever heard when he was growing up was "how Lodge's grandfather had helped put the stained-glass window in to the Gate of Heaven Church in South Boston."[55]

Nor did these deeds go unrewarded at the ballot box. Despite highly publicized stands against immigration, Lodge's grandfather did surprisingly well in Catholic wards when he ran statewide in 1916 and 1922. Lodge himself could make a similar claim with election victories over such formidable Irish Catholic opponents as Curley, Casey, and Walsh. In 1946 the Republican lawmaker even did his grandfather one better by carrying the predominantly Catholic city of Boston against David I. Walsh, an unusual feat for a Yankee politician of that era to accomplish.[56]

The challenge then facing Lodge in 1952 was whether he could come close to matching his earlier success among Catholic voters. Given Kennedy's appeal as an "Irish Brahmin" and his pro-Catholic voting record, this would be no easy task.

One ethnic group that Kennedy did draw skepticism from was Jewish American voters who feared the Democrat held anti-Semitic leanings. This belief stemmed mainly from Joseph P. Kennedy's well-deserved reputation as an anti-Semite. While serving as ambassador to Great Britain, the elder Kennedy had reportedly informed the German ambassador, Dr. Herbert von Dirkson, that he "understood" Nazi Germany's policy of racial persecution against the Jews. To embassy aide Harvey Klemmer, the ambassador was even more explicit: "Well, [the Jews] only have themselves to blame, they brought it on themselves." He later disdainfully noted that President Franklin Roosevelt had surrounded himself with a "crowd" of Jews and communists.[57]

"As a result," recalled Kennedy campaign worker Phil David Fine, "many of the sins of the father were visited on the son; and if you talked to some of the [Jewish American] community leaders, they would generally talk to you in negative terms."[58] Adding to Kennedy's difficulties was the traditional ethnic antagonism between Jewish Americans and Irish Americans.

For decades Jewish Americans living in Boston and surrounding areas had been "preyed" upon by gangs of Irish American street toughs from Dorchester, South Boston, and Charlestown who were roused to violence by the radio sermons of notorious anti-Semite Father Charles E. Coughlin of the Shrine of the Little Flower in Royal Oak, Michigan. One of their victims, Nicholas Henthoff, an impoverished tailor's son who went on to write for the *New Yorker* and become president of the American Civil Liberties Union, later recalled the humiliation of being beaten up by an Irish gang on his way to Hebrew school. "The shock and pain," Henthoff wrote, "are such that it takes a few moments for me to taste the blood and feel the space where, a second ago, there had been a tooth. [The gang's] leader, rubbing his fist with satisfaction, waits for a revengeful lunge and is not surprised when it doesn't come. So few of these kikes fight back. He and his sturdy companions move on, guffawing."[59] Indeed, such incidents were "horrible" but not uncommon in the supercharged, anti-Semitic climate of the 1930s and 1940s.

John Kennedy had opened himself up to charges of anti-Semitism in 1949, when he introduced a proposal in Congress to cut foreign aid to the Near East. Israel would have been particularly hurt by such cutbacks, and this led many Jewish American voters to interpret the move as anti-Israel. In his own defense, Kennedy said he did not intend to single out any one country in his proposal, only an entire region.[60]

Jewish American voters remained skeptical, however. Despite having responded "resoundingly to the message of social justice explicit in the Democratic party of Franklin Delano Roosevelt," the Jewish American community over the years was not averse to supporting liberal Republicans such as Lodge. For in Lodge they had a senator who supported issues important to Jewish American voters, such as the establishment of an independent state of Israel. Moreover, Lodge was an early and vocal advocate of giving "every material assistance" to the "new nation." "The army of Israel," he told a Boston audience of Jewish war veterans in 1948, "is sure to win, because all its men know what they are fighting for, and believe in what they know."[61]

Lodge continued to remind voters of this established track record in 1952, while instilling doubts about his opponent's commitment to the Jewish American cause. A week before the election, several reprints of a 1949 article, which had originally appeared in the *Jewish Weekly Times* under the provocative headline "German Documents Allege Kennedy held Anti-Semitic Views," were distributed by his campaign in Jewish American neighborhoods throughout the Boston area.[62] The article focused on the anti-Semitic remarks of Joseph P. Kennedy and mentioned nothing of his congressman son. Still, the intended implication was clear; John Kennedy was no different from his father.

In a counterattack the following day, the Kennedy campaign sent out 14-by-17-inch broadsheets with the inscription "Shame on You Mr. Lodge. You Endorse Senator McCarthy of Wisconsin and You Use His Tactics." "As a matter of fact," Fine claimed, "my recollection is that we hired the same goon squad [as Lodge had] to pass them out so we sent them to the same place" where the reprints of the inflammatory 1949 article were initially delivered.[63]

The efforts to reverse Kennedy's anti-Semitic image did not end there. A "blatant offer" of a financial nature was made to the Jewish American community in the form of a fifty-thousand-dollar donation to the Massachusetts Jewish Philanthropies from the Joseph P. Kennedy Jr. Foundation. Lavish ads were purchased in Jewish American newspapers extolling Kennedy's commitment to Israel along with published letters of endorsement from such prominent national Jewish American leaders as Benjamin G. Browdy of the Zionist Organization of America and U.S. Congressman Arthur G. Klein of New York. "KENNEDY, CHAMPION OF HUMAN RIGHTS!" screamed the banner headlines accompanying the ads.[64]

Personal meetings were also arranged between the candidate and influential members of the local Jewish American community such as Jackson J. Holtz, state commander of the Jewish Veterans of America, and Dewey D. Stone, the national vice president of the Zionist Organization of America, to dispel anti-Semitic fears. "Remember," he told them, "I'm running for the Senate, not my father."[65] To emphasize this point, Kennedy recruited Democrats with long-standing good relations with the Jewish American community such as Franklin Roosevelt Jr. and John McCormack to come into the Jewish American sections of Roxbury, Chelsea, and Dorchester and speak on his behalf.

McCormack, who was known as "the Rabbi" for his legislative efforts on behalf of Jewish American voters, particularly proved helpful. Addressing a large Boston rally, the senior lawmaker told a mostly Jewish American gathering that their concerns regarding Kennedy's alleged anti-Semitism were unwarranted. "I want you to know," he lectured, "there was a movement on foot in the Congress of the United States to strike out of the foreign aid bill money

Kennedy warmly receives Franklin Roosevelt Jr. and John McCormack in late October 1952. Roosevelt and McCormack were effective in allaying concerns among Jewish American voters that Kennedy was like his anti-Semitic father. Courtesy of the John F. Kennedy Library.

for Israel. And I looked around Congress for a man with courage and fortitude and stamina who would stand up. And I found young Jack Kennedy, and I gave him this amendment and I said, 'Jack, offer this amendment. It will cut the budget some, but we will save the remainder of the money for Israel.' And by offering the amendment he saved the remainder for Israel."[66]

The discussed incident was completely fabricated, but the Jewish American audience "bought the McCormack theory and story *in toto*." An appreciative Kennedy never forgot the gesture despite the many political differences he had had with McCormack over the years. "When the chips were down," he later told U.S. Congressman Thomas P. "Tip" O'Neill, McCormack "was in the line of fire for me because I was a Democrat. . . . He did something I never would have done for him."[67]

A common campaign stop was Boston's G & G Delicatessen on Blue Hill

Avenue, the epicenter of the state's Jewish American community, which boasted a total population of over two hundred thousand. Here Jewish Americans from all walks of life huddled over plates of kosher foods to discuss business deals, the latest gossip, and not least important of all, politics. According to Hillel Levine and Lawrence Harmon, historians of Boston's Jewish American community, Kennedy could often be seen at the establishment making "eye contact" and munching french fries "smothered in kishke grease with the best of them." Not to be outdone, Henry Cabot Lodge Jr. arranged for Republican presidential candidate Dwight D. Eisenhower to accompany him to the G & G when the latter was making a campaign swing through the state in early November.[68]

Yet when it came to courting Jewish American voters, no one could match the energy, drive, and determination of Kennedy. "Your continuous fight for aid to Israel, and your persistent battle for the rights of minorities," lauded Zionist leader Dewey Stone of Brockton in a published letter, "entitle you to the full and wholehearted support of the people of Massachusetts—for we know as Jews and Americans that the interests of Israel and of our country for the freedom and security of tomorrow are one."[69] Whether other Jewish American voters concurred with this sentiment would remain unknown until election day.

By summer's end, all the elements were in place for Kennedy to make a competitive run at Lodge's Senate seat. With the aid of his younger brother Robert and his father's thick wallet, the Democrat had built a highly effective campaign organization that allowed him to make inroads among women and Jewish American voters statewide as well as take tentative steps toward solidifying his support among Irish Catholics. "While it's a long road to November," reported the *Boston Herald* in late July, "it already has become evident that the toughest slugfest along the thorny path to Massachusetts ballot boxes will be fought by Senator Lodge and Rep. Kennedy in quest of U.S. Senate laurels." Describing the race as "nip and tuck," the paper went on to predict that voters would make a decision in the contest "independent of the presidential battle that overshadows Senate races in most states."[70] Given all the time and energy Lodge had spent campaigning for Eisenhower over the previous eight months, this was very bad news indeed.

Chapter FIVE

Enter Lodge, Exit Brewer

H ENRY CABOT LODGE JR. did not start actively campaigning until after Labor Day 1952. Why the Republican lawmaker waited until this late date to begin his reelection effort has long been a source of speculation. According to longtime Kennedy retainers Kenneth O'Donnell and Dave Powers, Lodge was guilty of the cardinal sin of politics: overconfidence. "He predicted that he would win by 300,000 votes and sent word to Ambassador Kennedy, through mutual friend Arthur Krock of *The New York Times,* that Jack's campaign would be a waste of money," O'Donnell claimed years later.[1]

While tantalizing and suggestive, O'Donnell's charge cannot be substantiated. A check of existing documentation fails to show that Lodge ever had a conversation with Krock or any other newspaper reporter in which he boasted of an easy victory. Indeed, the incumbent Massachusetts senator went out of his way during this period to tell interviewers that the contest was shaping up to be a "horse race." It is a position he later reiterated to historian Doris Kearns Goodwin. "From the beginning," he explained, "I knew it would be much harder than it had been against Curley, Casey and Walsh, for the people had nothing against Kennedy as they did against all the others. All along, I always knew if there came a man with an honest, clean record who was also of Irish descent, he'd be almost impossible to beat."[2]

Though Lodge did take a brief vacation to the Virgin Islands with his family shortly after the Republican National Convention in July, he nevertheless remained politically active the rest of the summer as chairman of Eisenhower's

Henry Cabot Lodge Jr. hits the campaign trail. Lodge got a late start because he was busy orchestrating Dwight Eisenhower's upset victory at the Republican National Convention in July. Courtesy of the Massachusetts Historical Society, Boston.

campaign advisory committee. "I recognized that I had started campaigning too late," Lodge later conceded, "but I really felt that . . . with my own attention back on Massachusetts, I could pull it off."[3]

To accomplish the latter feat, Lodge opted for a strategy of direct confrontation. He publicly challenged Kennedy to a series of debates to be held at various locations around the state "on the issues which so seriously affect this state and nation."[4] For his part, Kennedy was not averse to debating his senatorial opponent. Confidence in his own ability as an orator and an unwillingness to be seen as ducking a challenge undoubtedly accounted for this attitude.

The first debate took place on the night of September 16 at a junior high school auditorium in Waltham, an industrial city ten miles west of Boston. Before an overflow crowd of one thousand enthusiastic partisans and a radio audience of thousands of others, the two candidates addressed the topic "Issues Facing the Democratic and Republican Parties in the Coming Election."

Though a *Boston Herald* reporter described the proceedings as a "genteel political duel," the event was not without its share of verbal "fireworks."[5]

Indeed, a poised and confident-sounding Kennedy elicited the evening's biggest round of applause when he reprimanded Republicans for being excessively critical of the Democratic Party's record of domestic achievement over the previous two decades in the fields of social security and civil rights. "If we are to be held responsible for everything that went wrong," he declared, "we must be credited with everything that went right." Moreover, Kennedy asked rhetorically, "What hope for a better world lies in the leadership of [the Republican Party] which has opposed so much progressive legislation, foreign and domestic, for the last [twenty] years?"[6]

In his rebuttal, Lodge appeared taken aback by his challenger's clever yet spirited attack on the GOP. "I don't spend much time bemoaning the past," he said. "I agree one trouble with some Republicans is that they look back too much. There are good and bad features in both parties. Party sponsorship of a bill is not important. Politics is not a football game. I am not a narrow partisan. . . . If you send me back to the Senate, I will continue to work with men of good will regardless of party on all propositions that have merit." While reasoned and eloquent, Lodge's response failed to arouse the kind of raw emotional power his opponent's glib one-liners had registered. Remarked Kennedy staffer Ken O'Donnell, "You could feel the air going out of the Lodge people in the audience. I stood backstage watching Lodge nervously squeezing and flexing his hands behind his back, and I imagined him thinking, 'Why did I have to get a Democrat like this fellow?'"[7]

Newspaper coverage of the debate was more impartial. The local *Waltham News-Tribune* described the event as a "gentlemanly, tranquil forum" that was a "highly interesting exposition of opposition views that covered a wide range of national issues." The *Boston Globe* reported the debate was "extremely well-received" and reminded some of the Lincoln-Douglas presidential debates of a century before. "What reminded them," the paper noted, "were two statues of Lincoln and Washington, one on each side of the stage. Around the necks of Lincoln and Washington were draped cords connecting the loudspeakers."[8]

The *Boston Herald* offered that the tone of the debate "was polite enough to do credit to a Boston dining room." Perhaps the most honest and heartfelt appraisal of the event came from an attending Waltham resident who remarked, "I liked 'em both." The latter comment could not have come as encouraging news to Lodge. He had entered the debate hoping to knock down his younger, more inexperienced challenger a peg or two politically. Instead, Kennedy proved his equal throughout the course of the evening. Lodge may

Lodge and Kennedy listen intently to the moderator during a debate in Waltham on September 16, 1952. "Isn't this a hell of a way to make a living?" Lodge asked his opponent before the debate. Courtesy of the Massachusetts Historical Society, Boston.

have inadvertently summed up his own feelings on the matter when he accidentally crossed paths with Kennedy just before the debate. "Isn't this a hell of a way to make a living?" he asked his Democratic opponent.[9]

Though both candidates would debate again in October, this time on a televised public affairs program broadcast live out of New York City, there was apparently no interest on Lodge's part to stage a rematch in Massachusetts. Kennedy's strong performance in Waltham, in which he clearly matched his older and more distinguished rival, saw to that. To regain the political initiative, Lodge turned to the one issue where he thought his Democratic challenger to be most vulnerable: the latter's congressional absentee record.

Citing figures that showed Kennedy had missed more than half his roll-call votes over the previous six years, Lodge in late September took his opponent to task for "ducking every controversial issue in Congress," including tax relief, price controls, and immigration quotas, and for being a part-time legislator. The Senate, he asserted, "is a full time job, and one third of a Senator is no good." While essentially accurate, Lodge's charge failed to mention that

Kennedy had been unavailable for the majority of these roll-call votes because of poor health. "Now," Lodge later admitted, "I knew that he'd been sick a lot and I didn't like capitalizing on that, but I also knew that he had traveled a lot all over the world, so I didn't feel too guilty about it."[10]

To neutralize the absenteeism issue, Kennedy made brilliant use of Lodge's own woeful attendance record in the previous year when the Republican had been crisscrossing the country on behalf of Eisenhower. Citing statistics from the *Congressional Record,* Kennedy took out full-page newspaper advertisements showing how Lodge had been "ABSENT 98 out of 129 Roll-Call Votes in 1952."[11]

Supplying Kennedy with the needed "opposition research" to counter Lodge's charge of absenteeism was campaign aide Timothy Reardon Jr. A former advertising man and college football teammate of Joseph P. Kennedy Jr., Reardon was tapped early in the 1952 fight to compile an inventory of every public statement and vote Lodge had made during the course of his long career in the Senate. Entitled "Lodge's Dodges," Reardon's fully documented 162-page study provided Kennedy ammunition for the coming "two-front assault" on the incumbent Republican over the next two months. Observed Kennedy biographer Christopher Matthews: "It would appeal to the regular Democratic voter by showing Lodge as overly conservative on domestic issues and to anti-Communist conservatives in both parties by painting Lodge as a shirker in the global struggle against Russia and Red China."[12]

On the former count, Kennedy had already been active in downgrading his opponent's performance. "There is not only a crisis abroad but there is a crisis here at home in Massachusetts," the Democratic challenger had warned voters in his April 6 campaign announcement. "Our citizens who are out of work can testify to that out of their own experience. Our competitive industrial position with other states has been weakened. Unemployment, particularly in our textile and shoe manufacturing centers [read Lowell, Lawrence, Fall River, and Brockton], is on the increase." After suggesting that his political rival lacked the "definite goals" and "vigorous leadership" necessary to represent the state effectively in the U.S. Senate, Kennedy punctuated his remarks with a promise that, if elected, he would not waver in protecting Massachusetts economic interests.[13] "HE WILL DO MORE FOR MASSACHUSETTS," his campaign ads henceforward proclaimed, with the unspoken assurance that Kennedy would save existing manufacturing jobs in the state.

The notion that the Commonwealth was in a serious state of economic decline and that Lodge had done nothing as senator to correct the situation became a major theme of Kennedy's subsequent campaign. Since the end of

World War II, the leading industrial sectors of the state's economy had declined significantly owing to a combination of factors: cuts to the national defense budget due to demobilization, rising labor costs brought on by unionization, and stiff competition from the "cheap labor" South.

During the peak wartime production years of 1944 and 1945, for example, the combined total of industries in the state employed 711,727 and 667,551 persons respectively. These figures dropped to 585,776 by 1951.[14] Compounding the situation was the return of several thousand discharged servicemen to Massachusetts in search of jobs. Indeed, the departure of manufacturing jobs from Lowell, Lawrence, Peabody, Brockton, Fall River, and New Bedford to the South and other nonunionized parts of the country became a sore point for many state residents, and one that Kennedy deftly sought to exploit in stump speeches and in television appearances along the campaign trail.

"This State has lost much in the last few years," the young Democrat told a Boston television audience in early October. "We have seen our predominant position in cotton textiles whittled down by the competition of low-wage areas in the South. At one time we manufactured almost one out of every three pairs of shoes made in the United States. Today we make less than one of every five." As a congressman, Kennedy had voted to cut fourteen million dollars from a Tennessee Valley Authority (TVA) appropriation because of the belief it would give southern industries an unfair economic advantage in the form of cheap energy costs over its New England counterparts. "I do not believe that we should contribute our taxes to the support of an attempt to ruin us economically," he argued.[15]

The TVA funding vote was played up by Kennedy's campaign in newspaper ads as evidence of the candidate's overall determination to protect Massachusetts industry. In turn, Lodge was accused of shirking his duty on the issue. Interestingly enough, an examination of the Republican lawmaker's voting record during this period reveals that he had voted on two separate occasions significantly to reduce funding to federal projects designed to give cheap energy to competing out-of-state industries. Yet these votes were forgotten in the heat of the campaign as Lodge responded to his opponent's attacks by charging that Kennedy, along with Governor Paul Dever and Democratic House Majority Leader John McCormack should have had sufficient political clout to, as conservative *Boston Herald* columnist W. E. Mullins put it, "make a fight to protect our industry unnecessary."[16]

Rhetoric aside, on this issue, as with most dealing with labor and domestic economic concerns, there was little in the way of substance separating the two candidates. "Rarely in politics have hunter and quarry so resembled each other," historian and Kennedy biographer James MacGregor Burns has noted.[17] Both candidates favored increased spending on federal social programs, a continuation of postwar price controls, a higher minimum wage, better housing, and rent control. The one domestic issue over which there was significant disagreement was the Taft-Hartley Act of 1947, which outlawed specific unfair labor practices—including the closed shop and secondary boycotts—and permitted the president to delay strikes that posed a threat to the security and welfare of the nation. Kennedy opposed the Republican-sponsored measure, while Lodge supported it.

"The actual fact is—and I say this with restraint—this bill would in its present form strike down in one devastating blow the union shop, industry-wide bargaining with restraints and limitations as to make it ineffectual," admonished Kennedy at the time of the law's passage. Even more ominous from the congressman's perspective was the possibility that such repressive labor legislation would set off "a tide of left-wing reaction" throughout the country.[18] In such a worst-case scenario, the very survival of the free enterprise system would be placed in jeopardy.

For the purposes of the Senate race, however, Kennedy managed to put a local spin on the issue by linking Taft-Hartley to the loss of manufacturing jobs to the South. "To a large extent," he argued, "it is this act which has blocked the effort of the textile unions to organize the South and has left the New England mills with the unfavorable pay differential which is a most serious handicap today."[19]

To bring this message to voters, Kennedy targeted communities hard hit by the ravages of unemployment and industrial decline through a series of carefully staged personal appearances and an extensive media advertising campaign. Places such as Lowell, Lawrence, Fall River, Springfield, Worcester, and Pittsfield topped his list. Not only were these cities in the throes of economic recession, but a sizable segment of their populations consisted of unionized workers who could be counted upon to be less than enthusiastic about the restrictive Taft-Hartley legislation.

Pittsfield is a prime example. Located in the heart of the Berkshires, a scenic region of western Massachusetts that borders upstate New York, the once thriving city of fifty-five thousand had fallen on tough economic times since the end of World War II. Joblessness soared as many of the textile mills that had helped transform Pittsfield from an "isolated mountain town" into a prosperous industrial city in the late nineteenth century either closed their doors or "suspended operations." Causing further economic distress was an announcement by General Electric in early 1952 that it intended to build a new $25 million transformer plant in Rome, Georgia. The company already had a transformer plant in Pittsfield that employed over ten thousand people, approximately three out of every five employees in the city. Despite company claims to the contrary, the prevailing local fear was that G.E. intended to pull out entirely from Pittsfield and head south, where the siren's call of lower wages and little unionization beckoned.[20]

Kennedy did his best to exploit such fear. In June he publicly attacked G.E. for seeking a $25 million tax amortization certificate from the federal government for construction of the proposed Georgian plant. In a published letter to Henry Fowler, national production defense administrator, he argued that the granting of such a tax concession would encourage the "migration" of yet another New England industry to the South, "where labor can be hired more cheaply and companies can escape—at least temporarily [thanks to Taft-Hartley]—from the principles of trade unionism." Pittsfield, he noted, was "already suffering" from a "labor surplus." "What I fear," he warned, "is that with completion of the new plant at Rome, the Pittsfield plant will be closed down or its activities sharply curtailed. It would appear to me that the company should not be encouraged to move out of Pittsfield by the granting of tax favors by the federal government." Brushing aside assurances from G.E. management that the company had no plans to relocate its Pittsfield operation, Kennedy claimed that existing "evidence" suggested otherwise. "For instance," he asserted, "the projected employment at Rome is approximately the same percent employment at Pittsfield. After the peak demand for transformers is reached, would it not be possible for General Electric to close down at Pittsfield and supply its normal need from Rome?" Kennedy concluded his remarks by urging the NPD administrator not to grant G.E. tax relief until the facts in the case were "thoroughly heard and pondered."[21]

Echoing the Massachusetts congressman's sentiments was Pittsfield Democratic mayor Robert T. Capeless, Kennedy's campaign coordinator for Berkshire County. Capeless exhorted local union officials to protest the company's plans to representatives in Washington. "The threat posed by the plan," he declared, "is of no less concern to me as then it is to you and I am agreed that we should do all in our power to save ourselves from the harmful effects that might flow from it." One of the "harmful effects" included a "raid" by the South on northern industry, thanks in part to the "favorable position" the South enjoyed in the matter of federal expenditures. "New England tax dollars," he maintained, "have been utilized in part to build up the south to a point where it has a competitive advantage over New England to the extent that it can lure away the very industries which created the tax money in the first place." Kennedy, he added, "well expressed" this idea in Congress, and the issue "bears repeating in Washington as often as possible."[22]

In point of fact, Kennedy repeated this argument at a campaign appearance in nearby Lenox in early September. According to the local *Berkshire Eagle,* he told supporters that Massachusetts was receiving "only a fraction" of the federal aid due her, despite contributing "about five percent of the federal revenue." Southern states, he emphasized, got back far more in federal aid than they paid in taxes "despite the fact that they have been the leaders in resisting unions and minimum wage laws."[23]

Though the federal government granted G.E. the tax amortization benefit it desired in July, Kennedy's opposition helped cement his reputation as a "friend" of labor. Indeed, union newspapers across the state went out of their way to praise Kennedy's pro-labor voting record. A typical example came from the *New England Teamster,* a trade unionist monthly published in Lynn, an industrial community just north of Boston. "Kennedy," the paper exclaimed, "has fought the Taft-Hartley Act from the time it was introduced, and as a member of the House Labor Committee he has opposed all other measures to restrict the workingman in the exercise of his constitutional rights. There never has been any doubt in the minds of Massachusetts trade unionists as to where John Kennedy stands on labor-management issues. He's always been four-square for a fair deal for the worker and his family."[24]

As a result, Kennedy received the endorsement of every major union in the state from the International Brotherhood of Electrical Workers to the American Federation of Labor. At the same time, he portrayed his Republican opponent as being antiunion for his support of Taft-Hartley. "It is not understandable," he charged in a campaign press release, "how a Senator from the industrial state of Massachusetts could align himself with those who fathered a bill aimed at hurting his state and aiding some other section. When my opponent voted for the Taft-Hartley act, he and his friends closed the doors for textile workers here." Newspaper ads were also taken out by the Kennedy campaign, decrying the fact that Lodge "cast three votes FOR the Taft-Hartley Law and each one of them was a blow against New England textile industry."[25]

Lodge strenuously took issue with this characterization. Voting for Taft-Hartley, he told voters in a televised speech, had more to do with upholding the "health and safety" of ordinary citizens than any alleged scheme to weaken organized labor, thus inviting unfair economic competition from the South.

Lodge addresses workers at Fore River Shipyard in Quincy in late October 1952. Lodge had badly undermined his labor support by voting for the restrictive Taft-Hartley legislation in 1947, a decision of which Kennedy was only too willing to remind voters. Courtesy of the Boston Public Library, Print Department.

Kennedy, he said, "knows very well that my reason for voting in favor of the Taft-Hartley law was solely for one section which he himself once favored—that section which protects the Massachusetts public against nation-wide strikes which endanger their health and safety." A nationwide coal strike, he contended, had the potential of closing down all Massachusetts factories, schools, homes, and hospitals. "Protection of the public against this type of strike must rest in the Federal Government because it crosses state lines. I can see how a labor leader in the coal mines of Pennsylvania might oppose this provision, but surely no Massachusetts friend of labor is justified in doing so."[26]

On the anticommunism front, Kennedy was even more strident in his criticism of Lodge. "I'm going to use the same kind of stuff" that was used against Claude Pepper, he informed fellow Democrat George Smathers of Florida shortly before announcing his Senate candidacy. "I'm going to run an attack kind of campaign." Smathers had registered the political upset of 1950 by accusing his Democratic primary opponent, incumbent U.S. Senator Claude Pepper, henceforth known as the "Red Pepper," of being "an apologist" for Soviet dictator Joseph Stalin.[27] While Kennedy refrained from publicly making such outlandish statements about Lodge, he nonetheless did not shy away from portraying his opponent as being "soft" on communism.

How anticommunist a politician was had become the predominant concern of American voters by 1952. Since the end of World War II, relations had deteriorated between the United States and the Soviet Union, wartime partners in the "Grand Alliance" against fascism and leaders of the Western and communist blocs respectively. Disputes concerning foreign aid, war reparations, arms control, unsettled national boundaries, and the organization of postwar governments in Germany and Eastern Europe had resulted in a "Cold War." Americans now viewed their former allies not as trusted friends but as ruthless purveyors of "Red Fascism," a popular notion that suggested Russian expansionism was no different from the acts of aggression Nazi Germany had performed on Europe a decade earlier. Events seemed to confirm these fears. Beginning in the late 1940s, the Soviets installed puppet governments in Eastern Europe, cracked down on all internal dissent, exploded a nuclear device, and supported the communist takeover of mainland China under the leadership of Mao Tse-tung.

The most provocative action of all occurred on June 24, 1950. Without warning, Soviet-backed North Korean forces attacked south of the thirty-eighth parallel in a bold attempt to topple the weak, U.S.-backed Republic of Korea. Unwilling to see South Korea go the way of China and Eastern Europe, President Harry S. Truman committed U.S. combat troops to repel the invasion. In the months of fierce bloodletting that followed, American soldiers went about the grim business of fighting a limited defensive war against a determined communist opponent whose strength was augmented by at least two hundred thousand Chinese "volunteer" troops.[28] By the start of the 1952 campaign season, U.S. and communist forces were bogged down in a military stalemate with no foreseeable end in sight.

If events abroad convinced many Americans of an external communist threat, events at home suggested the existence of an internal communist threat. In 1948 a former senior State Department official named Alger Hiss stood accused of passing on classified government documents to the Soviets in the 1930s. The charge originated from Whittaker Chambers, a *Time* magazine editor who claimed to have once been a courier in a domestic Soviet spy ring. Hiss, a former law clerk to Supreme Court Justice Oliver Wendell Holmes and president of the Carnegie Foundation for International Peace, denied the allegations under oath before a federal grand jury. But corroborating evidence produced by Chambers discredited Hiss's testimony. Investigators, led by Congressman Richard M. Nixon of California, were taken to Chambers's Maryland farm, where they were shown a hollowed-out pumpkin containing microfilms of confidential government documents. Chambers explained that the "Pumpkin Papers" had been given to him by Hiss in the late 1930s to forward on to Soviet agents.[29] Unable to refute the allegations, Hiss was convicted of perjury, the statute of limitations having run out for an espionage charge, and sentenced to a five-year prison term.

The Hiss case sent shock waves throughout American society. Never in recent public memory had such a distinguished citizen, so closely linked to the so-called liberal, internationalist, eastern establishment, been exposed as a traitor. Republicans, eager since 1932 to win back the White House from the Democrats, seized upon the ruling as proof that Soviet agents had infiltrated the State Department and other executive branch agencies. The Truman administration, which in 1947 introduced a comprehensive Employee Loyalty Program to screen potential security risks from sensitive federal government areas, was now accused of harboring subversives and being insufficiently anticommunist.[30]

Suddenly the Soviet development of the atomic bomb, the "loss" of mainland China, and the invasion of South Korea took on newer, more sinister meanings. These perceived American setbacks were no longer seen as the result of complex geopolitical forces but as a product of an international communist conspiracy. Who lost China? "Red" traitors like Hiss, of course, who undermined American interests while sitting in the highest councils of power. Republican Senator Joseph R. McCarthy of Wisconsin, who was destined to play a singular role in the 1952 Massachusetts Senate race, became particularly adept at advancing this argument.

In February 1950 McCarthy gained national attention by telling a Wheeling, West Virginia, audience that he had in his possession a list of 205 State Department employees who were card-carrying members of the Communist Party. In the weeks and months that followed, McCarthy changed that figure enough times to indicate that he had no idea whether the foreign policy–making agency was riddled with communists.[31] But it did not seem to matter. His message that the country was under perilous assault by domestic communist subversives registered widespread support. Indeed, national opinion polls indicated that by the time McCarthy gave his Wheeling talk, a solid majority of the nation already believed in the existence of an internal communist threat.

New developments only served to reinforce this perception. The same month of the Wheeling speech, British physicist Klaus Fuchs confessed to authorities that he had transmitted classified information on the development of the atomic bomb to the Soviets. A few months later, a former civilian employee of the U.S. Army Signal Corps named Julius Rosenberg and his wife, Ethel, were arrested for atomic espionage. The Rosenbergs were eventually convicted of treason and, following an unsuccessful sentence appeal, executed in the electric chair.[32]

A less drastic fate awaited eleven American Communist Party officials from New York, including national secretary Eugene Dennis. In 1949 the so-called New York Eleven were tried and found guilty of conspiring to overthrow the federal government. The constitutionality of these convictions, which threatened long prison sentences, was upheld by the U.S. Supreme Court in 1951. "I guess that we'll always remember the fifties as the time when the cold war overshadowed everything," Harry Truman once observed.[33]

Massachusetts did not buck this national trend. Responding to public fears that communists had infiltrated American society and were clandestinely plotting "the forceful and violent overthrow of the government of the United States and the Commonwealth of Massachusetts," the state legislature created the Committee to Curb Communism. Formed in January 1951, the bipartisan legislative committee was charged with investigating all "Communist Party and communist-front organizations" within the state that were "actively engaged in communist indoctrination or in propaganda against the military efforts of the United States in support of the United Nations." Though no substantive evidence was ever found to suggest the existence of a serious subversive threat, the committee nevertheless concluded that there was a "clear and present danger" to the "democratic and constitutional form of government of the Commonwealth and the United States."[34]

Fanning the flames of local hysteria even higher were the shrill pronouncements of Archbishop Richard J. Cushing of Boston, a close friend of Kennedy and his family. Labeling communism as one of the "greatest evils" to "undermine western civilization," he regularly warned his flock to avoid "the spirit of Antichrist." Communism, he said, "is revealed as a false religion—the religion prophesied by the precursors of Stalin, namely, the religion of the Man-God in place of the religion of the God-man. The Christian symbol of this kind of religion, which is no religion at all, is Antichrist."[35]

Picking up on this theme, *The Pilot,* the official newspaper of the archdiocese, made a practice of publishing numerous anticommunist articles under such provocative headlines as "REDS SCOFF AT SOCIAL VISITS TO HOSPITALIZED" and "CHINESE COMMUNISTS EXPRESS FOND HOPE OF CONQUERING

AMERICA." "The Catholic Church," wrote one *Pilot* columnist, "declares that the State exists primarily to safeguard, and to further the exercise of natural rights. This is the very opposite of 'totalitarianism,' which is the arrogation of all human rights by a 'Politburo' under the domination of a Lenin or Stalin. It is the regimentation of the people, the denial of privilege of exercising their domestic, religious, educational, political and economic rights."[36]

Influenced by these findings and public outcries to do something about the "Red Menace," Governor Paul Dever signed into law a bill that outlawed membership in any group deemed "subversive" by the state attorney general's office. A subversive organization was defined as "any association of more than three persons . . . established for the purpose of advocating, advising, counseling, or inciting the overthrow by force or violence or any other unlawful means of the governments of the Commonwealth and the United States." Anyone found guilty of belonging to such an organization was subject to imprisonment and a one-thousand-dollar fine. Moreover, they were permanently barred from teaching at a "public or private educational institution" in the state.[37]

Civil libertarians were understandably outraged by the law's passage. John L. Saltonstall Jr., state chairman of the liberal Americans for Democratic Action, branded the legislation an affront to democracy. He wrote Governor Dever stating that his group felt concern and indignation over the new law, especially its abridgement of due process rights as guaranteed under the federal and state constitutions. "Regardless of how many individuals are convicted and sentenced under this section," Saltonstall explained, "in practice it will undoubtedly have a significant effect on freedom of association in discouraging citizens from joining all but the most conservative groups." Samuel H. Beer, a politically active member of the Harvard University faculty, echoed these sentiments by dismissing the legislation as "pure demagogy" aimed at winning votes and "hitting the headlines."[38]

Winning votes and hitting the headlines were exactly what John Kennedy had in mind when he attempted to hang the soft-on-communism label on Henry Cabot Lodge Jr. in 1952. Indeed, he accused Lodge of having the "number one record among Republicans" when it came to supporting the supposedly appeasing foreign policy of the Truman administration. Lodge, he further charged, had proven derelict in his duty as senator by failing to support legislation that would have "stopped" trade in war materials with communist China or Soviet Russia. "I saw this trade actually in operation when I was out in the British port of [Hong Kong] a year and a half ago," Kennedy claimed. "Trade of that type obviously must be stopped. Mr. Lodge now agrees with me in this political year of 1952."[39]

As for American policy toward Red China in general, he quoted Lodge as privately telling his Senate Foreign Relations Committee colleagues that he was "not one of those who is critical of our China policy." "I happen to have been among those who in 1949 were critical of our China policy," Kennedy reminded voters. "I believed then and have said since that our diplomats were frittering away the victories our young men won for us." An internal Kennedy campaign study of Lodge's voting record on foreign policy concluded that the Republican had "never raised his voice about the conciliatory and appeasing administration policy in China and the Far East."[40]

In contrast, Kennedy presented himself as an outspoken champion for the advancement of freedom and democracy throughout the world and at home. Citing America's superiority in nuclear weapons, the candidate told campaign audiences that the United States would "win" any military confrontation with the Soviet Union and that an aggressive foreign policy was required to prevent the underdeveloped regions of the world, such as the Middle East and the Far East, from being "swayed by the Communists." On the domestic side, he emphasized the need for all Americans to be "exact and responsible in dealing with the problem of Communist infiltration."[41]

Kennedy had been expressing such ardent views since the beginning of his public career. Running for Congress in 1946 from a heavily working-class district in the Boston-Cambridge-Charlestown-Somerville area, he stressed the "Red Menace" in many of his campaign appearances. "The candidate's political stance was almost ultraconservative," recalled Kennedy campaign secretary William Sutton. "Many of his speeches emphasized anticommunism as well as anticollectivism."[42]

In an October radio speech in Boston, Kennedy boasted about having told a group of "intellectual liberals" that the Soviet Union was "a slave state" run by "a small clique of ruthless, powerful and selfish men," who were bent on world conquest. "Many people will tell you that the Russian experiment is a good one, since the Russians are achieving economic security at a not too great loss of personal freedom," he stated. "The truth is, that the Russian people have neither economic security nor personal freedom." He also decried Soviet expansionism into Eastern Europe and Manchuria and expressed moral outrage at the existence of Siberian labor camps. "The world was incensed at Nazi Concentration Camps," he thundered. "What are we going to do about the Russian Concentration Camps now?"[43]

Kennedy continued to be an anticommunist hardliner after he became a congressman. In 1947, as a freshman member of the House Committee on Education and Labor, he publicly called for the perjury indictment of Harold

Christoffel, a United Auto Workers union official who was under suspicion of being a communist for having led a 1941 strike against the Allis-Chalmers Company in Milwaukee that disrupted vital defense production. Wisconsin congressman Charles J. Kersten, a devout anticommunist, later described this action as one of "the first shots fired against American communism in this country." In previous testimony before the Education and Labor Committee, Christoffel denied allegations that he was a member of the Communist Party and had organized the strike on party orders. But the testimony of ex-communist turned informer Louis F. Budenz, whom Kennedy later called one of the "ablest experts on Communism," convinced Kennedy and other committee members that Christoffel was lying. Budenz, an assistant professor of economics at Fordham University and the former managing editor of the *Daily Worker,* testified that Christoffel had been a party regular for several years and that as a result of directives issued by the party, he had orchestrated the 1941 strike against Allis-Chalmers in an attempt to disrupt important defense production there.[44]

Christoffel was eventually indicted and convicted of perjury in the district court for the District of Columbia. He received a five-year sentence that was upheld by the court of appeals. But upon further appellate review, this time before the U.S. Supreme Court, Christoffel's conviction was vacated on technical grounds. Kennedy was incensed by the Supreme Court's decision. He joined with conservative Republican Congressman Samuel McConnell of Pennsylvania in issuing a statement that condemned the ruling. "What a travesty on justice, that a Communist witness testifies untruthfully before a recognized committee of the House and then escapes the consequences of perjury by a technical claim," the statement read. "In war and peace, he [Christoffel] used his power, not for the benefit of members of his union, but in the interests of the Communist Party."[45]

According to Kennedy biographer James MacGregor Burns, Kennedy's diatribe against the Supreme Court "disturbed" civil libertarians, "who saw in the courts the last bulwark against violations of due process." But the Democrat's stand also earned him considerable public praise, particularly when Christoffel was again convicted and imprisoned in March 1950. Indeed, one local political columnist, W. E. Mullins of the *Boston Herald,* credited Kennedy with having been the first to "flush out" Christoffel as a traitor. "The recent conviction of Harold Christoffel for perjury," Mullins wrote, "must have been a source of satisfaction to the young Bay State politician because . . . he [Kennedy] made the motion that Christoffel be indicted."[46]

Kennedy maintained a steady drumbeat against communism throughout his congressional career. In 1948 he broke with his own party and voted for the Mundt-Nixon Bill, which required the registration of domestic communist front organizations as well as communist organizations and their members. Although vetoed by President Truman, the main provisions of the bill were incorporated into the Communist Control Act of 1950, the so-called McCarren Act, which Kennedy also supported. "We are faced with an enemy whose goal is to conquer the world by subversion and infiltration or, if necessary, by open war," he warned constituents during this period.[47]

On January 25, 1949, Kennedy received permission to address the House for one minute and proceeded to condemn the Truman administration for "losing China." "Mr. Speaker, over this weekend we have learned the extent of the disaster that has befallen China and the United States," he said of the communist victory over Chiang Kai-shek's Nationalist regime. "The responsibility for the failure of our foreign policy in the Far East rests squarely in the White House and the Department of State." He concluded his remarks by urging the House to "assume the responsibility of preventing the onrushing tide of communism from engulfing all of Asia."[48]

Kennedy repeated his accusations in a speech a few days later in Salem, Massachusetts. He stated that American policy with regard to China had "reaped a whirlwind" and faulted State Department diplomats and their advisors for giving insufficient support to Chiang's Nationalist government. "This is the tragic story of China whose freedom we once fought to preserve," he declared. "What our young men had saved, our diplomats and our President have frittered away." He also blamed "a sick Roosevelt" for giving away the Kurile Islands and other strategic ports to the Soviet Union during the Yalta Conference.[49]

Kennedy's intransigence deepened with the onset of the Korean War in June 1950. He vigorously supported American military action against communist North Korea and denounced the trade of strategic materials between the United States and its allies with communist China as "trade in blood." "Because of the fact that American casualties in Korea have reached a total of 60,000," he asserted in a speech on the House floor in May 1951, "such trade between Communist China and foreign countries is clearly a matter of grave concern to all Americans."[50]

Kennedy did not come by his stridency on the issue of communism by accident. He grew up listening to his father, self-made millionaire businessman Joseph P. Kennedy, deliver lectures on the evils of Marxist-Leninism. Stern and humorless, Joseph Kennedy lived with the fear that socialism might someday replace American capitalism, thereby eliminating all the material gains he had accumulated for himself and for his family. To help forestall the likelihood of such an event, the elder Kennedy adopted a militant anticommunist approach. He became a vocal critic of the Soviet Union and its policies and contributed large sums of money to anticommunist causes such as Francisco Franco's successful attempt to overthrow the socialist-led Republic of Spain. As U.S. ambassador to Great Britain in the late 1930s, he even urged British prime minister Neville Chamberlain to appease Nazi Germany rather than seek an alliance with the Soviet Union. His reasoning was that such a policy would encourage Hitler to march eastward against Russia, thereby bringing down the final curtain on Soviet communism. An FBI field report later described him as being "very well versed on communism and what it might mean to the United States."[51]

If Joseph Kennedy was important to the formation of his son's anticommunist philosophy, so too was Rose Fitzgerald Kennedy. She instilled in her son, as well as the rest of her nine children, a sense of individuality and moral purpose. "When I held my newborn baby in my arms," she once recalled, "I used to think that what I said and did to him could have an influence not only on him but on all whom he met, not only for a day or a month or a year, but for all eternity—a very challenging and exciting thought for a mother."[52]

A devout Roman Catholic, Rose also inculcated in her sons and daughters the major tenets of her religious faith, which included the belief that communism was "anti-Christian" and therefore to be reviled. Though not a deeply religious person himself, John Kennedy nevertheless showed indications that he was strongly influenced by this mother's teachings. In an Independence Day speech in 1946, he publicly lashed out against the "doctrine of collectivism" and the "twin pillars of atheism and materialism" on which he claimed all communist dogma rested. "You have been taught that each individual has an internal soul, composed of an intellect which can know truth and a will which is free," he told the 1950 graduating class of the University of Notre Dame. "Believing this," he concluded, "Catholics can never adhere to any political theory which holds that the state is a separate, distinct organization to which allegiance must be paid rather than a representative institution which derives its powers from the consent of the governed."[53]

Henry Cabot Lodge Jr. also firmly opposed the spread of communism, but unlike Kennedy, he did not view the issue in alarmist terms. He, for instance, attributed the rise of communism in Europe at the end of World War II more to adverse economic conditions than to any anti-Christian plot. "The Russians are not smart enough to have single-handedly created the Communists in Europe," he remarked in 1948. "Man's inhumanity to man, individually and collectively, had a large part in doing so." As for Western European governments adopting socialist legislative programs to combat poverty and massive unemployment, he opined that such countries did so "because they felt they had to and that their love for democracy is not any weaker for it."[54]

Above all, Lodge thought it was incumbent upon American policymakers not to oversimplify the Soviet challenge by demonizing communism. "It is not a holy war," he reminded colleagues on the Senate Foreign Relations Committee in 1947. "I hope it never becomes a holy war, because so long as you can keep it on the ground of national interest you can modify your course in accordance with the requirements of the situation. The minute it becomes a holy war, then you are in to the death and nothing can stop you."[55]

The danger, as Lodge saw it, was of U.S. and Soviet leaders misjudging the intentions of the other, thereby increasing the risks of war. "Maybe you are frightened of us," he told a Soviet delegation in a speech before the United Nations General Assembly in 1950. "Maybe you are frightened of the plain people in your own country. But I know that a frightened man can be dangerous. I am sorry that there is fright and I hope and believe that the time will come—and it is not far off either—when fear will disappear."[56]

To preserve peace in the interim, Lodge felt it was important for all Americans to back the Truman administration's efforts to contain perceived Soviet expansion in Europe and Asia. "The watchword now is cooperation with President Truman on all things which will bring a richer life and better future for ourselves and our children in a world of peace," he contended in 1948. "We have a big job ahead and there must be no sniping for partisan advantage."[57] True to his word, he helped lead a bipartisan drive in the Senate for passage of aid to Greece and Turkey, the Marshall Plan, and the North Atlantic Treaty. He also was a strong supporter of U.S. military action in Korea.

On the subject of domestic communism, Lodge evinced little concern. Though he publicly faulted the Truman administration for allowing several unscreened job applicants to enter the State Department before the Federal Loyalty Review Board had been established by executive order in 1947, he nonetheless refused to make the broader charge, as many of his Republican colleagues did, that the federal government was honeycombed with communist sympathizers. Indeed, he told a fall 1948 GOP gathering in Dayton, Ohio, that it "simply muddies the waters" for Republicans to say "all the Democrats are tools of the Communists." To Lodge such talk undermined the principle of bipartisanship, which he regarded as an essential prerequisite for meeting the communist challenge abroad. "Can't we all agree," he pleaded, "to stop this mudslinging and have the two parties compete for the votes of the people in a constructive way?"[58]

In general, Lodge maintained this scrupulous approach during the 1952 campaign. Though he was not above criticizing the Truman administration for allowing the city of Berlin to become "an island completely surrounded by Soviet territory," he stopped well short of the extreme red-baiting employed by other Republicans then running for office, such as Joseph McCarthy of Wisconsin. Responding to Kennedy's charges that he had not done enough to combat communism during his tenure in the Senate, Lodge reminded Massachusetts voters that he had been an early supporter of the Truman Doctrine and the Marshall Plan, bipartisan measures designed to keep the Soviet Union and her allies in check. In addition, he spoke of the importance of holding the line against perceived communist aggression in Asia. "I have asserted that our corps and divisions must remain," he said of America's continued military presence on the Korean peninsula.[59]

This failure to advocate more aggressive methods, as his opponent did, made Lodge vulnerable to attacks from state conservatives within his own party who questioned his commitment to the anticommunist cause and who were looking to "punish" Lodge for his part in denying Robert Taft the GOP presidential nomination. Leading this charge from the right was influential New Bedford and Cape Cod newspaper publisher Basil Brewer, the chairman of the Taft-for-President state committee. In terms of temperament, drive, and political ideology, he was ideally suited for the role of conservative avenger.

Born on July 23, 1884, in Rush Hill, Missouri, Brewer grew up under the strict and watchful eye of his father, Addison L. Brewer, a circuit rider of the Missouri Methodist Conference who studied the Bible in Hebrew. A pious advocate of self-reliance and personal discipline, Addison instilled in his son a sense that anything could be accomplished in life as long as one was willing to work hard and avoid sin. Earthly rewards, however, were few and far between for the elder Brewer. Unable to support his family on a minister's paltry salary, he operated a small print shop in upstate Kirksville to make ends meet. Young Basil worked long hours in this shop, acquiring an early appreciation for the printed word. A shy and awkward boy, he preferred reading books to playing sports or socializing with other children. He gradually became more outgoing and assertive, according to one family account, when he tried to "live up to the standards set by his father." This personal change was evident by the time he enrolled at Northeast Missouri Teachers College near the turn of the century. A popular figure on campus, Brewer endeared himself to students and faculty with his quick wit, ready smile, and energetic personality. He even wrote the words to the school fight song, "Old Missou."[60]

Upon graduation in 1901, he taught at the secondary school level for several years before poor health prematurely ended his classroom career. Undaunted, he landed a job with the Scripps-Howard newspapers in 1908 selling advertising space to local subcribers. Over the next two decades he rose steadily through a series of newspaper business office jobs to become publisher and part owner of a small Lansing, Michigan, daily called *Capital News.*[61]

Dissatisfied with being only a part owner, however, Brewer searched for an opportunity that would give him sole proprietorship of a newspaper. That opportunity came in 1931 when he learned through the journalism grapevine that the financially troubled *New Bedford Evening Standard* was for sale. Driven by a rage to succeed, he packed up all his belongings and moved halfway across the country to take on the challenge of turning around the struggling eighty-year-old southeastern Massachusetts daily. Within a year he had improved the paper's financial situation so markedly that he was able to buy a controlling interest in the *Standard*'s chief competitor, the *New Bedford Times.* The two papers were eventually merged into a single-edition *Standard-Times.* Brewer later founded the *Cape Cod Standard-Times,* purchased two radio stations, and obtained a license to operate a local television station. But he was not without detractors.

"He cut salaries in half," recounted former employee John H. Ackerman, "demanded that reporters turn in a stub of an old pencil to get a new one, slashed the staff and stopped giving away such premiums as china and glass to attract readers." Another former employee, reporter Jeremiah Murphy, who went on to become an award-winning columnist for the *Boston Globe,* remembered Brewer as a tight-fisted and inconsiderate man who demanded his newspaper staff work on Christmas Day, regardless of family obligations. For those unable or unwilling to go along with this policy, he would dock them a day's pay. "He was . . . a pain in the ass," Murphy explained.[62]

Editorially, Brewer also bought change by moving the paper in a decidedly rightward political direction.[63] This was by no accident. At heart a conservative Republican, Brewer believed the old aphorism that government working the least worked best. His own life experience seemed to confirm this. Coming from a relatively modest midwestern background, he had been able to pull himself up largely through his own pluck and personal initiative. Government had never entered the picture.

"He was a Republican hard-liner and a conservative," recalled former *Standard-Times* city editor Dick Early. "A lot of people working on the staff had trouble stomaching all that conservatism. He would have reporters leave because they couldn't identify with [the conservative thrust of] the paper." Brewer never outwardly let on he was bothered by such defections. To him the whole purpose of a newspaper was to express a particular viewpoint. "The American newspaper reader," he once said, "prefers to have his newspaper take a courageous stand to fight for what the paper believes, even though the reader may not himself agree." These instincts were ultimately proven correct. Despite a readership that was largely blue-collar in makeup, the paper posted healthy circulation totals of over fifty thousand by the early 1950s. "There were a lot of people in the community who didn't care for his views," Early explained. "But they did think it was a good newspaper. They respected it."[64]

Under Brewer's leadership the *Standard-Times* struck a consistently antiliberal, anti–New Deal tone. Federal poverty relief programs such as the Works Progress Administration and the Civilian Conservation Corps were criticized for being too costly and inefficient. Attempts at introducing progressivity to federal and state tax codes were routinely dismissed as soak-the-rich schemes. President Franklin Roosevelt came under attack for having allegedly caved in to pressures from liberal special interest groups attempting to undermine the free enterprise system. "This is not necessarily to say that Mr. Roosevelt is necessarily a radical," Brewer editorialized on the eve of the 1936 presidential election. "We have no sympathy with the charge that he has communistic leanings. But if he is elected, it will be by a combination that includes most of the country's radical elements; and while he may not have full sympathy with their objectives, he may find himself unable to control the situation arising out of their support of him."[65]

In the postwar years, Brewer focused his energies on fighting communism and promoting the presidential candidacy of Senator Robert Taft of Ohio. In his mind the two causes were not unrelated. Taft was a dedicated anticommunist who spent most of his political career warning Americans about the dangers of the "Red Menace." "There is no doubt," the Republican lawmaker told supporters in 1951, "that the liberty of this country is threatened at the present time, probably more seriously than at any time since the early days of the republic." Soviet expansionism, Taft maintained, had to be thwarted along with the "aggressive fanatical spirit of communism" in general.[66]

Such strident language, coming as it did from a fellow midwesterner, registered favorably with the New Bedford publisher. For he was an equally fervid anticommunist. When Senator Margaret Chase Smith of Maine denounced domestic witch-hunts for communists in her famed "Declaration of Conscience" speech of June 1, 1950, Brewer flew into an editorial rage. He chided his fellow Republican for being naive and uninformed. "The fact is," he wrote, "that what has been going on is an attempt to frustrate Communist designs by turning the spotlight on them and removing from government positions persons who have knowingly cooperated with the Communists or have been their dupes."[67]

To emphasize the threat posed by communism, Brewer ran a popular feature called "If I Were a Communist" on the editorial page of his newspaper. A daily reminder of the "Red Conspiracy," this unsigned diatribe informed readers that communists were attempting to undermine the nation's institutions through labor unrest, wasteful government spending, and biased propaganda against businessmen. "These three activities, carried on persistently and long enough," it cautioned, "would wreck any Democracy—any Republic."[68]

Brewer's anticommunism, like Taft's, stemmed from an innate fear of big government, the conservative belief that social welfare programs destroyed private enterprise by removing the possibility of personal gain. "The end result," he once informed a New Bedford audience, "is complete government control, Communist, fascist or Nazi, among which there is but little difference so far as the people are concerned."[69] The only way to avoid such an outcome, the scrappy Missourian believed, was to elect vigilant, tough-minded leaders who could safeguard American society from communist threats abroad and from the "creeping process of socialism" at home.

In Taft the New Bedford publisher was certain he had such a leader. The Ohio lawmaker was, in his opinion, "one of America's greatest statesmen" and a staunch defender of the free enterprise system. But Brewer's hopes of "Mr. Republican" becoming president were dashed at the 1952 Republican National Convention in Chicago. As a member of the Massachusetts delegation, he witnessed firsthand how Lodge "spearheaded" the drive to defeat Taft. Needless to say, the experience was unsettling. "I would not be honest if I did not say there are scars, deep ones, in the Republican Party as a result of the late primary campaign," he told an interviewer at the close of the convention.[70]

To make matters worse, a Lodge relative had rudely shoved Brewer when the latter took the Massachusetts standard to join a floor demonstration on behalf of Taft. A witness to the scuffle, Ed Martin, the brother of Massachusetts congressman Joseph Martin, later revealed that Brewer held Lodge solely responsible for the incident and never got over it.[71]

To gain a measure of political as well as personal revenge, the New Bedford publisher dedicated himself to ending Lodge's senatorial career. That there was no love lost between the two Bay State Republicans had been evident for several years. Though Brewer had endorsed the Massachusetts lawmaker for senator in 1936 and 1942, he had done so more out of party loyalty than any shared political beliefs. Indeed, Lodge, in terms of his pro-labor voting record and long-standing support of New Deal social programs, was considered too liberal by the conservative Missourian. "To Mr. Brewer," John Ackerman once observed, "such liberals as Henry Cabot Lodge Jr. were hardly Republicans at all."[72]

Given this predilection, it is not surprising that Brewer supported incumbent Democrat David I. Walsh over Lodge for the Senate in 1946. Walsh was by all accounts more conservative than his former Senate colleague, mounting vigorous opposition to many of the Roosevelt administration's domestic policies, such as wartime wage and price controls. "In his attack on government by bureaucracy," gushed Brewer in an editorial page endorsement, Walsh "showed a keen perception of an evil which should be terminated now that the war is over." No mention was made of Lodge, but the implication was that the Republican lacked a similar understanding.[73]

In the late 1940s political relations between the two Republicans deteriorated still further. When Lodge sponsored a constitutional amendment to replace the Electoral College with the direct election of the president and vice president, Brewer expressed stern opposition. The amendment, he argued, would bring negligible political gains to the Republican Party, particularly in the "solid South," where Democrats had enjoyed a virtual electoral stranglehold since the end of Reconstruction. "Obviously," he stated, "such Republican votes cannot come from the tight Democratic majority in these States, which facing the Truman civil rights program, still refused to vote" Republican. Not to be outdone, Lodge rejoined with a terse statement of his own. "Mr. Brewer assumes [the amendment] would not change the voting habits of the people," he told reporters. "But I believe voting habits would be changed."[74] When the amendment failed to secure the necessary two-thirds congressional approval, Brewer claimed personal vindication, thereby irritating Lodge and widening the political rift that already existed between the two Republicans. That rift would become unbridgeable following the 1952 Republican National Convention.

Furious at Lodge for having quashed Taft's bid to attain the presidency, Brewer began openly touting John Kennedy for senator over Lodge. At a September 25 press conference held at the Sheraton Plaza Hotel in Boston to explain his endorsement, Brewer characteristically minced no words. He told a throng of Boston-area newspapermen that he was supporting Kennedy because, in his opinion, Lodge had "long ago bolted his party by his votes for the Truman socialistic New Deal." That Kennedy was a Democrat made little difference. Kennedy would simply make "a better senator" than Lodge. "If a real Republican was running in this state," he concluded, "I'd support that Republican against Kennedy."[75]

Brewer's endorsement was given front-page coverage in Boston newspapers. Under the banner headline "BREWER BACKS KENNEDY, SAYS LODGE 'NEW DEALER,'" the *Boston Globe* noted that Brewer had been telling friends since the Republican National Convention in July that he could "not conscientiously support Lodge." No doubt taking stock in Brewer and Lodge's party affiliation, the paper concluded that the press conference was "unusual."[76]

Boston Herald columnist and Lodge supporter W. E. Mullins attempted to downplay the event's significance. "There is no desire to disparage the influence of this New Bedford publication," Mullins wrote. "If Lodge had his choice, of course, he would accept its support. Its political influence, however, is not vital and its loss not necessarily fatal to Lodge, even in a close election."[77]

The independent *Boston American* was less skeptical: "Fearful that Brewer, long known as a militant and influential conservative with a barbed tongue and a quick temper, would bolt the entire ticket if taken to task for his endorsement of Kennedy, Republican leaders [yesterday] maintained a mournful silence." Indeed, the latter's failure to take Brewer to task for his incendiary comments "indicated that they felt [Lodge] had suffered a severe setback in his campaign for re-election, and that open conflict with the fiery publisher would react adversely upon the entire Republican ticket."[78]

In actuality, the conservative Missourian would have been favorably disposed toward Kennedy whatever his party affiliation. Though differing in age, taste, style, religion, and family upbringing, Brewer nonetheless shared with Kennedy an abiding hatred of all things communist. The Democrat had been, he said, "in the forefront in the fight against Communism" in both word and deed. "As a freshman congressman and as a member of the powerful House committee on Labor and Education in 1947," Brewer enthused in an October 17 editorial, "Kennedy instigated the attack that was to land Harold Christoffel, the pro-Communist labor leader, in jail in February, 1950. His citation of Christoffel for perjury has been described as the 'opening skirmish between Congress and the American-Communist conspiracy.'" Kennedy's foreign policy views regarding perceived communist expansionism also drew praise. "He recognized the urgency of protecting Formosa from a Communist attack in 1949 while the [Truman] Administration was still asleep to the danger there," Brewer noted. As for the junior congressman's contribution to the "Who Lost China" debate, the New Bedford publisher credited him with having "pinpointed" the root cause of "our disastrous China policy"—the Truman ad-

New Bedford newspaper publisher Basil Brewer greets Kennedy in 1957. Brewer played a pivotal role in swinging conservative Republican support to Kennedy in 1952. Courtesy of the *New Bedford Standard-Times*.

ministration's alleged inability to meet the communist threat. "Kennedy," Brewer declared, "was not blinded by party ties when he said, 'the responsibility for the failure of our foreign policy in the Far East rests squarely with the White House and the State Department.'"[79]

Because of Kennedy's strong anticommunist record, Brewer was given the political excuse he had been looking for to support him over Lodge. "In these times when the United States is the leader of the free world against the onslaughts of Communist aggression," Brewer editorialized on October 24, "the voter has an obligation to pay particular attention to the qualifications of the senatorial candidates in the field of foreign affairs." Kennedy, he asserted, "has shown . . . a surer grasp of the problems and personalities involved in the nation's struggle for survival than has his opponent, Senator Henry Cabot Lodge Jr." Indeed, Lodge was faulted for being less than vigilant when it came to defending the nation against the "Red Peril." "Even after the outbreak of the Korean War," Brewer wrote, "Lodge voted against legislation which would have put a stop to the shipment of strategic war materials to the Iron Curtain countries—materials which found their way to Korea to be used against American soldiers." Kennedy, in contrast, was commended in the same editorial for having denounced the "trade in blood." Topping off Lodge's list of perceived sins was his support of the Truman administration's foreign policy, which the newspaper publisher considered weak and ineffectual. "So far as the records show," Brewer maintained, "Lodge never has criticized Secretary of State Dean Acheson, whose policies have contributed so heavily to the terrifying series of Communist diplomatic and practical victories."[80]

Brewer's efforts to "dislodge" the junior Massachusetts senator were not limited to holding press conferences and writing editorials. When the Lodge campaign attempted to place ads in the *Standard-Times* criticizing Kennedy's performance as a congressman, the New Bedford publisher refused to run them. This political blackout soon carried over into the paper's daily news coverage of the Republican candidate campaigning in the area. When Lodge attended a large political rally held in his honor at Hyannis, a small Cape Cod town within the *Standard-Times* circulation area, the paper gave scant mention of the event. "We were told [by Brewer] not to take any pictures of [Lodge]," reporter Jeremiah Murphy recalled. "I guess [the lack of overall press coverage] is linked to the fact that Lodge didn't do too well around New Bedford."[81]

For his part, Lodge tried to ignore the increasing ferocity of Brewer's attacks as best he could. "The truth of the matter is that Mr. Brewer is a man of deep convictions whose views on public questions are far closer to those of the Kennedy family than me," the Bay State senator commented diplomatically. Prior to this, he had tried to smooth over any lingering bad blood with Brewer and other disgruntled GOP conservatives by publicly claiming he was "with General Eisenhower more than I was against Senator Taft" at the Republican National Convention in July. Not many observers of the political scene, however, were impressed with this explanation.[82]

"With the senatorial contest rated as extremely close," the *Christian Science Monitor* predicted, "the Brewer position could be a serious factor in the Nov. 4 results if a sizable number of former backers of Senator Robert A. Taft of Ohio . . . follow the Brewer lead." The *Lynn Telegram-News* was somewhat less restrained in its analysis. "The growing anti-Lodge sentiment," the paper maintained, "which started to accrue against U.S. Senator Henry Cabot Lodge [following the Republican National Convention] undoubtedly will ensure the election of Cong. Kennedy to the important upper branch of the national government."[83]

Outside the state, the conservative but pro-Eisenhower *New York Herald Tribune* reported that Taft Republicans in Massachusetts were planning to vote for Kennedy "without giving up their franchise in the party by bolting the national ticket." Lodge's own straw polls showed that his support among "upper income groups" was dropping as a result of the split. "This may well reflect the bulk of the Taft defections," an internal Lodge campaign memo revealed. In later years, the Republican was privately less circumspect about his feelings on this subject. "If I had had the solid support of the Republicans in Massachusetts," he admitted to a confidant, "I would have been reelected, but [the conservatives] were determined to take it out on me and the official Taft chairman in Massachusetts [Brewer] openly supported my Democratic opponent just as my Democratic opponent's father had, it was said, contributed financially to the Taft campaign."[84]

There is no concrete evidence to support the charge that Joseph P. Kennedy aided Taft's unsuccessful presidential campaign directly. But the elder Kennedy, whom former Massachusetts Speaker of the House Thomas P. "Tip" O'Neill once described as "a tough and meddlesome father, especially when it came to Jack," had made a concerted behind-the-scenes effort to court Taft supporters. A retired wholesaler named T. Walter Taylor, who had previously been an office secretary for the Massachusetts Republicans for Taft committee, was tapped by the ambassador to head an Independents for Kennedy committee.[85]

Headquartered in Parlor B of the Sheraton-Plaza Hotel in Boston, the committee sent out letters to Taft supporters across the state asking them to "assure" Lodge's defeat by voting for Kennedy. "After what [Lodge] did to Senator Taft," one letter read, "we feel that he has forfeited all rights to expect right-thinking people to support him this fall in returning to office."[86] By "right-thinking" the letter implied that Lodge was lacking the same conservative, anticommunist values that Taft and, by extension, Kennedy possessed.

Although Taft openly discouraged such activities in the interest of preserving Republican unity, many of his Massachusetts supporters declined to follow suit. Unencumbered by national GOP leadership responsibilities, these "Taftites" maintained a steady barrage of political invective at Lodge. "We'll be happy to retire you to private life in favor of Congressman Kennedy this coming November for your actions" at the Chicago convention, was how one embittered Taft supporter, George Maroney of Boston, put it in a private note to the junior Massachusetts senator.[87]

Another Taft devotee, Cape Cod resident Carl Murchison, strongly urged Lodge, in an open letter published in the *Provincetown Advocate*, to "withdraw from the senate race" altogether. "It seems likely," he wrote the senator, "that a majority of the Taft supporters will not help you, as your chief occupation for some years has been to destroy their interest. . . . You have fallen further than Lucifer."[88]

The editorial page of the pro-Taft *Brockton Enterprise* was no less provocative in its own position. "In Massachusetts," the paper asserted, "every Republican who ever believed in the honesty and integrity of the party should bear in mind the treachery of Henry Cabot Lodge Jr. and vote against him on election day."[89]

On Boston's North Shore, a summer resort area for the region's oldest and wealthiest Republican families, automobiles began sporting "thousands" of window stickers emblazoned with the initials "O.G.," which stood for "Old Guard." A Kennedy supporter boasted to a local reporter that the stickers belonged to unhappy Old Guard Republicans, or Taftites, who were going to vote for the Democrat in the fall. "The campaign lieutenants of Cong. Kennedy," reported the *Lynn Telegram-News,* "can read in [the stickers] only certain victory."[90]

In Dartmouth, a midsize coastal community in southeastern Massachusetts, local Lodge campaign workers reported being accosted and ordered out of Taft-supporter homes while conducting routine door-to-door canvassing assignments. "As soon as [the Taftites] knew we were interested in you, they were quite rude before we could get out of the house," complained one couple to Lodge. "The gist of all that was said was that 'We shall never forgive him for what he did to Taft.'"[91]

A disgusted voter from central Massachusetts offered a similar assessment. "In circulating your nomination papers immediately after the convention," Townsend resident R. I. Harry claimed, "I found that some of the most steadfast Republicans were against you because they resented the part you played in Eisenhower's defeat of Senator Taft for the nomination. Some refused to sign your papers. These same people voted for Eisenhower as the choice 'between two evils,' but they did not vote for you. That is a shame, of course, but typical of many voters."[92]

It was certainly typical of Basil Brewer in 1952.

Chapter **SIX**

★ ★ ★ ★ ★ ★

Newspaper Endorsements, Television, and Joe McCarthy

B
ASIL BREWER would also play a minor but not unimportant role in securing Kennedy the endorsement of the influential *Boston Post*. Founded in 1831, the popular daily boasted a readership of over 300,000 and was considered by many to be the paper of record for the city's large Irish Catholic community.

Though traditionally Democratic—it endorsed Joseph E. Casey and David I. Walsh over Lodge in 1942 and 1946 respectively—the paper was not above crossing party lines. In 1948 the *Post* endorsed the reelection of Republican Congressman Christian A. Herter over Democrat Walter A. O'Brien, a supporter of the left-leaning presidential candidacy of Henry A. Wallace. "Mr. O'Brien," the paper noted, "stands on the same pro-Soviet platform as Mr. Wallace. He advocated the same policy of appeasement to Soviet Russia. This is a contest where party labels are misleading. You can serve yourself and your nation by voting next Tuesday for the re-election of Congressman Christian A. Herter."[1]

Indeed, Lodge, who had carried Boston by over twenty thousand votes in 1946 but who labeled the city a problem area in 1952 owing to Kennedy's unique personal appeal among Irish Catholic voters, was counting on a *Post* endorsement to negate his opponent's natural electoral advantage. "I knew it would be much harder this time [to carry Boston]," the GOP lawmaker later explained, "but I figured if I could get the endorsement of the *Post,* which in those days was worth forty thousand votes, I could hold my own in Boston."[2] Yet to win the *Post*'s endorsement required gaining the approval of the paper's mercurial owner and publisher, John J. Fox.

"If anyone was perfect grist for a gifted obituary writer," a perceptive journalist once noted, "it was John Fox." To be sure, Fox, who came from a modest Irish Catholic background, experienced enough highs and lows in his life
to fill the pages of any novel. Described as "brilliant" by some and an "ego-
maniac of extraordinary proportions" by others, this maverick entrepreneur
could always be counted on to elicit strong emotions from people. "He was so
unpredictable," recalled Herbert A. Kenny, a reporter who worked for the *Post*
when Fox came aboard as owner and publisher. "Many of us just kept out of
his way."[3]

Born on December 9, 1906, Fox grew up in a relatively poor Irish Catholic
neighborhood in South Boston. Though his family possessed limited financial
means, Fox never found himself wanting. This was in no small part due to the
efforts of Michael and Christian Fox, Fox's supportive but hard-driving parents, who at an early stage in their son's life instilled in him a fierce, unrelent-
ing desire to succeed. This enterprising young man did not disappoint, as he
excelled in his studies at school and showed a surprising aptitude for music. He
eventually went on to receive diplomas at the prestigious Boston Latin School
and Harvard University, where he acquired a reputation for being a heavy
drinker and "something of a ladies' man." To help finance his way through
Harvard, where he earned a bachelor's degree in English literature, Fox played
the piano at various local nightclubs and watering holes. In later years, when
he was financially broke and nearly destitute, this talent came in handy as he
supported himself by performing in bars of questionable repute in Boston's
old Scollay Square.[4]

Following his college graduation in the spring of 1929, Fox embarked on
a career in business. He landed a job selling securities with Ellis & Lane, a small
Boston firm. Then disaster struck. The stock market crashed in late October,
ushering in the Great Depression. "I thus caught the tail of the toboggan just
as it started over the top of the hill, and I hung on through the next three very
rough years," Fox later remembered.[5] Despite the dismal economic picture, he
was able to retain his twenty-dollar-a-week sales position by peddling securities door to door in small, backwater New England towns.

After three years on the job, however, it suddenly dawned on Fox that he
did not adequately understand the new federal laws governing securities. So
he enrolled full-time at Harvard University Law School to gain better insight.
Although he compiled a poor attendance record there—he still sold securities
by day—Fox was able to pass the Massachusetts Bar Exam six months before
graduation.[6]

After law school, Fox's business career flourished; he opened his own private securities firm and speculated heavily in the Boston and New York real estate markets. Over the course of the next decade, he was able to amass a personal fortune worth over $25 million. In his biggest financial move, he orchestrated the majority stock purchase of the Western Union & Telegraph Company at the beginning of 1952. "Nobody ever lost money investing with John Fox," he boasted to friends.[7]

It thus came as a surprise to many observers when Fox elected to buy the financially troubled *Boston Post* for $4 million on June 18, 1952. Although possessing the largest daily readership in Boston, the paper was reporting annual losses of over $500,000 in the early 1950s. The reasons given for this financial free fall were declining advertising revenues, an antiquated physical plant, and a nonexistent home delivery system.[8] So why then did Fox, for all his displayed business acumen, take on this journalistic white elephant? The answer has more to do with anticommunism than with any financial bottom line.

"I bought the *Post* for one reason—and one reason only—to fight communism," Fox revealed to employees in a private memo circulated around the newsroom months later. "It is my belief . . . it still is my belief . . . that if people like me, with the money, (however hard it may come), the health, the energy and whatever we may have of brains, toughness, and resources, are not willing, in the interests of preserving the freedom which made possible what we and our children are and may be, to give all that we have to fight the evil forces who would destroy us, then we do not deserve to survive. . . . On that basis, I bought the *Post*. I had to, or else consider myself degenerate."[9]

Thus Fox, a poor South Boston schoolboy turned millionaire wheeler-dealer, wanted to use the *Post* and all its attendant influence as a major metropolitan newspaper to combat what he considered to be the creeping influence of communism on American society. "He was obsessed with the idea of fighting communism," former Fox business associate Maurice H. Saval concluded years later. "He wanted to do his public part, and he was delighted to court publicity for it." Former *Post* employee Herbert Kenny agreed: Fox "was nutty on the subject of communism." According to Michael Fox, Fox's son, his father's move to buy the *Post* was "purely an emotional decision." The paper "was the first business that my father ever bought without being objective," he claimed.[10]

The question arises how Fox became so adamantly anticommunist in his personal outlook. On this issue, unfortunately, there is little documentary evidence to go on. Fox, who garnered a reputation for being a "mystery man" in Boston and New York financial circles, gave no indication of his true anticommunist leanings until the early 1950s. It could simply be, as *New England*

Monthly writer Charles P. Pierce once speculated, that Fox, as a newly established millionaire, "looked with antipathy upon communism's opposition to private wealth."[11]

Another explanation might be that Fox was somehow unduly influenced by his second wife, Olga dePolakova, whom he married in 1945 (he and his first wife, Isabel Murray, had divorced in 1940). The descendant of Russian aristocratic stock, dePolakova's family had to flee their homeland to avoid persecution at the hands of the Bolsheviks.[12] Though little is known of dePolakova or her political views, it would not be unreasonable to assume that she was strongly anticommunist and that this might have swayed him.

Regardless, Fox's anticommunism was a decisive factor in determining whom the *Post* endorsed for U.S. senator in 1952. Initially, Fox had planned on supporting Lodge, with whom he had enjoyed amicable social relations for several years. But a conversation three weeks before the election with Basil Brewer, the archconservative *New Bedford Standard-Times* publisher and confirmed Lodge hater, instilled doubts in Fox's mind as to the advisability of such an action. Though details remain sketchy as to what was actually said, it is clear from statements made later by Fox that Brewer had convinced him that Lodge had been "soft on the Communists for at least the past two or three years."[13]

According to Fox, this revelation came as a complete personal shock. Only a few days earlier, he had met privately with Lodge and two of his advisors to discuss the GOP candidate's views on communism. Fox, an avid Joe McCarthy supporter, revealed afterward that the impression he received from the meeting was that "Senator McCarthy, Senator Nixon and Senator Lodge were the effective influence in the Senate against Communists."[14] But the Brewer conversation made him revise this opinion.

"I was wrong in having that impression," Fox later confided to an associate on the night of October 23, two days before the *Post* publicly endorsed Kennedy. "I consider the information I received from Lodge last Sunday was erroneous. I was not in possession of all the facts that I now have." His paper would give *"an affirmative endorsement"* of Kennedy, but in deference to his earlier cordial relations with Lodge, Fox directed his staff not to "take a shot" at the Republican lawmaker. "We are going to be fair and will simply say that Kennedy is a great guy, a good Democrat, and, being a Democratic paper, we will support him," he said.[15]

Interestingly enough, nowhere in this account does Fox mention that Kennedy's father had loaned him half a million dollars around this time to help offset the enormous financial losses his paper was still experiencing. Fox had already poured most of his personal fortune into the paper, but to no avail. He

Boston Post newspaper publisher John Fox. "I bought the *Post* for one reason—and one reason only—to fight communism," he once claimed. He would provide a key endorsement to Kennedy under a cloud of controversy. Courtesy of the Boston Public Library, Print Department.

later insisted the loan was purely a commercial transaction with no connection whatsoever with the *Post*'s decision to endorse Kennedy. Joseph Kennedy "was merely a substitute for a bank," the Boston publisher told a House subcommittee investigating the relationship between Eisenhower aide Sherman Adams and Boston textile manufacturer Bernard Goldfine in 1958. As for Joseph Kennedy, he also denied any underlying political motives, claiming the loan was paid off on time with full interest.[16]

Nevertheless, the circumstances surrounding the *Post*'s endorsement, as Kennedy biographer Herbert Parmet has taken pains to point out, "encouraged skepticism." Lodge, for instance, told historian Doris Kearns Goodwin years later that he "never doubted for a moment" that Joseph Kennedy and his seemingly bottomless checkbook were responsible for turning Fox around, though he imagined that the ambassador handled the situation "pretty subtly, with all sorts of veiled promises and hints, rather than an outright deal."[17]

Lodge's suspicions aside, the charge that the Kennedys "bought" the *Post*'s endorsement cannot be substantiated. No documentation has turned up, as of yet, to determine whether a quid pro quo arrangement ever existed. In fact, Fox and Kennedy consistently maintained over the years that the loan was made after the endorsement had already been finalized.[18]

Fox endorsed Kennedy because he felt that Lodge had been unable to "explain himself" with regard to his anticommunism commitment. Kennedy, in contrast, with his strident Cold War rhetoric and proven track record against alleged domestic subversives (see the Christoffel affair), left no doubt as to where he stood on the issue. Indeed, the front-page October 25 *Post* editorial, which formally endorsed Kennedy, cited this record as the main reason why the paper supported him over Lodge. Kennedy "fired one of the first shots for the American people against communist infiltration away back in 1947 when he routed out the leader of a communist-inspired strike at a Wisconsin plant engaged in secret defense work," the editorial stated.[19]

Despite the *Post*'s endorsement, Kennedy lagged behind Lodge when it came to winning newspaper support. Indeed, five of the state's six most important dailies—the *Boston Herald,* the *Worcester Evening Gazette,* the *Lowell Sun,* the *Springfield Union,* and the *Berkshire Eagle*—enthusiastically backed Lodge's reelection. The sixth, the *Boston Globe,* a nominally Democratic paper, held fast to its long-standing tradition of not endorsing any political candidates.[20]

Still, the *Globe* found ways of letting its readers know where its true political sympathies lay. On September 25 the paper published a laudatory front-page story with accompanying photograph on the birth of Joseph P. Kennedy II, the son of Robert F. Kennedy. The article reported that Kennedy had "resigned a post as special assistant to the United States Attorney in Brooklyn, N.Y., to aid his brother, Congressman John F. Kennedy, in his Massachusetts Senatorial race. Uncle John," the paper enthused, "is scheduled to be godfather to young Joseph Patrick."[21] The *Globe* failed to mention, however, why this blessed event warranted special front-page coverage.

The *Globe* also gave prominent coverage on October 19 to a flattering letter Kennedy received from the former commander of the Japanese destroyer that "cut Kennedy's PT boat in two in the waters off the Solomon Islands nine years ago." Kohei Hanami, who commanded the destroyer *Amagiri* during World War II, wrote Kennedy to tell him he had read an interview Kennedy had given to *Time* magazine in August about the "battle" the PT-109 waged against his old ship. "I take this opportunity," he told Kennedy, "to pay my profound respect to your daring and courageous action in this battle and also to congratulate you upon your miraculous escape under such circumstances." So as not to miss the real purpose of the article, the *Globe* also included Hanami's expressed "wish" that Kennedy be successful "in the coming election in your country."[22]

In citing reasons for supporting Lodge over Kennedy, the Republican *Herald* found the Democrat's chronic absenteeism in the House to be the overriding factor. "It is known," the paper asserted, "that the Congressman has suffered some illness. And there are, of course, many other legitimate reasons why a Representative should fail to record himself on important votes. But when the number missed approaches half, it becomes a question of whether the public is being adequately served." Lodge, in contrast, "played a role not only in the most important deliberations of the upper chamber, but also in the dull routine of legislative work." He made it a point "to be on hand and to record himself on all issues, despite the pressure of other duties and interests." The issue before Massachusetts voters, then, was whether they wanted "a part-time or a full-time spokesman in the Senate for the next six years."[23]

The independent *Eagle* took a different approach, arguing that Lodge's exemplary record of service warranted him another term in office. In particular, the paper was impressed with Lodge's efforts to modernize the Republican Party. "Because the country so urgently needs the enlightened, responsible brand of Republicanism that Lodge represents," the paper explained, "it seems to us but common sense to support it at the ballot box." If Eisenhower won the presidency, Lodge, who was in line for chairmanship of the Senate Rules Committee, would be "an invaluable voice for liberalism in the intra-mural GOP jockeying for power that would almost certainly take place." Conversely, if Stevenson won, Lodge could be expected to serve "as a leader in the inevitable fight to keep the Republican machinery from domination by reckless and embittered Old Guardists." Kennedy, the paper maintained, "fumbled the ball badly" by failing to bring "his brand of integrity" to the fight for the governorship against what the *Eagle* perceived as the corrupt practices of the Dever administration. "Faced with the golden opportunity to lead a healthy revolt against the Dever forces," the paper concluded, "he chose instead to form tacit alliance with them in a relatively inglorious fight to unseat a deserving incumbent."[24]

Viewing Kennedy in an even harsher light, the Republican *Worcester Gazette* found the Democrat to be more at home in the "camp of the isolationists" than with committed internationalists such as Lodge. "Lodge," the paper noted, "has voted for aid to help our friends abroad." Kennedy, on the other hand, had demonstrated he was for "hobbling these neighborly gestures, when, indeed, he has risked a stand at all." His record for "non-voting" in Congress, the paper insisted, "reflects discredit on Massachusetts." Lodge, in comparison, had become "a distinguished successor for the late Senator Arthur Vandenberg in the role of the leading Republican exponent of extending a helpful hand to Europe and maintaining a bipartisan foreign policy."[25]

The independent *Lowell Sun* argued that Lodge's "brilliant leadership" in garnering Eisenhower the GOP presidential nomination earned him the paper's strongest possible endorsement. "The people of Massachusetts, men, women and children, Republicans, Democrats, and Independents can feel proud of Senator Lodge, and the fact that he comes from the old Bay State. Politicians have come and politicians have gone in Massachusetts in the last half century. But the statesmen have been few and far between. Senator Henry Cabot Lodge is certainly one of the few truly great statesmen, and never was he more deserving of election to the Senate than he is this year."[26]

The liberal yet Republican *Springfield Union* concurred. "Like Rep. Christian A. Herter, Republican candidate for governor, Sen. Lodge's reputation is nation-wide, and both records have appealed strongly to citizens who feel deep concern for the national welfare." The paper went on to quote extensively from an October 30 editorial in the pro-Eisenhower *New York Herald-Tribune* that praised Lodge for his advocacy of reform within the GOP and his firm grasp of international events. "No one represents better than he the liberal forces of the Republican Party," the excerpt read. "He has been on the good side in virtually every one of the crucial fights of the past years, an individual of audacity, imagination and courage. Foreign affairs and national defense he has made his specialties, studying them at first hand and mastering the intricacies as have few Senators of this or any epoch."[27]

Lack of newspaper support was not the only problem facing the Kennedy campaign as it entered the final leg of the Senate race. The interlocking issues of the candidate's health, his difficulties with the leadership of the state Democratic Party, and the specter of a Joseph McCarthy intervention all played their part in casting a shadow over the otherwise smoothly functioning Kennedy operation.

The question of the candidate's health had been an ongoing concern of the Kennedy camp. Since the end of the spring, when he injured himself by sliding down a fire pole in Springfield for a photo opportunity, Kennedy had experienced severe back spasms along with bouts of physical exhaustion caused by his continued struggle with Addison's disease. "He was in intense pain towards the end of the '52 campaign," confirmed Kennedy campaign publicist John Galvin. "I am convinced that there were times when he was walking around almost unconscious [from the pain] but he never, he never complained this guy."[28]

So delicate was the Democrat's physical condition that when he was scheduled to make a televised fifteen-minute speech on election eve, he had to bow out owing to extreme fatigue. No explanation was given to the newspapers. "We all had a feeling that to have him face up to the prospect of delivering on live television a fifteen-minute straight address was just too much to ask," explained campaign aide Joseph Healey.[29]

That Kennedy, for the most part, refused to give in to these ailments was a testament to his uncomplaining nature and an unremitting personal drive. Recalled campaign organizer Larry O'Brien, "I think that Jack's wartime experience, coming so close to death in his PT-boat mishap, had toughened him tremendously—not only physically but in his outlook toward life, so that he could withstand whatever came along including all the name-calling and backstabbing of Massachusetts politics."[30]

To prevent news of the Bay State lawmaker's health woes from going public and thus becoming a campaign issue, extraordinary measures were taken by the candidate and his staff to hide the truth. For instance, following the Springfield fire station incident, Larry O'Brien was enlisted to issue a cover story saying the congressman would have to cancel a string of campaign appearances in western Massachusetts owing to pressing legislative business in Washington, D.C. In reality, the Democrat was convalescing at a local hotel under a physician's care. "I doubted," O'Brien later confessed, "that Kennedy's sliding down the fire pole and injuring his back would stay secret long, however, so I called an editor of the Springfield paper and leveled with him and asked him to help us out. He did, and the paper went along with our story about Kennedy's return to Washington."[31]

The candidate himself contributed to this legerdemain. Concealing the crutches he used to relieve pressure from his back, Kennedy would arrive "erect and standing" at campaign events, giving no indication of the pain he was enduring. "When we got back to the hotel," Kennedy intimate Dave Powers later revealed, "out would come the crutches from the floor of the back seat [of the car] and he would use them to get upstairs, where I would fill the bathtub with hot water, and he would soak himself in the tub for an hour before going to bed."[32]

While Kennedy could mask his physical ailments through deft manipulation of the media and an almost superhuman tolerance for pain, he was less successful in papering over the differences he had with Governor Paul Dever, the reigning leader of the state's Democratic Party. Put simply, the two men did not see eye to eye politically, particularly when it came to coordinating their campaigns. "There was a bitterness between the two camps and, instead of running as a team, they were almost running against one another," remembered Edward J. McCormack, the future state attorney general who was beginning his active involvement in politics during this period.[33]

The bad blood stemmed from years of mutual distrust and recrimination. In 1946 Dever supported former Cambridge mayor Mike Neville over Kennedy in that year's hotly contested Eleventh Congressional District race, a move that earned Dever the lasting enmity of his fellow Democrat. "Not very good" was how Kennedy later described his relationship with Dever.[34]

This feeling of personal unease was reciprocated by Dever and his supporters, especially when Kennedy bested Neville in the Democratic primary. "They felt that we were trying to take away something from them which was justly theirs," related Kennedy campaign worker Joseph DeGuglielmo. "They had in January of that year, they had that congressional seat signed, sealed and delivered to Mike Neville. No if's, and's or but's about it. But as the thing developed, it turned out that both Mr. Neville and the others who were in the fight were doomed for a little disappointment."[35]

Exacerbating tensions between the two camps were the contrasting social background of each lawmaker. "I always respected Dever but, you know, we were from a different environment," Kennedy told biographer James MacGregor Burns in 1959.[36] Indeed, Kennedy was a millionaire's son who grew up in a world of wealth and privilege, while Dever came from a poor Irish Catholic family that had to struggle to make ends meet. That personal friction developed was perhaps inevitable.

Dever, envious of Kennedy's money and connections and fearful of his ambitions, was inclined over the years not to grant his younger political colleague any special favors. A case in point was the 1952 Democratic National Convention in Chicago. As the scheduled keynote speaker and de facto leader of the Massachusetts delegation, Governor Dever apparently saw nothing wrong with denying Kennedy an official spot in the delegation.[37] Though the snub undoubtedly rankled Kennedy, the three-term congressman wisely kept his own counsel. In the midst of a tough election battle for the U.S. Senate, he was not about to kick up a political hornet's nest over what amounted to a petty slight. To be sure, at this point in time he needed Dever more than Dever needed him.

The latter was particularly true in Boston, where Kennedy, hoping to capitalize on the governor's popularity among rank-and-file Democrats, entered into a limited political partnership with Dever that entailed the sharing of "certain expenses, staff and headquarters" for the upcoming fall election. But Dever's usefulness as a political ally diminished after he lost his voice in the middle of a nationally televised keynote address at the Democratic National Convention on July 21. "I felt so sorry for him," Dave Powers later said of the rotund lawmaker. "He was a great campaigner and a great talker too. I don't know what makes a fellow think his voice might come back. It got raspier and raspier. He was sweating like a pig and the press did an awful job on him. Somebody said all he needed was an apple in his mouth to look like a—you know."[38]

Indeed, one national publication later claimed that Massachusetts TV owners "were distressed at [Dever's] resemblance to any cartoonist's conception of an 1890 Republican plutocrat." Closer to home, the *Boston Herald* reported that Dever, "a tubby man in a blue suit," was "dripping with perspiration even before he began the speech." The *Berkshire Eagle* was equally harsh, calling the governor's performance "a repetitious rant that never paused, halted, changed its pace, its time or its roaring monotony." "At the end," the *Eagle* concluded, "the patience of the audience must have approached exhaustion; the speaker's voice had passed it."[39]

Humiliated by his performance in Chicago, Dever scrambled desperately to pick up the pieces of his shattered political reputation and to salvage what he could of his now troubled gubernatorial campaign against Republican Congressman Christian A. Herter of Boston. Hoping to benefit from Kennedy's own attractive political image, Dever started clamoring for joint Dever-Kennedy headquarters outside of Boston, along with a joint statewide advertising effort. The Kennedy camp not surprisingly balked at this proposed new arrangement. "We wished Dever well, but he was falling behind while we were pulling ahead, and we didn't intend to blow a year of work" in the closing weeks of the campaign, explained Kennedy strategist Larry O'Brien.[40]

Ignoring the decision, Dever supporters began erecting huge Dever-Kennedy campaign banners across Massachusetts. This action, however, only served to encourage an embarrassing series of vandalism incidents between the two camps. "Kennedy people in parts of the state would tear down the Dever signs and Dever people would tear down the Kennedy signs," remembered

Democrat Edward McCormack. "They were all supposed to be working [as] one."[41]

To straighten out the mess, Kennedy sent his trusted campaign manager, Robert F. Kennedy, into the Dever camp to speak on his behalf. His instructions to his eager yet politically inexperienced younger brother were clear and unambiguous. "Don't give in to them," he said, "but don't get me involved." Relishing the role of "bad cop" to his brother's "good cop," a role he would reprise several times over the course of his tragically abbreviated career, incidentally, Robert lashed into Dever for his alleged perfidy.[42]

Unnerved by the ferociousness of Kennedy's attack, Dever abruptly concluded the meeting. "I know you're an important man around here and all that," the Cambridge Democrat told Joseph Kennedy on the telephone afterward, "but I'm telling you this and I mean it. Keep that fresh kid of yours out of sight from here on in."[43]

Though deeply resentful of the strong-arm tactics employed by the Kennedys, Dever backed down and agreed to abide by the terms of the original arrangement he had with them, namely, a joint campaign operation in Boston. Fear of permanently alienating John Kennedy's supporters and thus effecting a split among state Democrats before election day no doubt accounted for this turnaround. "We succeeded in fuzzing over the situation," Larry O'Brien later boasted.[44]

While relations with Dever were a cause for concern, they still did not represent the kind of grave political threat to Kennedy's candidacy that Senator Joseph R. McCarthy of Wisconsin posed. Put succinctly, if the anticommunist firebrand came to Massachusetts to campaign on Lodge's behalf, Kennedy's hopes of reaching the Senate would have been severely impaired. For as was the case in other parts of the country in 1952, McCarthy was an extremely popular figure in Massachusetts, especially among the state's 750,000 Irish Catholic inhabitants.

"The influence of McCarthy on the Bay State was almost inevitable given the affinity that the Irish-American population had for one of its own who echoed their fears, even if he was a Republican," political historian Alec Barbrook has explained.[45]

Given this scenario, it is not surprising that prominent state Democrats such as John McCormack and "Tip" O'Neill refused to speak out against McCarthy or his increasingly controversial red-baiting tactics. "If you invited me here because you thought I would attack McCarthy or criticize the way he treats that kind of scum [communists], you've got the wrong man," O'Neill "icily" informed one local audience.[46]

Senator Joseph McCarthy of Wisconsin (left) with Massacusetts lawmakers (left to right) Leverett Saltonstall, Lodge, and Kennedy during a Boston banquet in 1947. "I'm going to teach that bastard of a Lodge to suck eggs," McCarthy once vowed.
Courtesy of the Boston Public Library, Print Department.

To be sure, conventional political wisdom of the day held that any stand taken against McCarthy was an open invitation for defeat come election day. This had been the case for Senator Millard E. Tydings of Maryland in 1950 and soon would be for Senator William B. Benton of Connecticut in 1952. Little wonder then that Kennedy and Lodge approached the subject of McCarthy cautiously during their Senate campaign. Neither candidate wanted to say or do anything that could be interpreted as being anti-McCarthy.

This caution was reflected in a memo Kennedy campaign aide R. Sargent Shriver sent Democratic presidential candidate and diehard McCarthy opponent Adlai Stevenson on the eve of the latter's planned visit to Massachusetts in late September. "Things to avoid—it would not be wise . . . to attack Joe McCarthy now," the memo read. "He is very popular up here with people of both parties."[47]

Old Joseph Kennedy associate and campaign advisor James Landis also urged caution on the McCarthy issue. "Why?" Landis later explained. "Because it's important in politics to win, and [Kennedy] would have lost a tremendous number of votes, especially in the [mostly Irish Catholic] South Boston area and so on, if he had taken on McCarthy. He avoided it. . . . He never justified McCarthy at any time. But '52 was a fairly conservative year and at that time McCarthy was riding pretty high."[48]

There was little danger of Kennedy's criticizing McCarthy or his politics. He had been on friendly terms with the Wisconsin senator for several years. According to McCarthy advisor Roy Cohn, this friendship began during World War II when the two men were stationed together in the Solomon Islands. At the time Kennedy was commanding the PT-59 (his first ship, the PT-109, had been sunk by a Japanese destroyer), and McCarthy was serving as a captain in the marines.

"On a hot, damp Sunday, Captain McCarthy got into conversation with young Lieutenant Kennedy, who took him for a ride," Cohn recounted. McCarthy appeared to have been very impressed by Kennedy. "I met this fellow Kennedy—a hell of a nice guy. His old man's the ambassador to Britain," he told marine acquaintance Penn T. Kimball, who later became a professor of journalism at Columbia University. Kennedy reportedly let McCarthy accompany him and his crew unofficially on two night patrol missions. "Joe McCarthy did that," Kimball later confirmed. "He knew who Jack was [the son of a famous ambassador]. He probably sought him out."[49] McCarthy, whose 1946 Senate campaign literature trumpeted him as "Tail-Gunner Joe," claimed that on one of these missions Kennedy let him test-fire the machine guns.

After the war, Kennedy and McCarthy found themselves serving together once again, this time as legislators on Capitol Hill. McCarthy became a frequent guest at Kennedy's brownstone apartment in Georgetown, and the two bachelors were often seen together making the rounds at various Washington, D.C., cocktail parties. "I got the idea that Jack liked McCarthy," recalled George Smathers, the veteran Florida politician who was a freshman congressman during this period. Kennedy "thought he was a pretty good guy. . . . He was friendly all the way through."[50]

The late Supreme Court Justice Willliam O. Douglas, a close Kennedy family friend, confirmed this observation in an oral history conducted for the Kennedy Library. Douglas stated that whenever he tried to discuss McCarthy and his increasingly controversial red-baiting tactics with the Massachusetts legislator, the latter would cut off all conversation on the subject. "Well, he's an old friend," he would usually say. "Known him for a long time."[51]

According to biographer Doris Kearns Goodwin, the personal closeness between Kennedy and McCarthy can be attributed to a shared "sense of fun and love of women."[52] Both were eligible bachelors at the time, and each had an abiding fondness for members of the opposite sex. Goodwin might also have added to her analysis that the two shared a strong sense of anticommunism. For Kennedy believed that McCarthy's overall goal of fighting communism at home was commendable, as befitted someone who had made an issue of domestic subversion during the Harold Christoffel investigation in 1947.

At a 1952 banquet commemorating the hundredth anniversary of the founding of the Harvard Spree Club, Kennedy's undergraduate final club, the young Democrat publicly berated a speaker for making a joke that linked Alger Hiss with McCarthy. "How dare you couple the name of a great American patriot with that of a traitor!" he shouted. Following an awkward silence, Kennedy, "visibly mad and very short," according to one witness, got up and walked out before dessert was served. He was also equally frank in comments made to a group of Harvard graduate students in the fall of 1950; he was quoted as saying that "he knew Joe [McCarthy] pretty well, and he may well have something."[53]

In later years, Kennedy staffers such as Theodore C. Sorenson and Arthur M. Schlesinger Jr. attempted to downplay their boss's relationship with McCarthy, claiming that Kennedy was personally turned off by the Wisconsinite's rough House style. But as historian Herbert Parmet has pointed out, such claims do not square with reality. "The fact is that in their younger days there was much compatibility." So much compatibility, in fact, that when liberal advisor Gardner "Pat" Jackson pressured the Bay State lawmaker to sign a newspaper advertisement condemning McCarthy late in the 1952 campaign, ("COMMUNISM AND MCCARTHY BOTH WRONG," the ad read), the candidate demurred.[54]

McCarthy also enjoyed close personal ties to the Kennedy family. A frequent visitor to the family's summertime retreat in Hyannis Port, McCarthy was known to participate in such time-honored family rituals as sailing, touch football, and softball, although he had to retire from the latter when he made four errors in a game. "In case there is any question in your mind," Joseph Kennedy informed a journalist in 1961, "I liked Joe McCarthy. I always liked him. I would see him when I went down to Washington and when he was visiting in Palm Beach he'd come around to my house for a drink. I invited him to Cape Cod." As a personal favor, McCarthy would later help Kennedy's second-youngest son, Robert, attain a staff assistant's position on the Permanent Subcommittee on Investigations of the Senate Government Operations Committee, a committee the Wisconsinite chaired.[55]

If McCarthy's relations with John Kennedy and his family could be described as warm and friendly, the same could not be said of his relations with Lodge. Bluntly stated, the two did not get along. "There was no great love between them," admitted Lodge staffer Maxwell Rabb. Barriers of social class, ethnic background, and personal temperament stood in the way. Lodge's reserved Brahmin demeanor simply did not mesh with what he thought to be McCarthy's brutish personality. "There's no question about it," recalled former *Boston Globe* political reporter Robert Healy, "Lodge would have had to hold his nose to appear on the same platform as him."[56]

The feeling was mutual. Longtime Lodge political aide and 1952 campaign advisor James J. Sullivan of Boston remembered being once approached by McCarthy in the U.S. Senate cloakroom. "What are you doing here?" McCarthy inquired after finding out Sullivan came from Boston. "I work for Lodge," Sullivan replied. "You work for Lodge! That Yankee [so and so]," responded McCarthy in a fit of rage. The conservative midwesterner was later equally as demonstrative of his dislike for Lodge when he heard a rumor that Lodge had been allegedly involved in a political scheme to discredit him. "I'm going to teach that bastard of a Lodge to suck eggs," McCarthy reportedly told his Senate office manager.[57]

Personalities aside, Lodge did come to McCarthy's defense in 1950 while serving on a special subcommittee of the Senate Foreign Relations Committee investigating charges by the Wisconsinite that the State Department was "riddled" with communists. On July 17 the subcommittee, which was chaired by conservative Democrat Millard E. Tydings of Maryland, filed a three-to-two majority report that characterized McCarthy's allegations as being "perhaps the most nefarious campaign of half-truths and untruth in the history of the Republic." Lodge, who had an eye toward placating his conservative Irish Catholic constituency back home in Massachusetts, predictably took issue with this conclusion and refused to sign the majority report along with fellow Republican Senator Bourke Hickenlouper of Iowa, a staunch McCarthy defender. In his thirty-four-page minority response, the Brahmin Republican faulted the subcommittee for producing a "superficial and inconclusive" study. "The fact that many charges have been made which have not been proven does not in the slightest degree relieve the subcommittee of the responsibility for undertaking a relentlessly thorough investigation of its own," he wrote.[58]

Accusing committee Democrats of letting partisan political concerns interfere with their own objectivity, he called for the establishment of an independent bipartisan commission to investigate McCarthy's charges. "This business will never end at all clearly or otherwise if the practice of having the majority party investigate the majority continues to hold sway," he reasoned.

"Nor will satisfactory results be obtained if the minority investigates the majority. The investigation must be non-political."[59]

In actuality, Lodge's position was consistent with earlier statements he had made on the subject. In April 1950 he had urged the appointment of a twelve-member commission, equally divided between Democrats and Republicans, to look into McCarthy's allegations. "We are dealing here with the foreign relations of the United States, which means all the men, women, and children of America," he said. "In such a life-and-death responsibility, there must be no politics."[60]

Then, as was later the case with the release of his Tydings minority report, Lodge received criticism in liberal circles for protecting McCarthy for what was believed to be partisan political reasons—despite personal differences, Lodge and McCarthy were still Republicans. The Bay State lawmaker brushed away such allegations. "Let me say that I am not trying to 'shield' Senator McCarthy," he wrote then–Harvard University professor and noted liberal savant Arthur M. Schlesinger Jr. of his actions. "Indeed there can be no one who feels more strongly opposed to besmirching the reputations of innocent people than I do."[61]

Nonetheless, it can be argued that Lodge's criticism of the Tydings investigation provided pro-McCarthy forces the political cover they needed to dismiss the majority report as "the most scandalous and brazen whitewash of treasonable conspiracy in our history." If Lodge had gone the other way and supported the majority Democrats' findings, the political case against McCarthy would have been immeasurably strengthened under a halo of bipartisanship. Thus, McCarthy dodged a bullet that had the potential of undermining his credibility as an anticommunist crusader and seriously damaging his political career. And for all that the Wisconsinite had Lodge, "that Yankee [so and so]," to thank.[62]

Although he still had no personal use for Lodge, McCarthy was appreciative that his fellow Republican had come to his aid in a moment of partisan political need. McCarthy expressed his gratitude in a telegram endorsement of Lodge on the eve of the 1952 Senate election, which, for reasons that will be discussed below, was never used by the veteran Massachusetts politician. Effused McCarthy, "YOUR DISSENTING REPORT IN WHICH YOU POINTED OUT WHEREIN THE TYDINGS COMMITTEE FAILED AND IN WHICH YOU SO CLEARLY STATED HOW THE INVESTIGATION COULD AND SHOULD HAVE BEEN CONDUCTED . . . WERE IN MY OPINION MASTERPIECES. AS I TOLD YOU AT THE TIME I DEEPLY APPRECIATED SUCH ACTION ON YOUR PART."[63]

Because McCarthy felt personally indebted to Lodge for saving him from political embarrassment during the Tydings subcommittee hearings, he was placed in an awkward position regarding the 1952 Massachusetts Senate race. If asked, McCarthy would be hard pressed not to campaign for Lodge, especially since both came from the same political party. But doing so ran the risk of upsetting his friendship with John Kennedy, not to mention the rest of the Kennedy family. The situation was further complicated by the fact that Joseph Kennedy had been a frequent and generous campaign contributor to McCarthy over the years.[64] Understandably, McCarthy hoped that Lodge would not seek his support. But the tide of political events dictated otherwise.

Since he had been away most of the previous eight months campaigning for Eisenhower, Lodge had, in the words of one friendly biographer, "neglected" his "political garden" back home. Of particular concern to Lodge was Kennedy's popularity in Boston with its majority Irish Catholic population. "Boston is recognized as a key to the state as a whole," the *Christian Science Monitor* claimed that fall. "Unless Republican candidates from Gen. Dwight D. Eisenhower on down can cut into the heavy Democratic majorities usually rolled up in Boston, G.O.P. victories are unlikely on Nov. 4." This was where McCarthy's importance came into play.[65]

"In some quarters it is felt that Senator McCarthy has a particular appeal for Boston, with its population makeup," the *Monitor* continued. "It is believed among these elements that Senator McCarthy's anticommunist drive, despite his much criticized methods, would win over the support of many Boston Democrats who are violently opposed to communism and fellow traveler groups, and those who are disturbed by charges of Communist infiltration in the national government."[66]

Private feelers were thus sent out from Lodge's camp to determine whether McCarthy would be willing to come to Massachusetts and speak on Lodge's behalf. A speech extolling Lodge's anticommunism was even drafted for McCarthy to give in the event the latter agreed to speak. "Elect as your Senator and Representatives in Washington men who by their records are vigorous, all-out foes of Communism—men who hold no brief political or social with fellow travelers or intellectual parlor pinks," the speech said. "On Nov. 4 go to the polls and get behind un-compromising American patriots such as your own United States Senator, Henry Cabot Lodge, Jr."[67]

But McCarthy never gave the speech. To avoid causing friction with the Kennedys yet still retain an appearance of party loyalty to Lodge, McCarthy devised an ingenious ploy. He informed the Lodge camp that he would be only too happy to stump for the Bay State lawmaker, provided that Lodge publicly asked for his help. These were terms that McCarthy shrewdly calculated Lodge would find unacceptable. "I cracked that one," McCarthy reportedly boasted to conservative supporter William F. Buckley Jr., the future editor and publisher of the *National Review.* "I told [the Lodge campaign] I'd go up to Boston to speak if Cabot publicly asked me. And he'll never do that— he'd lose the Harvard vote."[68]

The "Harvard vote" McCarthy referred to were the scions of Back Bay and Beacon Hill society who traditionally looked down their noses at the brass-knuckle tactics employed by politicians like McCarthy, even though the latter was a Republican. The Wisconsin senator "obviously had a definite following, but careful analysis convinced me that his support of me would lose me more votes than it would gain," Lodge later explained. Former Boston journalist Robert Healy agrees with this assessment. "All those North Shore WASPs, if Lodge campaigned on the same stage as McCarthy, they would have lost their breakfasts," he claimed.[69] Thus, McCarthy's offer was rejected. But Lodge did not abandon entirely the notion of securing McCarthy's assistance.

In the waning moments of the campaign, Lodge made a direct personal appeal to McCarthy to come to Massachusetts and campaign exclusively against Kennedy. "I became convinced that if [McCarthy] were to attack my opponent in his best rough and tumble manner, this would injure my opponent enough so as to make me win the election," Lodge later revealed. McCarthy flatly refused to go on the political offensive against Kennedy, but he did send off the previously mentioned telegram endorsing Lodge's candidacy three days before the election. The message read: "IN THE CLOSING DAYS OF THIS CAMPAIGN I WANT TO TELL YOU THAT YOU HAVE BEEN ONE OF THE REALLY GREAT FIGHTERS IN THE SENATE AGAINST COMMUNISM. . . . I BELIEVE IT IS UTTERLY VITAL THAT YOU BE REELECTED."[70]

Lodge never made use of the telegram.

"In the first place," commented Lodge confidant Maxwell Rabb, McCarthy "did this when it was late and when it was over. During the entire period it was clear he had been going to Hyannis Port. He had been part of that picture. He was a friend of Jack Kennedy's. He was a friend of the [Kennedy] boys all along the line. There's no question about that. He was their friend, and he desisted from putting himself forward. So part of this would be due to that. The other part was that Lodge was never impressed with him."[71] In any event, McCarthy stayed out of Massachusetts.

In retrospect, it seems clear that Lodge miscalculated when he rejected the Wisconsin lawmaker's terms for coming to Massachusetts. A McCarthy visit might have afforded Lodge the opportunity of neutralizing his Democratic

opponent's attacks concerning his alleged softness on the anticommunism issue. Moreover, the sight of McCarthy, the hero of the GOP's right wing, campaigning side by side with Lodge would have given conservative state Republicans second thoughts about swinging their support to Kennedy.

As for the argument advanced by Lodge that McCarthy would have cost
his candidacy more votes than it would have gained, this cannot be determined
from existing evidence. Eisenhower, who campaigned for McCarthy with outward enthusiasm in 1952, certainly was not hurt by this connection in Massachusetts. In fact, as political scientist Lawrence H. Fuchs pointed out in his
seminal 1957 study "Presidential Politics in Boston: The Irish Response to
Stevenson," the McCarthy affiliation, coupled with the Democratic presidential nominee's status as a divorcee, aided the general in picking up a substantial
number of Irish Catholic votes in Boston.[72]

Indeed, President Truman received 71.5 percent of the Boston vote in
1948, whereas Stevenson captured "only" 59.5 percent in 1952.[73] Little wonder,
then, that Kennedy kept his party's nominee at arm's length during the campaign. Irish Catholics represented a core constituency group, and the Democrat saw no reason to offend them by embracing the unpopular Stevenson.
The question becomes, then, whether Lodge could have similarly benefited,
as Eisenhower did, from the McCarthy connection. Given Lodge's previous
showings in the Irish Catholic community, it seems not unreasonable to think
he would have.

Noncompliance with McCarthy's terms for coming to Massachusetts was
not the only political blunder Lodge committed in the final weeks of the Senate race. He also failed to grasp the growing importance of television on mod-
ern campaigning.

By 1952 television had emerged as a powerful medium in which to convey
images and ideas. Network programs such as the *Texaco Star Theater* with Milton Berle and *I Love Lucy* with Lucille Ball and Desi Arnaz attracted millions of
viewers each week while making household names of its stars. Advertisers,
long accustomed to promoting their products in print and on the radio, now
embraced the new technology as a way of expanding their market base. Indeed, Hazel Bishop, a heretofore obscure manufacturer of lipstick, saw its annual sales skyrocket from $50,000 in 1950 to $4.5 million in 1952, thanks largely
to television advertising.[74]

Politicians and government officials were not slow in recognizing the
medium's potential. In 1950 Governor Thomas E. Dewey of New York placed
heavy emphasis on television in his successful campaign for reelection. On the

weekend before the election, for example, the twice-defeated GOP presidential nominee hosted an engaging eighteen-hour telethon that analysts later claimed garnered the candidate several thousand votes.[75]

Similarly, the "electric mirror" was credited with boosting the political fortunes of Senator Estes Kefauver of Tennessee. Little known and lightly regarded outside his home state, the Democratic lawmaker achieved overnight celebrity status in 1951 with his chairmanship of the televised Senate hearings on organized crime. According to journalist-historian David Halberstam, Kefauver came across as "a sort of Southern Jimmy Stewart, the same citizen-politician who gets tired of the abuse of government and goes off to do something about it."[76]

Though the same could not be said of Richard M. Nixon, the Republican vice-presidential candidate earned lasting notoriety in 1952 for his explanation of an alleged personal impropriety involving an eighteen-thousand-dollar expense fund. Addressing the charge that he accepted illegal cash contributions, the future president told a national television audience that he was innocent of any wrongdoing. In fact, he said, the only unsolicited gift he received was a little cocker spaniel dog his six-year-old daughter named Checkers. Public response to the so-called Checkers speech was overwhelmingly supportive, thus preserving the young Republican's place on the GOP ticket. Observed the *Christian Science Monitor,* "No other medium could have registered, pictured, relayed, and implanted the drama of Senator Richard M. Nixon's appeal and self-defense as television did."[77]

Massachusetts was not immune to the new technology. Since the end of World War II, television had made significant strides toward building a solid base of viewership in the Bay State. According to the "Preliminary Survey of Television Coverage for 1952 Senatorial Candidates" put out by the Radio-Television Division of the Republican National Committee in 1951, an estimated 48 percent of the state's 4.7 million population had access to 741,000 TV sets.[78]

Though existing data are too sparse to determine with any certainty the demographic makeup of who actually owned these sets, they most likely came from a moderate- to upper-income background, since the then relatively high price of a television set discouraged ownership by lower-income groups. In addition, these same owners were probably more inclined to live in the eastern half of the state: most communities in western Massachusetts lacked the technological facilities to receive and transmit television signals.

Moreover, there is no doubt about the interest the new medium engendered in local politicos such as Paul Dever, Leverett Saltonstall, and Christian Herter by the early 1950s. These individuals saw television as a potential vote-getting instrument. Indeed, no less a figure than perennial Boston mayoral candidate James Michael Curley made significant use of television in his unsuccessful 1949 reelection campaign against John B. Hynes. Showing film footage of the many municipal buildings, parks, and hospitals he had built during his four terms as mayor, Curley asked voters not to forget the public services he had rendered on their behalf. "Alert politicians have looked forward to television for many years," reported Courtney Sheldon of the *Christian Science Monitor* at the time. "Some of them are now convinced T.V. audiences are extensive enough to take the plunge."[79]

In 1952 both Democratic and Republican candidates for U.S. senator in Massachusetts took that plunge with varying degrees of success. John Kennedy, displaying a warm and engaging personality combined with movie star looks, was a natural for the new medium. Henry Cabot Lodge Jr., conveying a somewhat more stuffy, standoffish image, simply was not. Seeking an advantage, Kennedy's campaign purchased large blocks of advertising time from Boston-area television stations, since this was the principal broadcasting center in the state. In the three weeks leading up to the election, for example, Kennedy bought eight hours of TV advertising time, while Lodge, an apparently reluctant user of the new medium, purchased only four and a half hours. "John Kennedy knew that he was a television candidate," explained campaign aide Dave Powers.[80]

This awareness was ingrained in him by his father. As a former Hollywood movie mogul, Joseph P. Kennedy had a unique grasp of what it took to create a favorable image for mainstream consumption. "Mr. Kennedy was a genius about how Jack should be handled on television," recalled campaign speechwriter and the senior Kennedy's future son-in-law R. Sargent Shriver.

> He was the guy who really understood the tube. How Jack should appear on it. . . . He had a fantastic knack for knowing what the public was interested in. . . . He figured that television was going to be the greatest thing in the history of politics and set out studying it and how Jack could utilize it most effectively. Jack was on the early quiz shows and *Meet the Press*. [Joseph Kennedy] developed the local programs and got the right kind of questions. He knew how Jack should be dressed and how his hair should be, what his response should be and how to handle Lodge. He was really good on that. Super.[81]

Still, John Kennedy was not without initiative himself when it came to un-locking the mysteries of the new medium. A case in point was his making arrangements with CBS-TV to be a "guest student" at the network's "coaching school for political candidates" in Washington, D.C. Held on July 1, the one-day seminar gave Kennedy invaluable insight on "how to get the best advantage in television." Previous participants in the program included senators Estes Ke-fauver of Tennessee, William Benton of Connecticut, and Robert Kerr of Okla-homa. Headed by CBS director of public affairs William Wood and a team of seasoned network professionals, the school offered the candidate instruction on "how to distinguish among cameras in the studio and on the business end of the camera, so that when he wants to be eye to eye with his home audience he can be sure that he is." In the process of absorbing this information, Kennedy voiced agreement with a suggestion made by the CBS "faculty" that "if cir-cumstances permitted he could make a much more interesting presentation to televiewers with an extemporaneous talk than with a prepared one."[82]

At the conclusion of the session, Wood expressed satisfaction with his pupil's performance. "I believe we were able to clarify some of the principles and peculiarities of the TV medium for the Representative but beyond this there wasn't much for a teacher to do," the network official claimed. "Mr.

Kennedy with his sister Eunice during one of the well-received *Coffee with the Kennedys* television programs. "Mr. Kennedy has a natural approach which comes over television very well," a network television official observed in 1952. Courtesy of the John F. Kennedy Library.

Kennedy has a natural approach which comes over television very well. His good looks and strong personality lose nothing between studio and viewer and what's more he certainly doesn't have to worry about a receding hairline which is a problem with many a politician on TV."[83]

Lodge had a more difficult time with the new technology. Though handsome and well spoken, he could not translate these qualities onto the television screen. The problem, as TV ad producer Gene Wyckoff discovered when he worked with Lodge on the latter's 1960 vice-presidential campaign, was visceral. The Republican "looked like what you would expect an American statesman to look like," Wyckoff observed. "But when he opened his mouth and when he interacted with people on television, there was something not so attractive—something in his demeanor, a touch of hauteur, arrogance, aloofness, or condescension perhaps. His characterization did not ring true."[84]

This unflattering image came across when Lodge agreed to appear with Kennedy on the October 7 edition of *Keep Posted,* a national public affairs program that was broadcast live from a New York City studio and simulcast locally

Lodge looking less than comfortable in front of a television camera during the campaign. His difficulty with the new medium ultimately hurt his candidacy in 1952. Courtesy of the Massachusetts Historical Society, Boston.

on WNAC-TV in Boston. Addressing the show's main topic of discussion, "Who will do more for the country, Eisenhower or Stevenson?," the Republican lawmaker made a flat, uninspiring case for the general. He argued that Eisenhower's experience as NATO commander in Europe provided him the necessary managerial skills and insight to organize a "durable peace." Dressed in a dark, pin-striped suit, Lodge at times appeared distracted and bored with the proceedings. His fidgety body language seemed to tell viewers that he had better things to do than to sit around and spend time with them. This was in marked contrast to the image Kennedy projected. Alert and engaged, he gave a spirited yet lucid accounting of why he felt Stevenson was better qualified to be president. "I think his experience in bringing young, vigorous men into positions of responsibility in Illinois give[s] us hope" that he would do the same in Washington, D.C., the Bay State Democrat asserted. As an indication of who actually won this televised "debate," Kennedy can be seen smiling serenely into the camera as the credits begin to roll, while Lodge can be seen scowling conspicuously.[85]

Kennedy, confirmed one newspaper, "was in complete possession of all the facts he needed to support his contention that the Democratic party is better equipped to deal with the problems facing the country than the Republican party. His manner was unrestrained, and his poise never left him."[86]

Lodge's difficulties with television did not end with this broadcast. On election eve, Dwight Eisenhower came to Boston to conclude his presidential campaign with a rousing send-off rally at the Boston Garden on Causeway Street. The general's appearance was considered a major coup because Lodge was scheduled to introduce Eisenhower, thus gaining invaluable exposure for his Senate candidacy.

Unfortunately for Lodge, such well-laid plans went for naught. The Garden's audience's initial reaction to the GOP standard-bearer reached such a "sustained pitch" and got "so out of hand" that it forced "cancellation" of Lodge's scheduled introduction out of concern for running overtime with the networks.[87] Instead of basking in the reflected glow of the World War II hero's presidential candidacy, Lodge was left to ponder his missed opportunity. Exclaimed one exasperated Lodge supporter afterward, "We couldn't understand what happened to you, that you didn't introduce the General at the most important time . . . at the Boston Garden."[88]

It was, in many ways, a fitting epitaph for the lethargic television campaign Lodge waged against Kennedy in 1952.

Chapter SEVEN

Evening the Score

E LECTION day, November 3, 1952, brought months of hectic campaigning to a close. A record 2,422,548 persons went to the polls, and early returns suggested that a Republican sweep was in the making. Though clearly disturbed by the news, John F. Kennedy did his best to put on a brave face for the small gathering of family and friends that had assembled on election night at his parents' apartment on Beacon Street, a short distance from the Boston Common. A few days before in the same room, Joseph P. Kennedy had brashly predicted to a group of supporters that "the campaign is over and we have won."[1]

Such certitude now eluded John Kennedy. "One of the few times I remember seeing him really nervous was election night of '52," Rose Kennedy later wrote in her memoirs. "I remember especially he kept taking his jacket on and off and then soon putting it on again, sometimes pulling it off in such a way that the sleeves were inside out, then putting it on that way, and doing the same motion again, so that part of the sleeves were right side and part wrong side."[2]

Noting his son's unease, the ambassador suggested he and his college roommate, U.S. Congressman Torbert MacDonald of Massachusetts, take a walk across Boston Common to the Public Garden. Thankful for the distraction, John Kennedy readily complied. The crisp fall air outside seemed to restore some of his confidence as he thought aloud to his friend, "I wonder what sort of job that Ike will give Cabot." A surprised MacDonald laughed and replied, "What kind of job do you think Ike will give you?"[3]

Returning to the apartment, Kennedy learned that Dwight Eisenhower had won the presidency in a landslide over Adlai Stevenson but that his own Senate race was still very much in doubt. Television reports permitted the candidate to keep abreast of all the latest developments, as well as give him a glimpse of his not-so-distant future. For there on the tube flickered the jowl-faced image of Richard M. Nixon, the vice president–elect and Kennedy's 1960 Republican presidential opponent. "Imagine—he and I came into the Congress together and now he's Vice President of the United States," marveled the Democrat.[4]

Sometime before midnight, November 4, Kennedy departed for his campaign headquarters on Kilby Street with two of his sisters and MacDonald in tow. They were met there by the candidate's younger brother and campaign manager, Robert F. Kennedy, who looked nervous and agitated. "Bobby," MacDonald recalled, said things "didn't look any too great."[5]

Tempered by such negative reports, John Kennedy settled in for a long, expectant night of waiting. "I can't think of anything we could have done that we haven't," he claimed. At one point the candidate even lay across a desk to snatch a few moments of sleep. But Robert Kennedy, an emotionally intense

Lodge enthusiastically greets Dwight D. Eisenhower. The former had played a key role in convincing the general to seek the presidency in 1952. Courtesy of the Massachusetts Historical Society, Boston.

man by nature, refused to rest. As the latest returns trickled in, he mounted a desk and read off the results to the workers, friends, and hangers-on present. He grew angry and despondent over the possibility of defeat. "Bobby," Mac-Donald recounted, "was saying things about this guy and that and naming guys who hadn't done what they should have, including a lot of labor people— people who they felt should have been more helpful who really had given lip service and hadn't done what they should have for Jack." At dawn results broke in the Kennedy camp's favor, setting off a wild, impromptu celebration. The final vote tally read: Kennedy 1,211,984 (51.5 percent), Lodge 1,141,247 (48.5 percent).[6]

Not long after these results were announced, Kennedy received a long-distance phone call from an ambitious Democratic senator from Texas seeking votes to become the next Senate majority leader. "That was Lyndon Johnson

An obviously amused Kennedy is serenaded by Canadian bagpipers in Boston in late October 1952. Courtesy of the *New Bedford Standard-Times*.

of Texas," the surprised senator-elect told campaign aide Larry O'Brien. "He said he just wanted to congratulate me. The guy must never sleep."[7] Amid the fallen confetti and hoarse voices, attention began focusing down the street, where Lodge's campaign headquarters was located. Expectations were that the respected Republican lawmaker would come over and personally congratulate Kennedy on his victory.

The night's events had been bittersweet for Henry Cabot Lodge Jr. The man he had spent the better part of a year campaigning for around the country was now president-elect. Not only that, but Eisenhower easily carried Massachusetts, with 53 percent of the total vote for an impressive plurality of 208,800 votes.[8] The general's ascension meant that Lodge's tireless efforts to "modernize the GOP" had at last borne political fruit. Yet tempering these feelings of elation was the realization that he would not be returning to the Senate, where ironically a Democratic landslide had placed him in 1936, but a Republican one could not in 1952.

Defeat was a new, unsettling experience for Lodge, who had an unbeaten campaign record dating back to 1932. His feelings on the subject were later confided to Eisenhower in a private note. "I felt rather like a man who has just been hit by a truck," he wrote of his political loss. To his supporters on election night, however, he displayed an unflappable reserve. "You couldn't read Lodge, at least I couldn't," campaign aide James Sullivan reported. "What his real feelings were, that's another thing."[9]

Longtime Lodge friend and political lieutenant Maxwell Rabb found such reticence commendable. "I've never seen such calm in all my life," he recalled forty years later. "There was no backbiting. Nothing of the sort. I can remember I went away probably feeling prouder of him than at any other moment because it wasn't a question of 'Dammit, we could have had this thing, we should have started out long ago.' . . . It just struck me that this is a wonderful, wonderful way to be."[10]

Life magazine was less impressed, describing the Brahmin Republican's aspect that evening as "grim." Lodge later dismissed this account as an example of "what every managing editor thinks a defeated candidate should look like even though I do not even think I looked grim and I know I do not feel that way."[11] Still, with fifteen years of noteworthy service in the U.S. Senate ending so ingloriously, Lodge was entitled to a little grimness.

John Kennedy meanwhile patiently waited for his opponent to make an appearance at his campaign headquarters. Hailed by one newspaper as "the conqueror of Henry Cabot Lodge Jr.," the senator-elect sat leisurely with his brother Robert at a big table basking in the glow of his political triumph. On

Lodge and his wife, Emily Sears, cast ballots at the Cove School
in Beverly on election day. Courtesy of the Boston Public Library, Print
Department.

his suit jacket the young Democrat wore a 1912 John F. Fitzgerald mayoral
campaign button, a "good luck" charm from a supporter in Everett, a small
working-class community north of Boston.[12]

"Honey Fitz" had narrowly missed defeating Henry Cabot Lodge Sr. for
the same Senate seat back in 1916, the first year U.S. senators were chosen by
popular franchise. As a young boy, Fitzgerald had taken leave of his paper
route one wintery day and warmed his shivering body at the servants' quarters
of the Lodge family estate on Beacon Street. "In his wildest dreams that win-
ter's night," Rose Kennedy later told historian Doris Kearns Goodwin, "could
he ever have imagined how far he and his family would come?" Perhaps not,
but as a defeated senatorial candidate, Fitzgerald boldly predicted that "with

the proper work Massachusetts would land in the Democratic column for good."[13] His grandson had performed the "proper work," thus gaining a measure of political as well as familial revenge.

Around 7:30 A.M., a group of Kennedy supporters stationed at the windows overlooking Kilby Street spotted Lodge's tall, erect figure exiting from his campaign headquarters. "There he goes," they exclaimed in unison. "Everyone be polite to him," John Kennedy instructed. "Give him a hand when he comes in." The applause never came; Lodge got into a waiting limousine and sped past Kennedy's headquarters without slowing down. His concession remarks arrived via telegram at 7:34 A.M. "Son of a bitch," Kennedy spat bitterly. "Can you believe it?" The Fitzgeralds may have, as Rose Kennedy put it, "evened the score" with the Lodges, but the latter were loathe to admit it.[14]

News of Kennedy's victory was greeted with considerable interest around the country. Syndicated newspaper columnist Drew Pearson wrote in his diary afterward that he was unsure whether the outcome was "a plus or a minus." "Lodge was a good Senator," he attested. "Kennedy will probably revert to the thinking of his old man." The pro-Taft *Chicago Tribune,* which described Kennedy as a "fighting conservative," made no attempt to hide its delight: "Lodge, a well known trimmer and opportunist, tried to ride several political horses galloping off in different directions with the result that voters unseated him, both Republicans and Democrats taking part in the debacle."[15]

Former secretary of state George C. Marshall, an admirer of Lodge and his advocacy of a bipartisan foreign policy, grew depressed over the news and penned a letter of sympathy. "I am terribly sorry that the electorate failed you in your state," he wrote the Bay State lawmaker. "They made a great error for you were among the most conspicuous statesmen in public office. I anticipated great things for you and maybe in the curious workings of fate this mishap may be a turn for greater things."[16]

Closer to home, the *Boston Globe* reported that the "Republican tide which swept Gen. Eisenhower into the White House and gave him this state's [sixteen] electoral votes, was not strong enough to save Henry Cabot Lodge Jr." The Republican *Worcester Telegram* struck a more solemn tone: "There is no doubt that Mr. Kennedy will be an able senator, but it is regrettable that Massachusetts has refused to give Senator Lodge the endorsement which he deserved. It was far too soon to reject him, in view of the high standard of service which he had consistently maintained." Unsurprisingly, Basil Brewer's *New Bedford Standard-Times* offered the most acerbic yet brief commentary. "So the man who engineered the nomination of Eisenhower, failed to get himself elected," the paper sneered.[17]

A score evened. John F. Kennedy shakes the hand of Henry Cabot Lodge Jr. on November 10, 1952. Courtesy of the John F. Kennedy Library.

Lodge initially blamed his defeat on "those damned tea parties," which supposedly galvanized the women's vote on behalf of his Democratic opponent.[18] He may have been on to something. Though official election statistics from 1952 are frustratingly silent on the gender breakdown of voters, owing to the poor reporting methods of the times, some extrapolations can nevertheless be made.

To begin with, Kennedy's final victory margin of seventy thousand votes closely matches the number of guests, mostly women, who attended his tea receptions statewide during the campaign. Indeed, table one in the appendix shows that communities participating in large tea receptions recorded extraordinary increases in the number of voters who went to the polls in comparison to 1946, strongly suggesting that women might have picked up the electoral slack in 1952.[19]

"Everywhere," the *Boston American* reported on election day, "there was evidence that women for the first time were taking complete advantage of their political emancipation more than [thirty] years ago. They were turning out en masse, with babes in arms, in many cases."[20]

A record 90.94 percent of all eligible voters cast ballots statewide in 1952, an increase of more than 17 percent from previous totals compiled in 1946. "Of course," remembered Kennedy campaign volunteer Edward C. Berube, "his theme was to hit on the women['s] vote. Of course, he indicated this to me when I met him . . . that he figured the woman was the one that was going to put him in."[21] This strategy may well have paid off in 1952.

While existing evidence suggests Kennedy performed exceptionally well among women voters, he fared even better with Catholic voters. There were over two million Roman Catholics living in Massachusetts in 1952 (out of a total population of four million), and the prospect of voting for a young, handsome, and articulate candidate like Kennedy, who also happened to be of the same religion, may have proved too irresistible for many Catholic voters, in particular Irish Catholics. "Kennedy represented a new generation, a new kind of Irish politician, one who was rich and respectable and could do battle with the Lodges and other Yankee politicians on their own terms," maintained Kennedy campaign aide and future Democratic National Committee chairman Larry O'Brien in his memoirs.[22]

Unable to match Kennedy's "favorite son" appeal among members of his own religious faith, Lodge fared poorly in Catholic wards throughout Massachusetts. Nowhere was this trend more pronounced than in Boston, where 75 percent of the population was estimated to be Catholic. The incumbent senator dropped the city by 119,393 votes, while amassing only 33 percent of the overall vote.[23]

In specific Catholic areas such as Wards Three, Six, Seven, and Eight, Lodge performed exceptionally poorly, pulling down only 25.2, 18.8, 20.3, and 20.4 percent of the vote respectively. Though he dropped these wards in 1946, he amassed respectable voting percentages of 42.5, 41.4, 45.4, and 41.1 against David I. Walsh. In other words, Lodge saw his support in these areas roughly halved.[24]

The same pattern held true in places such as Salem and Woburn, where Catholics represented a large segment of the total population. Indeed, table two in the appendix suggests a causal link between Kennedy's religion and the percentage of votes he was able to secure in these communities.

Particularly striking is how support for Kennedy closely matched the amount of opposition referendum no. 4 generated in 1948. This controversial state ballot question, which asked voters if they approved of doctors disseminating birth control information to their patients, was staunchly opposed by the local Catholic Church led by Archbishop Richard J. Cushing. He urged all members of his flock to vote down the measure, which they did in record numbers on election day. Though Kennedy received no such formal sanction from the church in 1952, it can be persuasively argued that his religious affiliation, combined with his status as an "Irish Brahmin," allowed him to achieve similar results among Catholic voters. One Concord voter professed little surprise at this turn of events. "For those of us whose families have been here since the beginnings of our nation's history," Eleanor Spinney wrote Lodge shortly after election day, "it is hard to project ourselves into the thinking of nationality [read Catholic] groups. I do know the forces were at work."[25]

Another "ethnic" group that Kennedy performed well among was that of Jewish American voters. Despite his father's reputation as an anti-Semite, Kennedy was able to register impressive victories in Jewish American sections across the state through a combination of hard work, an attractive personality, and a massive public relations campaign. In Boston's Ward Fourteen, a representative sampling that encompassed parts of Roxbury, Dorchester, and Mattapan, the Democrat bested Lodge by 5,920 votes while accounting for 63.1 percent of the total ballots cast. In his Senate race against David I. Walsh in 1946, Lodge had captured the ward with 60.5 percent of the vote. The same trend occurred in precincts thirteen through eighteen of Boston's Ward Twelve, which constituted the bulk of the Jewish American vote in Roxbury. Table three in the appendix demonstrates that Kennedy thoroughly trounced Lodge in these areas, 60.5 to 39.5 percent.[26]

Making this outcome all the more impressive is the fact that Lodge had easily carried these precincts, 66.9 to 33.1 percent, over David I. Walsh in 1946. Thus, the dropoff in Lodge's support is a testament to the remarkable job the Kennedy camp did in turning around the perceptions of the Jewish American electorate. "We were in a real bind with regard to the Jewish people," Kennedy campaign aide Phil David Fine later confessed. "At first, we didn't have a single soul with us. . . .Then came many converts. . . .You had to have people meet Kennedy. They were impressed by the social prestige of the family and Jack's personality."[27]

Put another way, the "sins of the father" did not prevent John Kennedy from picking up valuable support from the Jewish American community.

Similarly impressive was the success that conservative state Republicans had under the leadership of newspaper publisher Basil Brewer in "punishing" Lodge for his championing of Dwight Eisenhower over Robert Taft for the GOP presidential nomination. A comparison of votes for Lodge and for Republican gubernatorial candidate Christian Herter reveals, for example, that 34,708 fewer ballots were cast for the incumbent senator. Except in Suffolk and Middlesex counties, Herter outpolled Lodge in every county of the state, in-

cluding the suburban Republican towns of western and southeastern Massachusetts, prime hotbeds of conservatism. A case in point was the rural Cape
Cod town of Barnstable, where Lodge's vote total was 11.6 percent lower than
Herter's. In 1946 Lodge had carried the town with the same vote percentage
that Herter had compiled in 1952: 77.3 percent.[28]

Even in the Back Bay and Beacon Hill sections of Boston, traditional areas
of GOP voting strength for Lodge, the Brahmin lawmaker performed below
expectations. In Ward Four the senator came out with only a three-hundred-
vote lead against Kennedy, while in Ward Five Lodge's lead was cut to less than
two to one, 10,999 to 6,615. Six years earlier, he had captured Ward Four by an
almost two-to-one margin and Ward Five by a three-to-one margin.[29]

The most telling example of conservative Republican defections, however, was Bristol County's New Bedford, where Brewer's influence was most
strongly felt. Lodge lost the city to Kennedy by 21,566 votes, which accounted
for almost a third of the Democrat's overall plurality. Herter, in contrast,
gained 10,564 votes over Lodge's aggregate in the city, which came to 28 percent of the total ballots cast, by far the lowest vote among GOP aspirants for
statewide office. In a much tighter Senate race in 1946, Lodge had lost New
Bedford to David I. Walsh by only 6,202 votes while tallying a respectable 40.7
percent of the overall vote.[30]

Defections from Republican ranks in 1952 undoubtedly accounted for this
electoral disparity. In traditionally Republican Ward Four, for instance, Lodge
could muster only 41.6 percent of the vote, while Herter garnered 60 percent.
In 1946 Lodge had taken the ward with 65.7 percent of the vote, meaning that
in six years he saw nearly a quarter of his support disappear. "You see, Brewer
could make the difference of thirty[-five] thousand votes," Lodge later
claimed. "That's what he did. I was beaten by seventy thousand. If thirty[-five]
thousand had gone the other way, I'd have been in the clear."[31]

Brewer had made a "difference" by using the resources at his disposal, his
newspaper and his prestige as state chairman of the Taft-for-President committee, to mobilize conservative Republican opposition to Lodge's candidacy.
Moreover, he was decisive in securing Kennedy the endorsement of John J.
Fox, the influential publisher of the *Boston Post*. Yet in order to justify supporting Kennedy over a fellow Republican, the New Bedford publisher needed a
ready-made excuse that he and other disgruntled Taftites could politically embrace without seeming disloyal to their party. The anticommunist issue provided just such a rationalization. It was acceptable for conservative Republicans to vote for Kennedy because the young Democrat had a standout
anticommunist record, while Lodge presumably did not. Given the "Red

Scare" atmosphere that was then prevalent in Massachusetts and the rest of the nation, this was a politically advantageous, if intellectually disingenuous, argument for Brewer to make.

As for Kennedy, he never forgot the political service the Missouri native had rendered on his behalf. "Mr. Brewer was really the key to whatever political success I have attained at this moment," he told a gathering of reporters and Democratic Party officials at his family's Hyannis Port home in the late 1950s. In a privately published history of the Brewer family, the late Given Brewer, Brewer's son, wrote that Kennedy confided in him in 1958 that he "never" would have beaten Lodge and become senator without his father's support.[32] The importance that the Democratic lawmaker placed on Brewer's assistance during the 1952 campaign was later underscored by the New Bedford publisher's presence as an invited guest of honor at Kennedy's White House reception following the 1961 presidential inauguration ceremony.

Equally damaging to Lodge's candidacy was his poor showing among blue-collar workers, who looked dimly on his votes for Taft-Hartley and his inability to stem the steady flow of manufacturing jobs leaving the state. Out of the seven cities in Massachusetts that had the largest labor union membership (Boston, Springfield, Lawrence, Fall River, Worcester, Lynn, and New Bedford), the Bay State Republican lost all but one (Springfield). The net loss from 1946, when Lodge defeated Democratic incumbent David I. Walsh for the same Senate seat, was considerable. He carried four of those cities in that race (Boston, Springfield, Worcester, and Lynn).[33]

Especially revealing is Lynn, which possessed a slumping shoe-making industry. Table four in the appendix shows that Lodge could secure only 33.6 percent of the vote in Wards Five, Six, and Seven, the traditional working-class enclaves of the city. In 1946 he had carried these wards by a cumulative total of 52.7 percent. Overall, he saw his support in these areas decline by nearly 20 percent, a disturbing trend for anyone professing to be a friend of labor.

To be sure, this outcome represented an ironic turnaround, since Lodge had for several years cultivated the goodwill of many labor groups statewide. As a member of the Massachusetts House of Representatives in the 1930s, he was instrumental in securing the passage of a reformed state workman's compensation law, which increased benefits for victims of industrial accidents, and voted for ratification of a federal constitutional amendment abolishing child labor. On January 28, 1952, he was even given a standing ovation for his efforts on behalf of working people at a Congress on Industrial Organization gathering in Boston.[34] Such ovations were not enough to secure labor support for his Senate candidacy, however.

Neither, did it seem, was the Lodge family checkbook large enough to secure victory over the bulging Kennedy coffers. There were three things, Joseph P. Kennedy once observed, that got a person elected to public office. "The first is money, the second is money and the third is money."[35] To be sure, John Kennedy obeyed this maxim to the letter in 1952, as he outspent his Republican opponent by a substantial margin.

Then-existing campaign finance laws specified that no individual could contribute more than one thousand dollars to a candidate or committee, but Kennedy skillfully circumvented this restriction by setting up a series of paper committees, such as the Committee for Improvement of Massachusetts Textile Industry and the Committee for Improvement of Massachusetts Shoe Industry, that allowed family members and friends to make multiple thousand-dollar donations. "Thus," wrote one analyst, "the seven members of the Joseph P. Kennedy family contributed a total of $35,000 to the five main Kennedy committees; members of the George Skakel family (Kennedy in-laws) were listed as giving $25,000; and John Dowdle III and his wife (a former Skakel) gave $10,000. This brings the family total not including the candidate's personal expenditure of $15,866 to $70,000." All told, the candidate reported expenses of $350,000, but even this figure fails to give an accurate accounting of the full amount spent.[36]

In addition, years before the Senate race, Joseph P. Kennedy, in expectation that his son would seek statewide office in 1952, donated large sums of money to local charitable and religious organizations such as the Boston archdiocese that had the potential of delivering valuable political assistance down the road. "The Kennedys don't spend money the way [former Boston mayor James Michael] Curley did and others do," acknowledged Mike Ward, a former Curley aide who went on to helm the Boston School Board. "They're smarter. Instead of making a contribution to the Jefferson-Jackson Day Dinner Committee [a traditional Democratic Party fund-raiser], they make a contribution in the sacred name of charity. It costs them only ten cents on the dollar. At the presentation or dedication they import hundreds of people — politically influential representatives of minority groups — and wine them and dine them at no expense to themselves."[37]

Sometimes these charitable deeds translated into some not-so-subtle displays of political support during the 1952 Senate campaign. In late September, when Ethel Skakel Kennedy, the wife of Robert F. Kennedy, gave birth to future U.S. Congressman Joseph P. Kennedy II of Massachusetts in a Boston hospital, none other than Archbishop Richard J. Cushing of the Boston archdiocese, a major benefactor of Kennedy largesse, turned up to baptize the baby in a special weekday ceremony. "That cut our hearts out," remembered Lodge aide James J. Sullivan ruefully.[38]

The extent of Kennedy family money did not end there. Close to $140,000 was spent on radio, television, and newspaper ads, while an additional $83,000 was expended on billboards and the production of a glossy eight-page campaign tabloid that was distributed to thousands of Massachusetts homes. Average persons "could live the rest of [their] lives on [Kennedy's] billboard budget alone," joked one political observer.[39]

Typically, the Kennedys sought to downplay the notion that money had any influence on the outcome of the race. "We had thousands of workers around the state," Robert Kennedy once commented, "and I don't think there were more than six paid employees in the entire campaign. I mean that. The other campaigns—the Dever campaign, for example—had many more paid employees. Actually, Dever probably spent a million dollars on his campaign, and we spent only about a third of that. I'm not pretending our campaign wasn't expensive. They're all expensive. Billboards and television and radio [costs add up] and there's no avoiding them."[40]

Dismissals aside, the perception lingered that the Kennedys were out to purchase a U.S. Senate seat. "I haven't got a doubt in my mind [that] they are going to try to buy the election," Henry Cabot Lodge Jr. complained to his campaign manager, Albert Cole, in early April. Indeed, evidence suggests that the Republican lawmaker was so sure of himself on this point that he considered filing a complaint with the Senate Subcommittee on Privileges and Elections, which supervised the conduct of campaigns. To this end he instructed his staff to monitor closely all the expenditures made by his opponent, especially those dealing with newspaper, billboard, and television advertising. "We would thus have an estimate of the amount of money being spent on those particular activities," he wrote. "Of course, this in itself would not give a complete picture of the campaign because there are many expenditures which cannot be seen." Nevertheless, he wanted to "have the facts with which to deal with it."[41]

Lodge never filed the complaint, perhaps because he lacked definite proof of an impropriety being committed, or more likely because his own campaign was not above reproach. For while he officially reported expenses of $59,000, he probably spent somewhat in excess of this amount, given his campaign indirectly benefited from a record $1,058,501 raised by the Republican State Committee. Still, John Kennedy held the decisive edge in fund-raising, as his creative use of loopholes in state campaign finance laws and the ambassador's own deep pockets (when it came to footing the bill for a lavish advertising campaign and lining up the support of key constituent groups through charitable donations) carried the day. As Dwight D. Eisenhower later observed, "Cabot was simply overwhelmed by money."[42]

Lodge might also have been overwhelmed by history. For while the Massachusetts Republican Party was able to secure the governorship, regain control of the House of Representatives, and add three seats to its majority in the state senate in 1952, the party was entering a period of long-term decline. From 1958 onward the Democrats easily maintained large majorities in both chambers of the state legislature. Moreover, apart from Eisenhower in 1952 and 1956, no Republican candidate for president would carry Massachusetts until 1984, when Ronald Reagan soundly defeated Democratic nominee Walter Mondale.

Several factors account for this new Democratic hegemony. First of all, unlike the 1930s and early 1940s, the party under the new leadership of Kennedy, John McCormack, and Thomas P. O'Neill was able to put forth a united front that minimized political and personal differences and ensured Democrats that there would be no repeat of the kind of destructive infighting that hamstrung party efforts in the days of James Michael Curley and David I. Walsh.

Second, the party was aided by the rise of ethnic voters, led by the Irish and supported by Jews, Italians, and other minorities. Long neglected by state Republicans, these ethnic groups voted en masse for Democratic candidates in the postwar period as they found the liberal social programs of the Fair Deal and later the New Frontier and Great Society to their political liking. It also didn't hurt Democrats that they were able to field high-caliber candidates such as Kennedy, a third-generation descendant of Irish immigrants, to lead their ticket, especially since Irish Americans constituted over 30 percent of the state's population, by far the largest ethnic group represented.[43]

Finally, there were the early rumblings of a trend that was to change the very face of Massachusetts politics: the postwar migration of Democratic voters to the five eastern counties that constituted the suburbs of Boston (Essex, Norfolk, Middlesex, Plymouth, and Bristol). For decades Republican candidates for statewide office had relied on these suburban boroughs for the bulk of their voting strength while conceding the "city vote" to the Democrats. According to one study, the counties "consistently accounted for [60 percent] of the Republican general election total, with the other [40 percent] roughly split [30] to [10] between the towns and Boston."[44]

But beginning with the postwar building boom in the late 1940s, which saw thousands of families (and voters) make the move from city to suburb, this political calculus changed. For the first time state Republicans saw their voting base begin to erode. These new suburbanites may have left Boston behind, but they carried with them their old attachment to the Democratic Party. At the same time, party affiliation in Boston remained steadfastly Democratic.

By 1948 these eastern suburban counties accounted for 52 percent of the total ballots cast for Democratic senatorial candidates, a marked increase in support over previous years. "The evidence," as one party position paper from this period concluded, "indicates that Democratic voters who are moving out of the cities into the suburbs are remaining loyal to the Democratic Party." Thus, when Kennedy ran for the Senate in 1952, he could legitimately claim 53 percent of his total support from these eastern suburban areas.[45] The tug of old party ties had triumphed over geography.

Yet this was not simply a victory for the Democratic Party. The 1952 Massachusetts Senate race marked the birth of a dynamic new political organization that would seize control of the state Democratic Party in 1956 and remain an influential force in state political affairs for several decades. Known simply as "the Kennedys," this organization was "more than a family affiliation." "It quickly developed into an entire political party, with its own people, its own approach, and its own strategies," recalled former Massachusetts congressman and U.S. House Speaker Thomas P. O'Neill in his memoirs.[46]

Starting in 1946 with John Kennedy's election to Congress from a small working-class district in the Boston-Cambridge area and continuing on through landslide reelection campaigns in 1948 and 1950, the Kennedys proved to be a highly successful political operation. But having a personal organization that was independent of the state party was not unique in Bay State politics. Indeed, four-time Boston mayor and one-time Massachusetts governor James Michael Curley had gone that route for most of his political career.

"What was new," according to Massachusetts political historian Alec Barbrook, "was the pragmatic combination of the old and new, wealth, personality, organization, an impression of integrity and ability, welded into an amalgam that possessed great elective potential."[47] This "great elective potential" was fully realized in the Senate campaign against Lodge. It would be realized again on a national scale in 1960, when Kennedy successfully challenged Richard M. Nixon for the presidency.

Chapter EIGHT

Men for All Seasons

ENRY CABOT LODGE JR. wasted little time dwelling on his 1952 Senate loss. Asked by a reporter to analyze the defeat, Lodge replied, "I don't believe in looking backwards. I have simply ended one phase of my career. Now I will embark on another."[1] Lodge was as good as his word.

Over the next decade he remained politically active as the U.S. representative to the United Nations, a post that occupied Cabinet status in the Eisenhower administration. Ironically, the United Nations represented the same kind of global collective security organization that Lodge's grandfather had so vociferously opposed three decades earlier. Lodge, however, saw no incongruity. His grandfather had been "essentially way ahead of his time," he argued, because the U.N. Charter contained all the reservations the Old Senator had voiced over the League of Nations, including the provision that reserved member nations the right to send troops into combat.[2]

Sensitive to the softness-on-communism charges that John F. Kennedy had leveled against him in 1952, Lodge gave no quarter to the Soviets or to their allies as ambassador. When Soviet delegate Semyon Tsarapkin sought recognition at a Security Council meeting, Lodge queried, "For what purpose does the gentleman from the Soviet Union take the floor?"

"I'm not a gentleman," Tsarapkin bristled, "I'm a delegate."

"I had hoped that the two were not mutually exclusive," Lodge responded, to the amusement of the chamber.[3]

Such testy exchanges were more the norm than the exception during

Lodge's stormy yet eventful seven-and-a-half-year tenure. Whether the issue was the Soviet invasion of Hungary in 1956 or the downing of a U.S. spy plane over Russian air space in 1960, Lodge was quick to point out the Kremlin's culpability. In his thinking, this was in keeping with what the United Nations stood for: the "headquarters for developing whatever united action the world is capable of taking at any given moment in the face of an aggressor's threat" to international peace and stability. Still, Lodge was not without his detractors. Broadcast journalist Joseph C. Harsch claimed that the American representative's outward belligerence toward the Soviets served only to alienate "friends of the West" who were put off by Lodge's confrontational style.[4]

Lodge's image as an intractable cold warrior did thaw somewhat in 1959 when President Eisenhower selected him to escort Soviet premier Nikita Krushchev on a goodwill tour of the United States. The tour got off to a bumpy start, however, when a Soviet security guard mistook Lodge for a journalist and rudely manhandled him at a train station in San Luis Obispo. Lodge responded by picking up the guard and tossing him into a corner. "Don't ever lay a hand on me again," he warned his assailant. Khrushchev could not help but be impressed by his host's display of raw physical courage. "I hear you have been beating up one of my guards," he jokingly admonished Lodge.[5] The diplomatic ice thus broken, Lodge and Khrushchev went on to have a cordial if not pleasant time together as they conversed with American union leaders in San Francisco, toured a farmer's cornfield near Coon Rapids, Iowa, and visited a steel mill in Pittsburgh, Pennsylvania.

This highly publicized goodwill tour, along with Lodge's years of dedicated public service at the United Nations, helped transform him into a national celebrity. Indeed, he became a familiar figure to millions of Americans tuning in to the U.N. proceedings on network television. Though he continued to be awkward and uncomfortable in front of a camera, Lodge nevertheless projected a kind of steely integrity that played well on the small screen, at least in an ambassador's role. "If Hollywood were casting Distinguished-Politician-as-Good-Guy," observed *Time* magazine, "it could hardly find a likelier looking specimen than Cabot Lodge. He is [fifty-eight], has gray hair and eight grandchildren, but he still has a youthfully athletic air about him. His voice is throatily masculine, with a kind of standard radio announcer accent that shows only faint traces of Boston and Harvard."[6]

The high-profile exposure was a crucial factor in Republican presidential candidate Richard M. Nixon's decision to choose Lodge as his running mate in 1960. Seeking someone who could bolster his weak political standing in the East and draw attention to international issues, a perceived GOP strength,

Nixon turned to Lodge. "If you ever let [the Democrats] campaign only on domestic issues, they'll beat us—our only hope is to keep it on foreign policy," Nixon said. Forgotten was the ignominy of Lodge's 1952 Senate defeat. "People's minds are short and all that they recall about Cabot is that for eight years he has been on television speaking against the likes of [Soviet foreign minister Andrei] Gromyko, etc.," Nixon explained. For Lodge's part, he left no doubt as to whom he owed this new honor. "If I hadn't lost to Jack [Kennedy]," he said, "I never would have had eight years in the U.N., and I might not be running for Vice President."[7]

John F. Kennedy, of course, headed the Democratic presidential ticket opposing Nixon and Lodge. Over the previous eight years he had become something of a political child of destiny as he moved inexorably toward a White House run in 1960. But before embarking on any political crusades, he had first to resolve some unfinished personal business. During the 1952 campaign he had begun dating an attractive young socialite from Southampton, New York, named Jacqueline Bouvier. Witty, accomplished, and reserved, Jacqueline possessed a joie de vivre that the new senator found appealing.

Asked later by a reporter whether it was love at first sight, Kennedy politely demurred. "Well, I don't know," he said. "I don't know how you describe love anyway, but I was very interested."[8] The two were married at St. Mary's Church in Newport, Rhode Island, on September 12, 1953, in a lavish wedding ceremony that captured the imaginations of people nationwide. The union would eventually produce three children, Caroline Bouvier in 1957, John Fitzgerald Jr. in 1960, and Patrick Bouvier in 1963. Born prematurely, Patrick Bouvier died less than thirty-nine hours after entering the world. The cause of death was a severe respiratory condition.

Just a month after marrying Jacqueline Bouvier, John Kennedy appeared with his young bride on Edward R. Murrow's *Person to Person* television program. Quoting from a letter written by Alan Seeger, a famous American poet who had been killed during World War I, Kennedy told a nationwide audience that success in life to him meant "doing that thing then which nothing else seems more noble or satisfactory or remunerative. And then being ready to see it through to the end."

Whether Kennedy was ready to see a future presidential campaign through to the end had yet to be decided. He nevertheless began accepting speaking engagements around the country, just as he had in Massachusetts before 1952. The purpose again was to increase his name recognition and to set up a network of political contacts for use in a possible Kennedy-for-President campaign organization down the road. "Suddenly," fellow Bay State lawmaker

A radiant couple: Jacqueline Bouvier and John F. Kennedy on their wedding day, September 13, 1953. Courtesy of the *New Bedford Standard-Times.*

"Tip" O'Neill observed, "he became an active person. Suddenly he became a person with a future in the Democratic Party. 'Will you go to Missouri and speak for the party?' You can't go to those places unless you have a knowledge of what is taking place in the Congress of the United States. He started to do his homework."[9]

There were some setbacks. In 1954 he had an unsuccessful corrective surgical procedure performed on his back that nearly cost him his life. As he lay in bed recovering from the surgery, he was confronted with perhaps the greatest moral issue of his political career: whether to support a Senate motion to censure Joseph McCarthy for his increasingly disruptive personal behavior. Much to the dismay of liberal Democratic Party leaders such as Eleanor Roosevelt, Kennedy declined to go on the record against the Wisconsin senator, refusing even to pair his vote with that of another absent senator in opposition to the censure. Kennedy later claimed that poor health resulting from his back surgery prevented him from voting for the censure motion, but this falls short of the truth. "I was caught in a bad situation," Kennedy privately confessed. "My brother [Robert] was working for Joe. I was against it, I didn't want him to work for Joe, but he wanted to. And how the hell could I get up there and denounce Joe McCarthy when my own brother was working for him? So it wasn't so much a political liability as it was a personal problem."[10]

This refusal to censure McCarthy was not without political calculation. The Republican was still revered by Irish Catholics in Massachusetts for his staunch anticommunism, and the idea of publicly denouncing him, however justified, risked alienating this all-important constituency group. "Hell, half my voters . . . looked on McCarthy as a hero," Kennedy told Arthur Schlesinger Jr. after the Harvard historian had lobbied him unsuccessfully to break with the Wisconsinite.[11]

Kennedy's reluctance to take a moral stand against McCarthy belied the message he was trying to convey in his Pulitzer Prize–winning book *Profiles in Courage,* which he wrote while recuperating from back surgery in 1954. *Profiles* told the story of eight U.S. senators—John Quincy Adams, Daniel Webster, Thomas Hart Benton, Sam Houston, Edmond G. Ross, Lucius Quintus Cincinnatus Lamar, George Norris, and Robert A. Taft—who defied the wishes of their constituents at critical periods in American history. While liberal critics found irony in Kennedy's failure to show the courage he was writing about, the work nevertheless served the purpose of enhancing his image as a serious-minded lawmaker.

Such visibility proved useful when Kennedy made a surprisingly strong bid to attain the vice presidency at the 1956 Democratic National Convention in Chicago. Initially he had no intention of seeking the number two spot on the Democratic ticket, but when convention delegates and television viewers nationwide saw him deliver a rousing nomination speech for the party's eventual standard-bearer, Adlai E. Stevenson of Illinois, a Kennedy-for-Vice-President boom developed. Ever the opportunist, Kennedy attempted to make the most of his newfound celebrity by lining up the support of northern political bosses and meeting with delegates from key western and southern states.

In the end, his effort fell short, as the prohibitive vice-presidential favorite going into the convention, Senator Estes Kefauver of Tennessee, was able to parlay his strength in the Middle West and Rocky Mountains into a third-ballot victory. Still, the near miss convinced Kennedy that he had what it takes to make a successful presidential run the next time around. "If I work hard for four years," he told aide Dave Powers after the convention, "I ought to be able to pick up all the marbles."[12]

Before launching a concerted presidential bid, he had first to win reelection to the Senate in 1958. His Republican challenger was Vincent J. Celeste, the same obscure Boston attorney who had unsuccessfully run against him for Congress in 1950. "Precisely because Celeste was such a weak opponent," historian Doris Kearns Goodwin has concluded, "Kennedy believed that only a majority of at least half a million votes would constitute a clear enough victory to boost his chances for the presidency."[13]

The Democrat achieved this goal and then some as he captured over 73 percent of the total senatorial vote, the greatest margin then achieved by a candidate for statewide office in Massachusetts history.[14] Making the difference was not only himself but also his superior and well-financed field organization, which oversaw the door-to-door distribution of over one million glossy campaign pamphlets. Not content with resting on his own political laurels, Kennedy maintained a punishing schedule of personal appearances throughout the state.

In his first day of campaigning alone, he hit every major community on Boston's North Shore, including Marblehead, Salem, Swampscott, Beverly, Gloucester, Danvers, Peabody, and Lynn. Again, as in 1952, nothing was left to chance. Once while passing through South Boston, he ordered his campaign driver to a stop so he could personally escort an elderly woman across the street. "You really want all the votes, don't you?" campaign advisor Dave Powers injected. Kennedy answered, "How would you feel if you lost South Boston by one vote and then remembered that you didn't bother to help this lady across the street?"[15] Such single-mindedness in achieving victory would be on display again in 1960, this time on a national stage.

Coasting through a Democratic presidential primary field that included such party notables as Hubert H. Humphrey of Minnesota, Stuart Symington of Missouri, and Lyndon B. Johnson of Texas, Kennedy went on to secure a first-ballot victory at the Democratic National Convention in Los Angeles, California, in July. Now, as his party's standard-bearer at the tender age of forty-three, he had only Vice President Richard M. Nixon, his GOP opponent, standing between him and the White House.

But Nixon was no Vincent J. Celeste. Working in the Republican's favor was his more than seven years of exemplary service in the executive branch, his highly publicized stands against communism, and public trepidations regarding Kennedy's religion. On the latter score, many Protestant voters voiced the concern that a Catholic president might be unduly influenced in his decision making by the pope and other high church officials.

To counter these popular fears, Kennedy addressed the Greater Houston Ministerial Association, an influential Protestant group that had been openly hostile to the idea of a Catholic becoming president. "I believe in an America," he told the clergymen, "where the separation of church and state is absolute—where no Catholic prelate would tell the President, should he be a Catholic, how to act, and no Protestant minister would tell his parishioners for whom to vote." A virtuoso performance, Kennedy's talk did much to allay Protestant concerns about where his true loyalties lay. "Martin Luther himself would have welcomed Senator Kennedy and cheered him," assessed one Lutheran minister in attendance. "By God, look at him—and listen to him!" exclaimed elderly Texas power broker Sam Rayburn as he watched the event on television. "He's eating 'em blood-raw! This young feller will be a great President."[16]

Having so effectively addressed the religious issue, Kennedy next trained his political sights on Nixon. Taking a page from his 1952 campaign playbook, he accused Nixon and by extension the Eisenhower administration of lying down before the onslaught of international communism. "In the election of 1860," he lectured, "Abraham Lincoln said the question is whether this nation could exist half slave or half free. In the election of 1960, and with the world around us, the question is whether the world will exist half slave or half free, whether it will move in the direction we are taking, or whether it will move in the direction of slavery."[17]

Kennedy claimed that a "missile gap" favoring the Soviet Union had been allowed to occur, endangering the security of the United States and the entire West. If this wasn't bad enough, he said, the Republican administration had acquiesced to the Soviets by letting them set up a puppet communist regime in Cuba, just ninety miles south of Florida. Yet there was more at stake than mere strategic advantage. "This is not a struggle for supremacy of arms alone," Kennedy pointed out. "It is also a struggle for supremacy between two conflicting ideologies: freedom under God versus ruthless, godless tyranny."[18]

As in 1952, the Kennedy family played a prominent role in the campaign. Robert Kennedy once again took the controls as campaign manager while Joseph P. Kennedy worked behind the scenes paying the bills, hiring consultants, and lining up the support of Democratic bosses in key states. The rest of the clan, including radiant newcomer Jacqueline Bouvier Kennedy, did their part by attending rallies, delivering speeches, holding teas, shaking hands, and making themselves generally available for television and newspaper interviews.

The turning point in the campaign, however, came during the first of four televised debates before a nationwide audience on the night of September 26. Looking tan, fit, and robust, Kennedy simply outperformed Nixon, who admittedly was still showing the effects of a painful infection that had caused him to be hospitalized for several days with a 102-degree temperature. "It didn't really come down to the better man," television producer and debate coordinator Don Hewitt later concluded. "It came down to the better performer. The matinee idol won."[19]

People listening to the debate over the radio felt that Nixon had clearly bested his Democratic challenger in terms of the substantive points he made on issues ranging from U.S.-Soviet relations to the reduction of the federal debt. Yet the unforgiving glare of the "electric mirror" was not interested in substance, only style. And in this all-important category Kennedy excelled, as his inviting smile, handsome face, and smooth delivery made him appear the more presidential of the two candidates. Nixon, in contrast, looked like a grotesque caricature of a back-room politician with his heavy jowls, shifty eyes, and sweat-stained forehead. Watching his running mate's disastrous showing on television with increasing irritation, Lodge exclaimed, "That son of a bitch just lost the election."[20]

In truth, Lodge's own lackluster campaign efforts did nothing to endear voters to the GOP either. Refusing to campaign around the clock as Kennedy and Nixon did, the vice-presidential candidate instead opted for a restful hour of sleep after lunch. Needless to say, this laid-back approach did not sit well with anxious local campaign chairmen. "We didn't mind him having a nap in the afternoon," complained one hardened Republican veteran, "but why did he have to put on his pajamas?" In his own defense, Lodge argued that he needed the rest to maintain his energy level for the already demanding campaign schedule he kept. "There are really two essential things in campaigning," he explained. "First, you must be in good humor. If you're going to be irascible, you ought to stay home. Second, you ought to make sense in your speeches. These are the two things you must do. Unless you're a saint, you can't be in good humor when you're exhausted."[21]

Fear of personal fatigue was not the only concern facing Lodge during these hectic days. In early October he told a Harlem rally that the GOP ticket was committed to placing "a Negro in the Cabinet." The only problem was that he had failed to clear his remarks in advance with his running mate or any official at the Republican National Committee. "It hurt us in the South unquestionably," Nixon later claimed. "And it did us no good in the North. To Negroes as well as other voters it appeared to be a crude attempt to woo the support of Negroes without regard to the qualifications an individual might have for high office—something that Lodge had never remotely intended to suggest."[22]

Lodge appeared unmoved by the controversy. "I did not discuss this specific speech with the Vice President," he admitted to reporters, "but I am confident that he agrees with me that there should be no discrimination of any sort with respect to hiring Federal officials, from Cabinet offices on down."[23]

The Massachusetts Republican was equally adamant in his denunciation of religious intolerance. Asked by a reporter to comment on the issue of Kennedy's Catholicism, Lodge could barely keep his indignation in check. "I absolutely refuse to admit that my three Roman Catholic grandsons [his younger son, Henry, had married a Catholic woman] will be debarred from the presidency on those grounds, or, for that matter, my two Episcopalian grandsons."[24]

Echoing his 1952 performance, Lodge refused to engage in the kind of base partisan sniping that usually marred such high-stakes political contests. Explained Lodge, "I won't attack the Democrats as such; I want and expect to get some of their votes. I've never been narrowly partisan. Let them present their case and we ours, and let the voters decide. There's no point in rebutting campaign oratory. You've got to stay fluid—in tactics, not in principle. Otherwise, it's disaster."[25]

Unfortunately for Lodge, disaster struck for him on election day; Kennedy and his running mate, Senate Majority Leader Lyndon B. Johnson of Texas, edged the Republican presidential ticket by less than 1 percent of the popular vote. For the second time in less than a decade, the Kennedys had proven they could "even the score" with the Lodges. Yet the bitter taste of defeat did not prevent Lodge from congratulating John Kennedy upon his hard-earned victory.

He wired his former 1952 Senate combatant: "SINCERE CONGRATULATIONS ON YOUR ELECTION AS PRESIDENT OF THE UNITED STATES. YOU HAVE MY VERY EARNEST AND GENUINE GOOD WISHES FOR AN ADMINISTRATION FILLED WITH USEFUL AND VALUABLE ACCOMPLISHMENTS FOR THE AMERICAN PEOPLE. NOW THAT THE VOTERS HAVE SPOKEN AMERICANS SHOULD CLOSE RANKS AND PRESENT A UNITED FRONT BEFORE THE WORLD."[26]

Perhaps remembering the personal slight Lodge had paid him on election night eight years earlier, Kennedy neglected to reply in kind. He did joke to supporters that Lodge looked as if he was having a "hard time" staying awake during an election night television interview, an obvious dig at the Republican's well-documented sleep habits.[27]

While the newly elected president went about the business of governing the nation, Lodge busied himself with doing part-time consulting work for Time, Inc., and heading a new transatlantic think tank organization called the Atlantic Institute. Formed for the purpose of fostering closer political and economic ties between the United States and Western Europe, the France-based institute had the enthusiastic support of several world leaders, including Kennedy. So intrigued was the president by the idea that he invited his old political foe to the White House on December 12, 1961, to discuss the organization's long-term goals and programs.

"He appeared to take great interest in it and said he hoped the Atlantic Institute would make a special study on the effect of the Common Market on our trade with Latin America," Lodge recounted in a memo afterward. As the thirty-five-minute meeting came to a close, Kennedy took the opportunity to discuss the looming Massachusetts Senate battle between his brother Edward and Lodge's son George. The president "said that it looked as though George and Teddy would be campaigning hard, adding that he was glad that he wasn't doing it and that he really didn't think he could ever bring himself to do it again." Lodge "echoed" this feeling and offered the opinion that his son "was off to a very good start."[28]

A "good start" was not enough to gain victory, however. Running under his brother's 1952 Senate campaign slogan, "He Can Do More for Massachusetts," Edward M. Kennedy easily defeated George Cabot Lodge with 57 percent of the vote. "The smashing Kennedy victory climaxed almost two months of feverish campaigning by both senatorial candidates, who roamed the length and breadth of the commonwealth from early morning to late at night virtually seven days a week in search of votes," the *Boston Herald* reported.[29]

What made Edward Kennedy a decisive winner was a superb field organization and long presidential coattails. "And I ask you," charged Massachusetts attorney general Edward McCormack, who had unsuccessfully challenged Kennedy in the Democratic primary, "if his name was Edward Moore—with his qualifications, with your qualifications, Teddy . . . your candidacy would be a joke."[30] Though overstated, McCormack's analysis was essentially correct. Unlike his Republican opponent, who had served several years as an assistant secretary of labor, the younger Kennedy had virtually no governmental experience.

This aside, neither John Kennedy nor Henry Cabot Lodge became actively involved in the Senate fight, Kennedy because he had more pressing affairs of state to attend to and Lodge because he was equally busy as head of the Atlantic Institute. In any event, it would have made little difference, as the outcome was already a foregone conclusion. The Kennedys would "even the score" with the Lodges once again.

The old rivals crossed political paths one final time in 1963. On the advice of Secretary of State Dean Rusk, Kennedy appointed Lodge to one of the most challenging posts in the U.S. Foreign Service, the ambassadorship of South Vietnam. Under the authoritarian leadership of Ngo Dinh Diem, the small Southeast Asian country had been waging a losing three-year battle against North Vietnamese communists, who were conducting large-scale guerrilla warfare operations in the south. Unless the military situation showed marked improvement, the former French colony appeared destined for communist subjugation, a prospect that deeply offended the Cold War sensibilities of the president.

In recommending a distinguished Republican such as Lodge for the Saigon post, Rusk hoped to win bipartisan support for the administration's Vietnam policy, which called for massive amounts of military and economic aid to the south. Kennedy wasted little time in signing off on this choice, perhaps sensing as well that the GOP leader would act as "asbestos against the heat of possible future criticism of his foreign policy."[31] Only the president did not phrase it that way when he met with Lodge on June 12 to discuss the latter's availability for the job. "Cabot," he said, "I am beginning to spend more of my time on Vietnam than anything else. The Diem government seems to be in the terminal phase. . . . I'd like to persuade you to go out there as Ambassador and as my personal representative."[32]

The request did not come as a surprise to the former U.N. ambassador. Earlier in the year he had passed word on to Kennedy that he was interested in taking on an "important and difficult" assignment for the administration. "When President Kennedy said in June that he was going to try to persuade me to go to Saigon," Lodge later recalled, "he had every reason to believe that I would say yes. So I did say that I was very much honored to have him ask me and that I wanted to consult my wife, because it had been some time since the matter had come up. I did consult her, and wrote the President the next day saying that I would be glad to go."[33]

The South Vietnam Lodge went to was a seething cauldron of political unrest. In previous months, Diem, a devout Roman Catholic, had embarked on a ruthless campaign of oppression against the country's majority Buddhist population. Measures taken included the arrest and torture of several hundred monks and nuns and the wanton destruction of religious shrines and pagodas. The raids were carried out by Diem's brother, Ngo Dinh Nhu, whose reputation for brutality was surpassed only by his appetite for power.

To correct the situation, Kennedy instructed Lodge to put pressure on Diem to reform his ways. "If, in spite of your efforts, Diem remains obdurate and refuses," the president cabled his ambassador on August 24, "then we must face the possibility that Diem himself cannot be preserved." Lodge, who

The new U.S. ambassador to Vietnam confers with an old political rival in the Oval Office on August 15, 1963. Courtesy of the John F. Kennedy Library.

had a thinly disguised contempt for the Vietnamese leader, found no fault with this policy, especially when Diem refused to make the requested changes to his regime. "We are launched on a course from which there is no responsible turning back: the overthrow of the Diem government," Lodge wrote Kennedy five days later. "We should make an all-out effort to get the generals to move promptly."[34] The "generals" Lodge referred to were disgruntled field commanders in the South Vietnamese army who had grown weary of Diem's excesses and his failure to decisively meet the communist threat from the north.

Under the direction of Major General Duong Van Minh, the military leaders staged a successful coup d'état on November 1 that resulted in the executions of Diem and Nhu. Though Lodge made a half-hearted effort to secure Diem's safety during the crisis, he shed no tears over the Vietnamese leader's passing. "When we read in our newspapers here about a coup in Vietnam," he told journalist Charles Bartlett in 1965, "we think in terms of a coup in the White House, and we're horrified. But it doesn't horrify the Vietnamese. In fact, when the coup came there were smiles on everybody's faces, and they just wanted to be sure that some of these officials, who'd been torturing people and incarcerating them, were going to get punished." As for Kennedy's handling of the affair, Lodge opined, "I think he was sophisticated in his realization that he was dealing with a different kind of civilization, with a different kind of culture."[35] However patronizing and culturally insensitive these remarks now appear, they are representative of the type of paternalistic mind-set that dominated Washington policy-making circles in the early 1960s. The Vietnamese were viewed as children, supposedly not sufficiently schooled in the tenets of democracy to know the difference between liberty and dictatorship.

Such sentiment did not preclude a peaceful resolution to the conflict, however. "I thought from the beginning," Lodge wrote in his memoirs, "that an exclusively military solution to the Vietnam problem was impossible. . . . I eventually reached the conclusion that we should withdraw our troops from Vietnam as fast as could be done in an orderly way and try to negotiate a settlement."[36]

John Kennedy never got the opportunity to oversee such a settlement. On November 22, 1963, Kennedy was struck down by an assassin's bullet while on a routine political visit to Dallas, Texas. Lodge, who was en route to Washington, D.C., to brief the president on the Vietnam situation two days later, first learned of the tragedy during a stopover visit to San Francisco. "My thoughts were shock and horror," he later said.[37]

Kennedy's death may have brought the curtain down on the "New Frontier," but it did not end Lodge's political career. He stayed on as ambassador to

Lodge is sworn in by Secretary of State Dean Rusk as ambassador to Vietnam for his
second go-round on August 12, 1965. President Lyndon B. Johnson is to his immediate right. Photo by Yoichi R. Okamoto, courtesy of the Lyndon Baines Johnson Library Collection.

South Vietnam through the spring of 1964, until events within the Republican Party forced him to resign his post and return stateside. Conservative Senator Barry Goldwater of Arizona was in the process of winning the GOP presidential nomination, and this development greatly alarmed Lodge. To him,
Goldwater represented the kind of outmoded conservative thinking that had
cost the Republicans national elections in the 1930s and 1940s.

Though Lodge won the New Hampshire primary by an overwhelming
margin of write-in votes, he steadfastly refused to accept a draft for president.
"I don't think [Lodge] would have turned [the presidency] down," remembered one close friend, "but he wasn't willing to go out and fight for it himself."[38] Lodge instead threw his support to Governor William W. Scranton of
Pennsylvania, a fellow moderate who ultimately lacked the organization to
compete with Goldwater.

Man for all seasons. A retired Henry Cabot Lodge talks about the late President John F. Kennedy to a high school gathering in Salem, Massachusetts, on October 20, 1979.
Courtesy of the *Salem Evening News*.

Following President Lyndon B. Johnson's landslide victory over Gold-water in that fall's general election, Lodge returned to South Vietnam for a second tour of ambassadorial duty. His efforts to bring stability to the wartorn land were largely unsuccessful. According to biographer Anne Blair, Lodge fell victim to the same false assumptions that plagued Johnson and his advisors throughout this period. He saw "U.S. honor and the fate of the free world [as] the stakes in Vietnam, without a commitment to total war, and in full knowledge of the weakness of both the South Vietnamese government and the American popular will to persist year after year."[39] Resigning yet again on April 25, 1967, Lodge continued to remain active in diplomatic circles as ambassador to Germany in 1968–69 and special envoy to the Vatican, 1970–77. He also held the post of chief U.S. negotiator at the Paris Peace Talks in 1969.

Lodge's final years were spent largely outside the political arena. Returning home to Beverly, he worked on his memoirs, taught a course on international affairs entitled "The Nation and the World" at neighboring North Shore Community College, and took in a family of South Vietnamese refugees at his private estate on Hale Street. Asked by a local reporter whether other citizens should become involved in the resettlement of foreign émigrés, the retired lawmaker was characteristically blunt. "I'm past the point of telling people about their moral commitments," he replied. "Our offer to sponsor the family was a personal decision. We just thought it was a nice thing to do."[40]

When the John F. Kennedy Library and Museum, a $12 million memorial to the late president, opened its doors in Boston in 1979, Lodge was tapped to give a talk to area high school students on his impressions of Kennedy. Calling him "a man for all seasons," Lodge praised Kennedy for his displayed wit and personal charm. "He was a master of the repartee," he assessed. "Nothing will get you a bunch of votes as quickly as coming back with a quick reply."[41]

Despite the activity, Lodge's health had begun to deteriorate, and on February 27, 1985, he passed away at his Beverly home at the age of eighty-two. Condolences poured in from all parts of the country, but perhaps none were as poignant as the statement made by Senator Edward Kennedy upon hearing the news. "Henry Cabot Lodge was one of the greatest statesman from one of the great families in the history of the Commonwealth," he noted. "He will be honored and remembered most for his extraordinary achievements as a senator and diplomat, but he is also remembered by all of us in the Kennedy family for the warmth and friendship that endured despite our political rivalry."[42]

There was no longer any need for the Kennedys to "even the score" with the Lodges. That issue, like the 1952 Massachusetts Senate race, had long since been settled.

Appendix

Table One
1952 Women's Vote

Communities participating in large teas	Percentage of voters going to polls in 1946	Percentage of voters going to polls in 1952	Percentage Difference
Brockton	73.9	91.8	+17.9
Fall River	79.1	90.9	+11.8
Fitchburg	73.1	92.5	+19.4
Haverhill	70.5	90.7	+20.2
Holyoke	76.8	91.8	+15.0
Lowell	78.2	91.3	+13.1
Taunton	70.7	91.3	+20.6
Waltham	76.3	90.6	+14.3
Totals	74.8	91.3	+16.5

Source: Commonwealth of Massachusetts, *Massachusetts Election Statistics, 1946, 1952.*

Table Two
1952 Catholic Vote

Community	Percentage of two-party vote for Kennedy in 1952	Percentage voting "No" on referendum no. 4 in 1948	Percentage of Catholics in total population (1950)
Salem	60.8	65.4	62.5
Woburn	60.7	61.06	60.4

Source: Commonwealth of Massachusetts, *Massachusetts Election Statistics, 1948, 1952;* Parish records, Boston archdiocese; U.S. Bureau of the Census, *Census of Population (1950)* (Washington, D.C., 1952).

Table Three
1952 Jewish American Vote in Boston Ward 12

Precincts	Percentage of two-party vote for Kennedy	Percentage of two-party vote for Lodge
13	63.9	36.1
14	67.0	33.0
15	53.4	46.6
16	52.5	47.5
17	57.7	42.3
18	68.6	31.4
Totals	60.5	39.5

Source: City of Boston, *Report of the Board of Election Commissions for the Year 1952.*

Table Four
Lodge Performance in Lynn Labor Wards, 1946–1952

Wards	Percentage of two-party vote for Lodge in 1946	Percentage of two-party vote for Lodge in 1952	Percent Difference
5	52.3	31.9	−20.4
6	44.4	26.7	−17.7
7	61.6	42.3	−19.3
Totals	52.7	33.6	−19.1

Source: City of Lynn, *Lynn Election Commission Records, 1946, 1952.*

Notes

Introduction: A Decisive Moment

1. Dave Powers Oral History, John F. Kennedy Library (hereinafter cited as JFKL), Boston, Massachusetts.

2. Alonzo L. Hamby, *Liberalism and Its Challengers: F.D.R. to Reagan* (Oxford, 1985), 191.

3. Commonwealth of Massachusetts, *Massachusetts Election Statistics, 1958* (Boston, 1958).

4. James N. Giglio, *The Presidency of John F. Kennedy* (Lawrence, Mass., 1992), 2.

5. Patrick J. Mulkern Oral History, JFKL.

6. *Boston Globe,* November 2, 1916.

7. Ibid.

8. Ibid., October 31, 1916.

9. *Assessed Polls, 1916* (Boston, 1916).

10. James MacGregor Burns, *The Crosswinds of Freedom: From Roosevelt to Reagan: America in the Last Half Century* (New York, 1989), 312.

Chapter 1: Two Households

1. James Sullivan, interview with author; Camman Newberry interview, Nigel Hamilton Papers, Massachusetts Historical Society (hereinafter cited as MHS), Boston, Massachusetts.

2. Fletcher Knebel, "Pulitzer Prize Entry John F. Kennedy" in Eric Sevareid, ed., *Candidates, 1960* (New York, 1959), 201; Joseph P. Kennedy quoted in William Shannon, *The American Irish* (New York, 1963), vii; John Kennedy quoted in Paul B. Fay Jr., *The Pleasure of His Company* (New York, 1966), 108.

3. Arthur Krock, *Memoirs: Sixty Years on the Firing Line* (New York, 1968), 357; William Sutton, interview with author.

4. John F. Kennedy to Henry Cabot Lodge Jr., February 24, 1949, General Correspondence 166 (hereinafter cited as GC 166), Henry Cabot Lodge II Papers, MHS; Henry Cabot Lodge Jr. to John F. Kennedy, February 28, 1949, GC 166, Henry Cabot Lodge II Papers, MHS.

5. Excerpt from *Congressional Record,* 78th Cong., 1st sess., July 7 1943–October 21, 1943, GC 166, Henry Cabot Lodge II Papers, MHS.

6. Henry Cabot Lodge Jr. to John F. Kennedy, May 14, 1948, Henry Cabot Lodge II Papers, MHS.

7. Sutton, interview.

8. William J. Miller, *Henry Cabot Lodge: A Biography* (New York, 1967), 139.

9. *Boston Post,* April 14, 1938; Joseph P. Kennedy to Edward Dunn, April 27, 1938, Joseph P. Kennedy Papers, JFKL.

10. Joseph P. Kennedy quoted in David E. Koskoff, *Joseph P. Kennedy: A Life and Times* (Englewood Cliffs, N.J., 1974), 320.

11. Richard J. Whalen, *The Founding Father* (New York, 1964), 364.

12. Commonwealth of Massachusetts, *Massachusetts Election Statistics, 1942* (Boston, 1943).

13. Joseph P. Kennedy to Henry Cabot Lodge Jr., July 25, 1947, GC 166, Henry Cabot Lodge II Papers, MHS.

14. Whalen, *The Founding Father,* 434; *Boston Herald,* October 29, 1952.

15. John F. Kennedy, interview with James MacGregor Burns, March 22, 1959, Nigel Hamilton Papers, MHS; John F. Kennedy, interview, Ralph Martin Collection (hereinafter cited as RMC), Department of Special Collections, Boston University, Boston, Massachusetts.

16. Gardner Jackson, interview, RMC; John F. Kennedy Library Introductory Film, Peter Davis Productions, 1993.

17. Norman MacDonald, interview, RMC.

18. William O. Douglas Oral History, JFKL; Hank Searls, *The Lost Prince: Young Joe: The Forgotten Kennedy* (New York, 1969), 60; Arthur Krock Oral History, JFKL.

19. Whalen, *The Founding Father,* 401; David E. Koskoff, *Joseph P. Kennedy,* 33.

20. Camman Newberry, interview, Nigel Hamilton Papers, MHS.

21. *Boston Herald American,* May 29, 1978; Seymour St. John and Richard Bode, " 'Bad Boy' Jack Kennedy," *Good Housekeeping,* September 1985.

22. *The Kennedys: The Early Years, 1900–1961,* video documentary, WGBH-Television, September 20, 1992; Joan Meyers, ed., *John Fitzgerald Kennedy as We Remember Him* (New York, 1965), 17.

23. Rip Horton Oral History, JFKL.

24. Maurice Shea Oral History, JFKL; Doris Kearns Goodwin, *The Fitzgeralds and the Kennedys: An American Saga* (New York, 1987), 488.

25. Ibid., 489; Herbert S. Parmet, *Jack: The Struggles of John F. Kennedy* (New York, 1980), 40.

26. John F. Kennedy, interview with James MacGregor Burns, March 22, 1959, Nigel Hamilton Papers, MHS.

27. Joseph P. Kennedy to Delmar Leighton, August 28, 1936, John F. Kennedy Personal Papers, box 2, JFKL.

28. Torbert MacDonald Oral History, JFKL.

29. John F. Kennedy, interview, RMC.

30. David Burner and Thomas R. West, *The Torch Is Passed* (New York, 1984), 27.

31. John F. Kennedy Library Introductory Film.

32. John F. Kennedy, "Appeasement at Munich," March 15, 1940, John F. Kennedy Personal Papers, box 2, JFKL; H. Yeomans, "Report on Thesis for Distinction," John F. Kennedy Personal Papers, box 2, JFKL.

33. Arthur Krock, interview, Joan and Clay Blair Papers (hereinafter cited as JCBP), University of Wyoming, Laramie, Wyoming.

34. Ronald Kessler, *The Sins of the Father: Joseph P. Kennedy and the Dynasty He Founded*

(New York, 1996), 219; James MacGregor Burns, *John F. Kennedy: A Political Profile* (New York, 1960), 44.

35. *The Kennedys: The Early Years, 1900–1961.*

36. *Harvard Crimson,* September 20, 1939; John F. Kennedy to Joseph P. Kennedy, n.d. [December 1940], John F. Kennedy Personal Papers, box 4A, JFKL.

37. Goodwin, *The Fitzgeralds and the Kennedys,* 627.

38. Joan Blair and Clay Blair, *The Search for J.F.K.* (New York, 1976), 135; Goodwin, *The Fitzgeralds and the Kennedys,* 634.

39. *Boston Globe,* January 11, 1944.

40. John Hersey, "Survival," *New Yorker,* June 17, 1944.

41. *Boston Globe,* January 11, 1944; Charles Harris, interview, JCBP.

42. *Boston Globe,* June 22, 1939.

43. Robert Donovan, *PT-109: John F. Kennedy in World War II* (New York, 1960), 203.

44. *Boston Globe,* January 11, 1944.

45. Peter Collier and David Horowitz, *The Kennedys: An American Drama* (New York, 1984), 483.

46. Official Citation for Navy and Marine Corps Medal for Valor, May 19, 1944, John F. Kennedy Personal Papers, box 11A, JFKL.

47. *New Yorker,* June 17, 1944; Parmet, *Jack,* 112.

48. Goodwin, *The Fitzgeralds and the Kennedys,* 693.

49. *Chicago Herald American,* April 28, 1945.

50. Meyers, ed., *John F. Kennedy as We Remember Him,* 46.

51. Jack Beatty, *The Rascal King: The Life and Times of James Michael Curley* (Reading, Mass., 1992), 456.

52. *Boston Post,* April 23, 1946.

53. Anthony Gallucio Oral History, JFKL; Kenneth P. O'Donnell and David F. Powers with Joe McCarthy, *Johnny, We Hardly Knew Ye: Memories of John F. Kennedy* (Boston, 1972), 67.

54. Charles Garabedian Oral History, JFKL.

55. Thomas P. O'Neill with William Novak, *Man of the House: The Life and Political Memoirs of Speaker Tip O'Neill* (New York, 1987), 83.

56. Anthony Gallucio Oral History, JFKL.

57. Meyers, ed., *John F. Kennedy as We Remember Him,* 48.

58. Ibid., 49; Ralph Martin, *Seeds of Destruction: Joe Kennedy and His Sons* (New York, 1995), 138.

59. Collier and Horowitz, *The Kennedys,* 155; J. Anthony Lukas, *Common Ground: A Turbulent Decade in the Lives of Three American Families* (New York, 1986), 380.

60. Steve Buckley, "The Other Joe Russo," *Boston Magazine,* June 1993.

61. Ibid.

62. O'Neill, *Man of the House,* 88; Mike Neville, interview, RMC.

63. Commonwealth of Massachusetts, *Massachusetts Election Statistics, 1946* (Boston, 1946).

64. Thomas P. O'Neill, quoted in *J.F.K.: The Man, The President* (Boston, 1979), 27.

65. O'Neill, *Man of the House,* 100; John F. Kennedy, interview with James MacGregor Burns, March 22, 1959, Nigel Hamilton Papers, MHS.

66. William O. Douglas Oral History, JFKL; William Sutton, interview, RMC.

67. Pamela Churchill Harriman, interview, JCBP.

68. Camman Newberry, interview, Nigel Hamilton Papers, MHS.

69. Frank Waldrop, interview, JCBP.

70. Roger Kahn, *The Boys of Summer* (New York, 1972), 427–28.

71. Blair and Blair, *The Search for J.F.K.,* 567.

72. Mary Davis, interview, RMC.

73. Burns, *A Political Profile,* 74.

74. Ted Reardon, interview with Christopher Matthews, by permission of Christopher Matthews; Burns, *A Political Profile,* 76.

75. *Person to Person,* CBS Television Network, September 29, 1960.

76. *Congressional Record,* January 25, 1949; Christopher Matthews, *Kennedy and Nixon: The Rivalry That Shaped Postwar America* (New York, 1996), 75.

77. Richard Thaler, "John F. Kennedy in Massachusetts: A New Generation's Leader," Thesis, Princeton University, 1973; John F. Kennedy, interview with James MacGregor Burns, March 22, 1959, Nigel Hamilton Papers, MHS.

78. John F. Kennedy, interview with James MacGregor Burns, March 22, 1959, Nigel Hamilton Papers, MHS.

79. Thomas H. O'Connor, *The Boston Irish: A Political History* (Boston, 1994), 218; David Burner, *John F. Kennedy and a New Generation* (Boston, 1988), 23; O'Neill, *Man of the House,* 98.

80. Burner, *John F. Kennedy and a New Generation,* 23.

81. Joseph Healy Oral History, JFKL.

82. Ibid.; Matthews, *Kennedy and Nixon,* 76.

83. Robert Curran, *The Kennedy Women* (New York, 1964), 2.

84. Alec Barbrook, *God Save the Commonwealth: An Electoral History of Massachusetts* (Amherst, Mass., 1973), 113.

85. *Time,* July 11, 1960; John Galvin Oral History, JFKL.

86. Barbrook, *God Save the Commonwealth,* 87.

87. Ibid., 88.

88. O'Neill, *Man of the House,* 64.

89. Ibid.

90. James M. O'Toole, "Prelates and Politicos in Massachusetts, 1900–1970," in Robert E. Sullivan and James M. O'Toole, eds., *Catholic Boston: Studies in Religion and Community, 1879–1970* (Boston, 1983), 49.

91. James M. O'Toole, *Militant and Triumphant: William Henry O'Connell and the Catholic Church in Boston, 1859–1944* (London, 1992), 232; William E. Kelly, "Richard J. Cushing: The Cardinal and Politics," January 17, 1975, research paper, Boston Archdiocese Archives, Boston, Massachusetts; *The Pilot,* August 7, 1948.

92. Sullivan and O'Toole, eds., *Catholic Boston: Studies in Religion and Community,* 52.

93. O'Neill, *Man of the House,* 67.

94. *Springfield Republican,* November 3, 1926.

95. National Council of the Churches of Christ in the United States of America, Bureau of Research and Survey, *Churches and Church Membership in the United States, 1958–1960,* series C, no. 3.

96. J. Joseph Huthmacher, *Massachusetts People and Politics, 1919–1933* (Cambridge, Mass., 1959), 263.

Chapter 2: Striking High

1. Henry Cabot Lodge, *The Storm Has Many Eyes* (New York, 1973), 17.

2. Stephen Hess, *America's Political Dynasties* (Garden City, N.J., 1966), 453–54.

3. Henry Cabot Lodge to Henry Cabot Lodge Jr., January 13, 1919, Henry Cabot Lodge Papers, MHS.

4. Henry Cabot Lodge to Henry Cabot Lodge Jr., May 24, 1922, Henry Cabot Lodge Papers, MHS.

5. Henry Cabot Lodge Jr. to Henry Cabot Lodge, March 1, 1924, Henry Cabot Lodge II Papers, MHS.

6. *Boston Globe,* January 8, 1933, July 24, 1932.

7. William J. Miller, *Henry Cabot Lodge,* 57, 49.

8. *Boston Globe,* November 8, 1936.

9. *Boston Evening Transcript,* July 25, 1923.

10. Emily Sears Lodge quoted in Huntley-Brinkley interview, September 24, 1960, *Senate Reports,* vol. 13 (Washington, D.C., 1961), 69.

11. John A. Garraty, *Henry Cabot Lodge: A Biography* (New York, 1965), 416; Beatty, *The Rascal King,* 238.

12. Henry Cabot Lodge Jr., *The Cult of Weakness* (New York, 1932), 158.

13. Ibid., 33–34; Anne E. Blair, *Lodge in Vietnam* (New Haven, Conn., 1995), 2; Lodge, *The Cult of Weakness,* 163.

14. Indeed, the October 23, 1932, issue of the *New York Times Book Review* called Lodge's work "incisive" and "vigorous" and praised the author for having "a precious gift of clear, virile and interesting expression."

15. *Beverly Evening Times,* September 10, 1932; Thaler, "A New Generation's Leader," 59.

16. Henry Cabot Lodge Jr. to Governor Joseph B. Ely, December 21, 1934, GC 166, Henry Cabot Lodge II Papers, MHS; *Boston American,* May 8, 1933.

17. Miller, *Henry Cabot Lodge,* 121.

18. Henry Cabot Lodge Jr. to Richard C. Storey, June 16, 1939, GC 166, Henry Cabot Lodge II Papers, MHS; *Boston Advertiser,* November 18, 1936.

19. Henry Cabot Lodge Jr. to Elizabeth Davis Lodge, December 20, 1935, Henry Cabot Lodge II Papers, MHS.

20. Miller, *Henry Cabot Lodge,* 127; Alden Hatch, *The Lodges of Massachusetts* (New York, 1973), 198.

21. *Boston Herald,* August 2, 1960; *Boston Advertiser,* August 9, 1936.

22. Beatty, *The Rascal King,* 370.

23. *Boston Advertiser,* August 9, 1936.

24. Beatty, *The Rascal King,* 396, 397; Commonwealth of Massachusetts, *Massachusetts Election Statistics, 1936* (Boston, 1937).

25. Beatty, *The Rascal King,* 397.

26. Miller, *Henry Cabot Lodge,* 133.

27. *Boston Herald,* October 23, 1936.

28. *Beverly Evening Times,* September 25, 1936.

29. Miller, *Henry Cabot Lodge,* 150.

30. John Henry Cutler, *Honey Fitz: Three Steps to the White House* (New York, 1962), 33.

31. *Beverly Evening Times,* October 2, 1936.

32. Commonwealth of Massachusetts, *Massachusetts Election Statistics, 1936.*

33. Ibid.

34. *Boston Advertiser,* November 8, 1936.

35. *Boston Globe,* September 9, 1937.

36. *Boston Advertiser,* November 8, 1936; *Boston Herald,* June 15, 1937.

37. *Boston Globe,* June 23, 1937.

38. *Boston Post,* August 18, 1937.

39. Newspaper clipping, October 26, 1937, Henry Cabot Lodge II Papers, MHS.

40. *Boston Globe,* September 14, 1939.

41. Ibid.

42. Ibid., March 9, 1941; Henry Cabot Lodge Jr. to Alvan T. Fuller, March 11, 1941, Henry Cabot Lodge II Papers, MHS.

43. *Boston Herald,* December 8, 1941; Leigh White, "He Runs the Show for Ike," *Saturday Evening Post,* May 31, 1952.

44. *Boston Globe,* October 23, 1942; *Boston Herald,* October 29, 1942.

45. Newspaper clipping, October 7, 1941, Henry Cabot Lodge II Papers, MHS.

46. Henry Cabot Lodge Jr., "The Enemy in Africa," as told to the editorial staff of the *Calvary Journal,* Military Papers 166, n.d., Henry Cabot Lodge II Papers, MHS.

47. *Boston Globe,* July 6, 1942; Lodge, "The Enemy in Africa," Military Papers 166, Henry Cabot Lodge II Papers, MHS; Hatch, *The Lodges of Massachusetts,* 217.

48. Henry Stimson to Henry Cabot Lodge Jr., July 7, 1942, Henry Cabot Lodge II Papers, MHS.

49. *Boston Globe,* July 6, 1942.

50. *Boston Herald,* October 29, 1942.

51. Commonwealth of Massachusetts, *Massachusetts Election Statistics, 1942.*

52. Ibid.; Alec Barbrook, *God Save the Commonwealth,* 51.

53. *Boston Globe,* October 1, 1943, June 10, 1943.

54. Henry Cabot Lodge Jr. to Hon. D. Worth Clark, February 3, 1944, Military Papers 166, Henry Cabot Lodge II Papers, MHS.

55. Franklin D. Roosevelt to Henry Cabot Lodge Jr., February 1, 1944, GC 166, Henry Cabot Lodge II Papers, MHS.

56. Miller, *Henry Cabot Lodge,* 174.

57. Bronze Star Citation from Willis D. Crittenberger, Major General, U.S. Army, n.d., Military Papers 166, Henry Cabot Lodge II Papers, MHS.

58. Hatch, *The Lodges of Massachusetts,* 224.

59. Miller, *Henry Cabot Lodge,* 177.

60. Henry Stimson to Henry Cabot Lodge Jr., November 20, 1945, GC 166, Henry Cabot Lodge II Papers, MHS.

61. *Boston Herald,* April 22, 1946.

62. Ibid., April 24, 1946.

63. Dorothy G. Wayman, *David I. Walsh, Citizen-Patriot* (Milwaukee, 1952), 311; *New York Post,* May 6, 1942.

64. Wayman, *David I. Walsh,* 318.

65. *Boston Herald,* October 25, 1946.

66. Goodwin, *The Fitzgeralds and the Kennedys,* 764; Commonwealth of Massachusetts, *Massachusetts Election Statistics, 1946.*

67. Lodge, *The Storm Has Many Eyes,* 61.

68. *Saturday Evening Post,* May 31, 1952.

69. Ibid.

70. *Berkshire Eagle,* February 8, 1950.

71. Henry Cabot Lodge Jr., "A Foreign Aid Program Which Will Aid Americans," May 14, 1947, speech copy, Essex Institute, Salem, Mass.

72. Lodge, *The Storm Has Many Eyes,* 62.

73. Neil MacNeil and Harold W. Metz, *The Hoover Report, 1953–1955* (New York, 1956), 10; Bradley D. Nash and Cornelius Lynde, *A Hook in Leviathan: A Critical Interpretation of the Hoover Commission Report* (New York, 1950), 224.

74. *New York Times,* February 2, 1950; Hatch, *The Lodges of Massachusetts,* 244.

75. Henry Cabot Lodge Jr., "Modernize the G.O.P.," *Atlantic Monthly,* March 1950.

76. *Berkshire Eagle,* February 8, 1950.

77. Henry Cabot Lodge Jr., "Think and Act Anew," *Saturday Evening Post,* January 26, 1949.

Chapter 3: Laying the Groundwork

1. O'Donnell and Powers with McCarthy, *Johnny, We Hardly Knew Ye,* 79.

2. "JFK Appearances, 1946–1952," JFKL.

3. *Boston American,* March 6, 1951.

4. *Boston Post,* December 8, 1951.

5. Joseph DeGuglielmo Oral History, JFKL.

6. Ralph Martin and Ed Plaut, *Front Runner, Dark Horse* (New York, 1960), 159.

7. Joseph DeGuglielmo Oral History, JFKL.

8. John F. Kennedy, interview, RMC; Lawrence F. O'Brien, *No Final Victories: A Life in Politics from John F. Kennedy to Watergate* (Garden City, N.J., 1974), 26.

9. John F. Kennedy, interview with James MacGregor Burns, March 22, 1959, Nigel Hamilton Papers, MHS.

10. Barbrook, *God Save the Commonwealth,* 94.

11. Commonwealth of Massachusetts, *Election Statistics, 1952.*

12. O'Donnell and Powers with McCarthy, *Johnny, We Hardly Knew Ye,* 82.

13. Ibid.

14. Mark Dalton, interview with Christopher Matthews, by permission of Christopher Matthews.

15. Whalen, *The Founding Father,* 420; O'Donnell and Powers with McCarthy, *Johnny, We Hardly Knew Ye,* 83.

16. John Spiegel, interview, RMC.

17. Ralph Coghlan, interview, RMC; *Dorchester Citizen,* August 14, 1952.

18. Mark Dalton, interview, RMC.

19. R. Sargent Shriver, interview, JCBP.

20. John Spiegel, interview, RMC; John F. Kennedy to John Ford, June 4, 1952, Pre-Presidential Papers, box 106, JFKL.

21. John F. Kennedy to T. J. Reardon and R. Sargent Shriver, August 21, 1952, Pre-Presidential Papers, box 103, JFKL.

22. John F. Kennedy, interview, RMC.

23. Robert F. Kennedy, interview, RMC.

24. Jean Stein and George Plimpton, eds., *American Journey: The Life and Times of Robert F. Kennedy* (New York, 1970), 41; Lester David and Irene David, *Bobby Kennedy: The Making of a Folk Hero* (New York, 1986), 64.

25. Arthur Schlesinger Jr., *Robert F. Kennedy and His Times* (Boston, 1978), 23.

26. Ibid., 45.

27. Writers, Editors, and Photographers of Associated Press, *Triumph and Tragedy: The Story of the Kennedys* (New York, 1968), 61.

28. O'Brien, *No Final Victories,* 30; O'Donnell and Powers with McCarthy, *Johnny, We Hardly Knew Ye,* 86.

29. Stein and Plimpton, eds., *American Journey,* 41–42.

30. O'Neill with Novak, *Man of the House,* 95; James W. Hilty, *Robert Kennedy, Brother Protector* (Philadelphia, 1997), 67; *Newsweek,* April 1, 1957.

31. Dave Powers Oral History, JFKL.

32. O'Brien, *No Final Victories,* 30.

33. O'Connor, *The Boston Irish,* 218.

34. Ken O'Donnell, interview, RMC.

35. *John F. Kennedy for United States Senator,* Campaign Tabloid, Robert F. Kennedy Pre-Administration Papers, box 1, JFKL.

36. Robert F. Kennedy, interview, RMC.

37. Hilty, *Robert Kennedy,* 70; Robert F. Kennedy, interview, RMC.

38. John Droney Oral History, JFKL; O'Brien, *No Final Victories,* 27; Thaler, "A New Generation's Leader," 87–88.

39. Robert F. Kennedy Oral History, JFKL.

40. Thaler, "A New Generation's Leader," 89–90.

41. *Boston Post,* June 24, 1952.

42. O'Donnell and Powers with McCarthy, *Johnny, We Hardly Knew Ye,* 90.

43. Camman Newberry, interview, Nigel Hamilton Papers, MHS.

44. Hatch, *The Lodges of Massachusetts,* 258.

45. Henry Cabot Lodge Jr. to Al Cole, June 13, 1952, Henry Cabot Lodge II Papers, MHS.

46. Maxwell Rabb, interview with author.

47. Henry Cabot Lodge Jr., "A Challenge to Republicans," typescript, February 12, 1947, Henry Cabot Lodge II Papers, MHS.

48. *Boston Globe,* January 13, 1949.

49. *Boston Herald,* September 19, 1952.

50. *Boston Herald–Boston Traveler,* May 1, 1952, Newsclip File, Boston University, Boston, Mass.; *Boston Herald,* May 7, 1952.

51. James T. Patterson, *Mr. Republican: A Biography of Robert A. Taft* (Boston, 1972), 427.

52. Miller, *Henry Cabot Lodge,* 201.

53. Eleanora W. Schoenebaum, *Political Profiles: The Truman Years* (New York, 1978), 535.

54. Hamby, *Liberalism and Its Challengers,* 104.

55. Patterson, *Mr. Republican,* 429.

56. Arthur H. Vandenberg Jr., *The Private Papers of Senator Vandenberg* (Boston, 1952), 466–67.

57. *Boston Globe,* January 13, 1952.

58. Dwight D. Eisenhower, *The White House Years: Mandate for Change, 1953–56* (New York, 1963), 18.

59. Hatch, *The Lodges of Massachusetts,* 248; Eisenhower, *The White House Years,* 18.

60. Lodge, *The Storm Has Many Eyes,* 75–76.

61. *Haverhill Gazette,* August 8, 1952.

62. Herbert S. Parmet, *Richard Nixon and His America* (Boston, 1973), 75–76.

63. *Boston Herald–Boston Traveler,* May 12, 1952.

64. *Boston Globe,* August 16, 1976.

65. *Boston Herald,* July 3, 1952; Maxwell Rabb, interview with author.

66. Lodge campaign memo, n.d., Ann Whitman File, Administration Series, box 23, Dwight D. Eisenhower Library, Abeline, Kansas.

67. *Boston Globe,* August 16, 1976.

68. *Boston Herald,* July 12, 1952.

69. Miller, *Henry Cabot Lodge,* 251.

70. Mason Sears to James F. Shea, December 8, 1953, Henry Cabot Lodge II Papers, MHS.

Chapter 4: Kennedys on the Move

1. John F. Kennedy, interview, RMC.

2. Joe McCarthy, *The Remarkable Kennedys* (New York, 1960), 136.

3. O'Brien, *No Final Victories,* 32.

4. McCarthy, *The Remarkable Kennedys,* 136.

5. Robert P. Cramer Oral History, JFKL.

6. Ibid.

7. Ibid.

8. Robert Capeless, interview, RMC.

9. Edward C. Berube Oral History, JFKL.

10. Anna Mae Arsenault, interview with author.

11. Ibid.

12. Robert P. Cramer, interview, RMC.

13. John E. Powers, interview, RMC.

14. Harold Vaughn, interview, RMC.

15. Robert F. Kennedy quoted in Paul F. Healy, "The Senate's Gay Young Bachelor," *Saturday Evening Post,* June 13, 1953.

16. Joseph Alsop Oral History, JFKL.

17. Leo Damore, *The Cape Cod Years of John Fitzgerald Kennedy* (New York, 1993), 124; Ralph Martin, *A Hero for Our Time: An Intimate Story of the Kennedy Years* (New York, 1983), 55.

18. Damore, *The Cape Cod Years,* 124; John F. Kennedy, interview, RMC.

19. Newsclipping, October 18, 1952, Pre-Presidential Papers, box 119, JFKL.

20. *Lynn Telegram-News,* October 26, 1952.

21. McCarthy, *The Remarkable Kennedys,* 135.

22. John E. Powers, interview, RMC.

23. *Lynn Telegram-News,* November 2, 1952.

24. Writers, Photographers, and Editors of the Associated Press, *Triumph and Tragedy,* 100.

25. O'Neill, *Man of the House,* 89.

26. Writers, Photographers, and Editors of the Associated Press, *Triumph and Tragedy,* 100; Goodwin, *The Fitzgeralds and the Kennedys,* 718.

27. *Congressional Quarterly News Feature,* October 3, 1952, Pre-Presidential Papers, box 101, JFKL; Pauline Fitzgerald, interview, JCBP.

28. *Berkshire Eagle,* September 8, 1952.

29. Gail Cameron, *Rose* (New York, 1971), 163.

30. Ibid.; Dave Powers, interview, JCBP.

31. John Henry Cutler, *Ed Brooke: Biography of a Senator* (New York, 1972), 48.

32. Whalen, *The Founding Father,* 432.

33. *Haverhill Gazette,* October 7, 1952.

34. *Berkshire Eagle,* September 8, 1952.

35. *Lynn Telegram-News,* September 22, 1952.

36. Pauline Fitzgerald, interview, JCBP.

37. *Saturday Evening Post,* September 14, 1953.

38. Writers, Photographers, and Editors of the Associated Press, *Triumph and Tragedy,* 113.

39. Cabell Phillips, "Case Study of a Senate Race," *New York Times Magazine,* October 26, 1952.

40. *Lynn Telegram-News,* September 22, 1952.

41. *Boston Globe,* October 19, 1952.

42. *New Bedford Standard-Times,* October 15, 1952.

43. Phillips, "Case Study."

44. *Boston Herald,* October 13, 1952.

45. Matthews, *Kennedy and Nixon,* 77.

46. Thomas H. O'Connor, *Bibles, Brahmins, and Bosses: A Short History of Boston* (Boston, 1984), 115.

47. Ibid.

48. *Boston Herald,* January 21, 1916; O'Connor, *Bibles, Brahmins, and Bosses,* 135.

49. Barbrook, *God Save the Commonwealth,* 12.

50. *Boston Globe,* November 2, 1952.

51. Whalen, *The Founding Father,* 419.

52. PMS Analysis Poll, September 5, 1952, Senate Campaign 1952 166, Henry Cabot Lodge II Papers, MHS.

53. Martin and Plaut, *Front Runner, Dark Horse,* 154–55; *The Pilot,* March 18, 1950.

54. Lodge, *The Storm Has Many Eyes,* 256.

55. McCarthy, *The Remarkable Kennedys,* 25.

56. Commonwealth of Massachusetts, *Massachusetts Election Statistics, 1946.*

57. Koskoff, *Joseph P. Kennedy,* 137; *The Kennedys: The Early Years, 1900–1961;* Michael Beschloss, *Kennedy and Roosevelt: The Uneasy Alliance* (New York, 1980), 257–58.

58. Phil David Fine Oral History, JFKL.

59. Nat Henthoff, *Boston Boy* (New York, 1986), 21.

60. *Jewish World,* November 1952.

61. Hillel Levine and Lawrence Harmon, *The Death of an American Jewish Community: A Tragedy of Good Intentions* (New York, 1992), 24; *Boston Herald,* December 13, 1948.

62. Parmet, *Jack,* 254.
63. Phil David Fine Oral History, JFKL.
64. Ian J. Bickerton, "Kennedy, the Jewish Community, and Israel," in *John F. Kennedy: Person, Policy, Presidency,* ed. J. Richard Snyder (Wilmington, Del., 1988), 102; *Jewish Advocate,* October 2, 1952.
65. Ronald Kessler, *The Sins of the Father,* 337.
66. Thomas P. O'Neill Oral History, JFKL.
67. Ibid.
68. Levine and Harmon, *The Death of an American Jewish Community,* 25; *Boston Globe,* November 3, 1952.
69. *Brockton Enterprise,* October 16, 1952.
70. *Boston Herald,* July 27, 1952.

Chapter 5: Enter Lodge, Exit Brewer
1. O'Donnell and Powers with McCarthy, *Johnny, We Hardly Knew Ye,* 90.
2. *Boston Herald,* August 16, 1952; Goodwin, *The Fitzgeralds and the Kennedys,* 757–58.
3. Ibid., 764.
4. *Boston Herald,* September 9, 1952.
5. Ibid., September 17, 1952.
6. Ibid.; *Boston Globe,* September 17, 1952.
7. Ibid.; O'Donnell and Powers with McCarthy, *Johnny, We Hardly Knew Ye,* 91.
8. *Waltham News-Tribune,* September 17, 1952; *Boston Globe,* September 17, 1952.
9. *Boston Herald,* September 17, 1952; *Boston Globe,* September 17, 1952; Joseph Rosetti Oral History, JFKL.
10. *Boston Record,* October 18, 1952; *Boston Herald,* September 19, 1952; Goodwin, *The Fitzgeralds and the Kennedys,* 764.
11. *Boston Herald,* October 23, 1952.
12. Matthews, *Kennedy and Nixon,* 77.
13. *Boston Post,* April 7, 1952.
14. Commonwealth of Massachusetts, Department of Labor and Statistics, *Report of the Division of Statistics* (Boston, 1952).
15. "WNAC Keynote Speech," October 5, 1952, Pre-Presidential Papers, box 94, JFKL; Timothy J. Reardon, "John F. Kennedy's Positions on Campaign Issues," n.d., JFKL.
16. Lodge, *The Storm Has Many Eyes,* 260; *Boston Herald,* April 11, 1952.
17. Burns, *John F. Kennedy: A Political Profile,* 102.
18. "J.F.K. Comments on Labor-Management Act," April 16, 1947, in *John F. Kennedy: A Compilation of Statements and Speeches Made during His Service in the United States Senate and House of Representatives* (Washington, D.C., 1964), 4; *Boston Herald,* April 15, 1947.
19. Ibid., October 13, 1952.
20. George F. Willison, *The History of Pittsfield, Massachusetts* (Pittsfield, Mass., 1957), 226, 230.
21. *Berkshire Eagle,* June 6, 1952.
22. Ibid., June 10, 1952.
23. Ibid., September 8, 1952.
24. *New England Teamster,* November 1952.

25. Press release, n.d., Pre-Presidential Papers, box 105, JFKL; *Boston Herald,* October 23, 1952.

26. "WBZ-TV Speech," October 17, 1952, Henry Cabot Lodge II Papers, MHS.

27. George Smathers, interview with Christopher Matthews, by permission of Christopher Matthews; David Caute, *The Great Fear* (New York, 1978), 37.

28. Melvyn Leffler, *The Specter of Communism: The United States and the Origins of the Cold War, 1917–1953* (New York, 1994), 107.

29. Greg Mitchell, *Tricky Dick and the Pink Lady: Richard M. Nixon vs. Helen Gahagan Douglas: Sexual Politics and the Red Scare, 1950* (New York, 1998), 44.

30. M. J. Heale, *American Anticommunism: Combatting the Enemy Within, 1830–1970* (Baltimore, 1992), 138.

31. David Halberstam, *The Fifties* (New York, 1993), 50–51.

32. Heale, *American Anticommunism,* 163.

33. Harry S. Truman quoted in Ray Robinson, *The Home Run Heard round the World* (New York, 1991), 2.

34. Commonwealth of Massachusetts, *Report of the Committee to Curb Communism,* March 30, 1951 (Boston, 1951).

35. Richard J. Cushing quoted in J. Anthony Lukas, *Common Ground* (New York, 1986), 380; *The Pilot,* July 5, 1952.

36. Ibid., March 15, April 19, August 23, 1952.

37. Commonwealth of Massachusetts, Chapter 805 of the Acts of 1951, Civil Liberties Union of Massachusetts Papers, MHS.

38. *Christian Science Monitor,* November 26, 1951; *Harvard Crimson,* November 23, 1951.

39. *New Bedford Standard-Times,* October 30, 1952; Press release, October 30, 1952, Pre-Presidential Papers, box 105, JFKL.

40. Ibid.; "Kennedy-Lodge Waltham Debate Background Book Draft," in Pre-Presidential Papers, box 102, JFKL.

41. "WNAC Keynote Speech," October 5, 1952, Pre-Presidential Papers, box 94, JFKL.

42. William Sutton, interview with author.

43. "Radio Speech on Russia," Pre-Presidential Papers, box 94, JFKL.

44. *Boston Herald,* March 3, 1950; Victor Lasky, *JFK: The Man and the Myth* (New York, 1963), 111; *New York Herald-Tribune,* March 14, 1947.

45. "The Christoffel Case: Factual Background," Pre-Presidential Papers, box 98, JFKL; *Congressional Record,* June 29, 1949.

46. Burns, *John F. Kennedy: A Political Profile,* 133; *Boston Herald,* March 3, 1950.

47. Donald F. Crosby, S.J., "The Angry Catholics: American Catholics and Senator Joseph R. McCarthy" (Ph.D. dissertation, Brandeis University, April 1973), 247; John F. Kennedy quoted in Damore, *The Cape Cod Years,* 114.

48. *Congressional Record,* January 25, 1949.

49. "China: Salem, Massachusetts, Jan. 30, 1949," in Pre-Presidential Papers, box 95, JFKL.

50. "British Shipment to Communist China," May 9, 1951, in *John F. Kennedy: A Compilation of Statements and Speeches,* 78–80.

51. Whalen, *The Founding Father,* 265; Athan Theoharis, *From the Secret Files of J. Edgar Hoover* (Chicago, 1991), 318.

52. Martin, *Seeds of Destruction*, 1.

53. Independence Day oration, July 4, 1946, Pre-Presidential Papers, box 94, JFKL; "Notre Dame Speech," January 29, 1950, Pre-Presidential Papers, box 94, JFKL.

54. "Lodge Comments to New York Star," Henry Cabot Lodge II Papers, MHS; *Christian Science Monitor*, May 1, 1948.

55. Stenotype report on executive session, U.S. Foreign Affairs Committee, April 2, 1947, Henry Cabot Lodge II Papers, MHS.

56. *New York Times*, October 29, 1950.

57. "Possible Statement for Publication," November 1948, speeches, Henry Cabot Lodge II Papers, MHS.

58. "Remarks at Montgomery County Republican Rally, Dayton, Ohio," October 25, 1948, speeches, Henry Cabot Lodge II Papers, MHS.

59. *New Bedford Standard-Times*, October 15, 1952; "WBZ-TV Speech," October 17, 1952, radio and television speeches, Henry Cabot Lodge II Papers, MHS.

60. Given A. Brewer, *History of the Brewer, Lanius, Given, Perrin, and Ankeny Family* (n.p., 1981), 218, 201.

61. Ibid., 209–10.

62. *New Bedford Standard-Times*, November 20, 1988; Jeremiah Murphy, interview with author.

63. *New Bedford Standard-Times*, November 20, 1988.

64. Dick Early, interview with author; Minna Littmann, "Basil Brewer, Editor-Statesman," *Nemoscope*, fall 1947, *New Bedford Standard-Times* Library, New Bedford, Mass.

65. *New Bedford Standard-Times*, November 2, 1936.

66. *Boston Herald*, July 30, 1951.

67. *New Bedford Standard-Times*, June 3, 1950.

68. Ibid., January 5, 1947.

69. Ibid., May 25, 1950.

70. Ibid., July 30, 1951, July 12, 1952.

71. Brewer, *History of the Brewer, Lanius, Given, Perrin, and Ankeny Family*, 71.

72. *New Bedford Standard-Times*, November 20, 1988.

73. Ibid., November 1, 1946.

74. Ibid., March 9, 1949.

75. "Stenographic Record of Press Conference of Basil Brewer on His Support of Mr. Kennedy," September 25, 1952, Pre-Presidential Papers, box 104, JFKL.

76. *Boston Globe*, September 26, 1952.

77. *Boston Herald*, September 26, 1952.

78. *Boston American*, September 26, 1952.

79. *New Bedford Standard-Times*, October 17, October 31, 1952.

80. Ibid., October 24, 1952.

81. Jeremiah Murphy, interview with author.

82. *Boston Globe*, September 26, 1952.

83. *Christian Science Monitor*, September 26, 1952; *Lynn Telegram-News*, August 10, 1952.

84. *New York Herald-Tribune*, September 9, 1952: PMS Analysis Poll, September 5, 1952, Senate Campaign 1952 166, Henry Cabot Lodge II Papers, MHS; Undated Lodge letter, Henry Cabot Lodge II Papers, MHS.

85. O'Neill, *Man of the House,* 81; Ralph Blagden, "Cabot Lodge's Toughest Fight," *The Reporter,* September 30, 1952.

86. *Lowell Sun,* August 1, 1952.

87. Miller, *Henry Cabot Lodge,* 252.

88. *Provincetown Advocate,* July 31, 1952.

89. *Brockton Enterprise,* July 18, 1952.

90. *Lynn Telegram-News,* September 8, 1952.

91. Francis S. Winsper to Henry Cabot Lodge Jr., November 5, 1952, Henry Cabot Lodge II Papers, MHS.

92. R. I. Harry to Henry Cabot Lodge Jr., November 17, 1952, Henry Cabot Lodge II Papers, MHS.

Chapter 6: Newspaper Endorsements

1. *Boston Post,* October 26, 1948.

2. PMS Analysis Poll, September 5, 1952, Senate Campaign, 1952 166, Henry Cabot Lodge II Papers, MHS; Goodwin, *The Fitzgeralds and the Kennedys,* 488.

3. Charles Pierce, "Nobody Ever Loses Money Investing with John Fox," *New England Monthly,* March 1986; Herbert A. Kenny, interview with author.

4. Pierce, "Nobody Ever Loses"; *Boston Globe,* January 23, 1985.

5. *Boston Herald,* July 8, 1956.

6. Ibid.

7. Pierce, "Nobody Ever Loses."

8. Herbert A. Kenny, *Newspaper Row: An Anecdotal History of the Flamboyant Age of Boston Journalism, 1890–1956* (Chester, Mass., 1987), 219–20.

9. John Fox, memorandum to employees, June 10, 1953, Boston Globe Library, Boston, Mass.

10. Pierce, "Nobody Ever Loses"; Herbert A. Kenny, interview with author.

11. Pierce, "Nobody Ever Loses."

12. Duncan Norton Taylor, "Money Man from South Boston," *Fortune,* July 1952.

13. *Boston Globe,* June 27, 1958.

14. Transcription of John Fox, conversation with Tim Clark, October 23, 1952, Henry Cabot Lodge II Papers, MHS.

15. Ibid., emphasis in source.

16. *Christian Science Monitor,* June 27, 1958; *Boston Globe,* June 27, 1958.

17. Parmet, *Jack,* 242; Goodwin, *The Fitzgeralds and the Kennedys,* 765.

18. *Boston Globe,* June 28, 1958.

19. *Boston Post,* October 25, 1952.

20. Altogether, the five papers had a total circulation of over 372,000. The *Boston Herald* led the pack with 133,497 readers, with the *Worcester Evening Gazette* (99,811), *Springfield Union* (75,966), *Lowell Sun* (38,729), and *Berkshire Eagle* (24,900) following suit. While the *Eagle* possessed a comparatively small circulation, the paper was nevertheless the most-read daily in the westernmost part of Massachusetts. The *Boston Globe,* incidentally, had an overall circulation of 151,503.

21. *Boston Globe,* September 25, 1952.

22. *Boston Globe,* October 19, 1952.

23. *Boston Herald,* September 2, 1952.

24. *Berkshire Eagle,* October 29, 1952.

25. *Worcester Evening Gazette,* October 4, 1952.

26. *Lowell Sun,* September 29, 1952.

27. *Springfield Union,* November 1, 1952.

28. John Galvin Oral History, JFKL.

29. Joseph Healey Oral History, JFKL.

30. O'Brien, *No Final Victories,* 32.

31. Ibid.

32. O'Donnell and Powers with McCarthy, *Johnny, We Hardly Knew Ye,* 79.

33. Edward J. McCormack Oral History, JFKL.

34. John F. Kennedy, interview with James MacGregor Burns, March 22, 1959, Nigel Hamilton Papers, MHS.

35. Joseph DeGuglielmo Oral History, JFKL.

36. John F. Kennedy, interview with James MacGregor Burns, March 22, 1959.

37. Undeterred by Dever's action, Kennedy attended the convention as a nondelegate and garnered much favorable media attention through a series of television appearances shrewdly arranged by press aide Ralph Coghlan, formerly of the *St. Louis Post-Dispatch.*

38. Parmet, *Jack,* 233; Dave Powers, interview, JCBP.

39. *Time,* September 29, 1952; *Boston Herald,* July 22, 1952; *Berkshire Eagle,* July 22, 1952.

40. O'Brien, *No Final Victories,* 36.

41. Edward J. McCormack Oral History, JFKL.

42. Collier and Horowitz, *The Kennedys,* 186; James W. Hilty, *Robert Kennedy,* 69.

43. Collier and Horowitz, *The Kennedys,* 186.

44. O'Brien, *No Final Victories,* 36.

45. Barbrook, *God Save the Commonwealth,* 94.

46. *Boston Post,* November 29, 1953.

47. "Information from Sargent Shriver," September 17, 1952, Adlai Stevenson Papers, Manuscripts Division, Princeton University, Princeton, N.J.

48. James Landis Oral History, Columbia University, New York.

49. Roy Cohn, *McCarthy* (New York, 1968), 16; Penn T. Kimball, interview, JCBP.

50. George Smathers Oral History, JFKL.

51. William O. Douglas Oral History, JFKL.

52. Goodwin, *The Fitzgeralds and the Kennedys,* 723.

53. Robert Amory Oral History, JFKL; John Mallan, "Massachusetts: Liberal and Corrupt," *New Republic,* October 13, 1952.

54. Parmet, *Jack,* 174; Gardner Jackson, interview, RMC.

55. *New York Post,* January 9, 1961; Donald F. Crosby, S.J., *God, Church, and Flag* (Chapel Hill, N.C., 1978), 110.

56. Maxwell Rabb, interview with author; Robert Healy, interview with author.

57. James J. Sullivan, interview with author; Thomas C. Reeves, *The Life and Times of Joe McCarthy* (Briarcliff Manor, N.Y., 1982), 443.

58. *New York Times,* July 18, 1950.

59. Ibid.

60. *Boston Globe,* April 3, 1950.

61. Henry Cabot Lodge Jr. to Arthur Schlesinger Jr., March 16, 1950, Arthur Schlesinger Jr. Papers, box P-18, JFKL.

62. Reeves, *The Life and Times of Joe McCarthy*, 311; Sullivan, interview.

63. Joseph R. McCarthy to Henry Cabot Lodge Jr., November 1, 1952, Henry Cabot Lodge II Papers, MHS.

64. Parmet, *Jack*, 244.

65. Hatch, *The Lodges of Massachusetts*, 257; *Christian Science Monitor*, September 25, 1952.

66. *Christian Science Monitor*, September 25, 1952.

67. "Draft of Suggested Remarks for Senator McCarthy," Henry Cabot Lodge II Papers, MHS.

68. *Boston Globe*, September 30, 1962.

69. Henry Cabot Lodge Jr. to Joseph M. Dailey, July 11, 1974, Henry Cabot Lodge II Papers, MHS; Healy, interview.

70. Henry Cabot Lodge Jr. to Joseph M. Dailey, July 11, 1974; Joseph R. McCarthy to Henry Cabot Lodge Jr., telegram, November 1, 1952, Henry Cabot Lodge II Papers, MHS.

71. Rabb, interview.

72. Lawrence H. Fuchs, "Presidential Politics in Boston: The Irish Response to Stevenson," *New England Quarterly*, December 1957.

73. Ibid.

74. Erik Barnouw, *Tube of Plenty: The Evolution of American Television* (New York, 1990), 114.

75. Sig Mickelson, *The Electric Mirror* (New York, 1972), 93.

76. Halberstam, *The Fifties*, 191.

77. *Christian Science Monitor*, October 11, 1949.

78. "Preliminary Survey of Television Coverage for 1952 Senatorial Candidates," Radio-Television Division, Republican National Committee, August 30, 1951, Henry Cabot Lodge II Papers, MHS.

79. Beatty, *The Rascal King*, 491; *Christian Science Monitor*, October 11, 1949.

80. Kennedy and Lodge television schedules, October 17, 1952, Pre-Presidential Papers, box 106, JFKL; Dave Powers, interview with author.

81. R. Sargent Shriver, interview, JCBP.

82. *Boston Globe*, July 2, 1952.

83. Ibid.

84. Gene Wyckoff, *The Image Candidates: American Politics in the Age of Television* (New York, 1968), 49.

85. *Keep Posted*, CBS Television Network, October 7, 1952, Audio-Visual Archives, JFKL.

86. *Lynn Telegram-News*, October 8, 1952.

87. *New Bedford Standard-Times*, November 4, 1952.

88. Charles Eliot Worden to Henry Cabot Lodge Jr., November 8, 1952, Henry Cabot Lodge II Papers, MHS.

Chapter 7: Evening the Score

1. Joseph Healey Oral History, JFKL.

2. Rose Fitzgerald Kennedy, *Times to Remember* (New York, 1974), 327.

3. Torbert MacDonald Oral History, JFKL.

4. Joseph Healey Oral History, JFKL.

5. Torbert MacDonald Oral History, JFKL.

6. O'Brien, *No Final Victories,* 36; Torbert MacDonald Oral History, JFKL; Commonwealth of Massachusetts, *Massachusetts Election Statistics, 1952.*

7. City of Boston, *Annual Report for the Board of Election Commissioners, 1946* (Boston, 1947); O'Brien, *No Final Victories,* 37.

8. Commonwealth of Massachusetts, *Massachusetts Election Statistics, 1952.*

9. Henry Cabot Lodge Jr. to Dwight D. Eisenhower, November 6, 1952; Eisenhower Correspondence 166, Henry Cabot Lodge II Papers, MHS; James J. Sullivan, interview with author.

10. Maxwell Rabb, interview with author.

11. *Life,* November 17, 1952; Henry Cabot Lodge Jr. to Abraham Glovsky, November 24, 1952, Henry Cabot Lodge II Papers, MHS.

12. *Boston Globe,* November 6, 1952.

13. Rose Fitzgerald Kennedy quoted in Goodwin, *The Fitzgeralds and the Kennedys,* 768; *Boston Globe,* November 9, 1916.

14. O'Brien, *No Final Victories,* 37; Whalen, *The Founding Father,* 364.

15. Tyler Abell, ed., *Drew Pearson Diaries* (New York, 1974), 227; *Chicago Tribune,* November 1, 1952.

16. George C. Marshall to Henry Cabot Lodge Jr., November 6, 1952, Henry Cabot Lodge II Papers, MHS.

17. *Boston Globe,* November 5, 1952; *Worcester Telegram,* November 6, 1952; *New Bedford Standard-Times,* November 5, 1952.

18. Camman Newberry, interview, Nigel Hamilton Papers, MHS, by permission of Nigel Hamilton.

19. Commonwealth of Massachusetts, *Massachusetts Election Statistics, 1952.*

20. *Boston American,* November 4, 1952.

21. Ibid.; Edward C. Berube Oral History, JFKL.

22. O'Brien, *No Final Victories,* 23.

23. Commonwealth of Massachusetts, *Massachusetts Election Statistics, 1952.*

24. City of Boston, *Annual Report for the Board of Election Commissioners, 1952* (Boston, 1953); City of Boston, *Annual Report for the Board of Election Commissioners, 1946.*

25. Eleanor Spinney to Henry Cabot Lodge Jr., November 14, 1952, Henry Cabot Lodge II Papers, MHS.

26. City of Boston, *Annual Report for the Board of Election Commissioners, 1952.*

27. City of Boston, *Annual Report for the Board of Election Commissioners, 1946;* Phil David Fine, interview, RMC.

28. Commonwealth of Massachusetts, *Massachusetts Election Statistics, 1946–1952.*

29. City of Boston, *Annual Report for the Board of Election Commissioners, 1952, 1946.*

30. Commonwealth of Massachusetts, *Massachusetts Election Statistics, 1946–1952.*

31. *New Bedford Standard-Times,* November 5, 1952; Henry Cabot Lodge Oral History, JFKL.

32. Brewer, *History of the Brewer, Lanius, Given, Perrin, and Ankeny Family,* 214, 24.

33. Commonwealth of Massachusetts, *Massachusetts Election Statistics, 1946–1952.*

34. *Boston Herald,* January 29, 1952.

35. Martin, *A Hero for Our Time*, 53.

36. Hugh D. Price, "Campaign Finance in Massachusetts in 1952," *Public Policy* 6 (Cambridge, Mass., 1955), 38–39.

37. Mike Ward, interview, RMC, by permission of Ralph Martin.

38. James J. Sullivan, interview, RMC, by permission of Ralph Martin.

39. Mallan, "Massachusetts: Liberal and Corrupt."

40. Robert F. Kennedy, interview, RMC, by permission of Ralph Martin.

41. Henry Cabot Lodge Jr. to Al Cole, April 12, 1952, Henry Cabot Lodge II Papers, MHS.

42. Price, "Campaign Finance in Massachusetts in 1952"; Miller, *Henry Cabot Lodge*, 253.

43. Edgar Litt, *The Political Cultures of Massachusetts* (Boston, 1965), 115.

44. Thaler, "A New Generation's Leader," 20.

45. "Town Influence Up in Population Shift," Robert F. Kennedy, Pre-Administration Political Files, box 1, JFKL; Thaler, "A New Generation's Leader," 20.

46. O'Neill, *Man of the House*, 87.

47. Alec Barbrook, *God Save the Commonwealth*, 110.

Chapter 8: Men for All Seasons

1. *Beverly Times*, February 28, 1985.

2. *Life*, September 14, 1953.

3. Hatch, *The Lodges of Massachusetts*, 268.

4. *Beverly Times*, February 28, 1985; *New Republic*, October 24, 1960.

5. Lodge, *The Storm Has Many Eyes*, 170.

6. *Time*, September 26, 1960.

7. Stephen E. Ambrose, *Nixon: The Education of a Politician, 1913–1962* (New York, 1987), 553–54; *Newsweek*, August 8, 1960.

8. John F. Kennedy Library Introductory Film.

9. *The Kennedys: The Early Years, 1900–1961*.

10. John F. Kennedy, interview, RMC.

11. Arthur Schlesinger Jr., *A Thousand Days* (Boston, 1965), 12.

12. O'Donnell and Powers with McCarthy, *Johnny, We Hardly Knew Ye*, 128.

13. Goodwin, *The Fitzgeralds and the Kennedys*, 793.

14. Ibid.

15. Ibid., 143–44.

16. *Time*, September 26, 1960; O'Donnell and Powers with McCarthy, *Johnny, We Hardly Knew Ye*, 210.

17. Matthews, *Kennedy and Nixon*, 150.

18. Michael Beschloss, *The Crisis Years: Kennedy, Khrushchev, 1960–1963* (New York, 1991), 25.

19. David Hochman, "Kennedy Out-Glams Nixon," *Entertainment Weekly*, September 27, 1996.

20. Fawn M. Brodie, *Richard Nixon: The Shaping of His Character* (New York, 1981), 427.

21. *Washington Post*, April 15, 1964; *Time*, September 26, 1960.

22. *New York Times,* October 13, 1960; Richard M. Nixon, *Six Crises* (New York, 1962), 351.

23. *New York Times,* October 13, 1960.

24. *Time,* September 26, 1960.

25. Miller, *Henry Cabot Lodge,* 328.

26. *New York Times,* November 10, 1960.

27. O'Brien, *No Final Victories,* 96.

28. Memorandum of meeting with President Kennedy, n.d., Henry Cabot Lodge II Papers, MHS.

29. *Boston Herald,* November 7, 1962.

30. Whalen, *The Founding Father,* 477.

31. Blair, *Lodge in Vietnam,* 13.

32. Richard Reeves, *President Kennedy: Profile of Power* (New York, 1993), 526–27.

33. Lodge Oral History, JFKL.

34. Matthews, *Kennedy and Nixon,* 229.

35. Lodge Oral History, JFKL.

36. Lodge, *The Storm Has Many Eyes,* 206.

37. Henry Cabot Lodge to Jim Bishop, April 13, 1973, GC 166, Henry Cabot Lodge II Papers, MHS.

38. *Beverly Times,* February 28, 1985.

39. Blair, *Lodge in Vietnam,* 135.

40. *Beverly Times,* February 28, 1985.

41. Ibid., October 20, 1979.

42. *Beverly Times,* February 28, 1985.

Selected Bibliography

Nearly a half century has passed since John F. Kennedy beat Henry Cabot Lodge Jr. in the race for the U.S. Senate. This seminal political event has been relegated to footnotes in the lives of the two combatants. Scholarly accounts by such noted historians as Arthur Schlesinger Jr., James MacGregor Burns, Richard J. Whalen, Doris Kearns Goodwin, and Herbert S. Parmet have touched on this topic. Yet none has ever addressed the 1952 Massachusetts Senate race in a comprehensive manner. Indeed, Schlesinger devotes only a few perfunctory sentences to the campaign in his massive study *A Thousand Days* (1965). He writes that in 1952 he and other staff members of the Adlai Stevenson presidential campaign were "impressed by the cool efficiency of the Kennedy campaign operation and by Kennedy himself, slim, careless and purposeful against the sodden background of old-time Boston politicians."

In his groundbreaking biography *John Kennedy: A Political Profile* (1960), Burns characterizes the contest as "essentially a battle between Yankee Republicans and Catholic immigrant Democrats," with the latter prevailing thanks to their superior numbers. Whalen can count himself among the most fervid supporters of this argument. In his best-selling book *The Founding Father* (1964), he claims that Lodge had been defeated by a "young politician whose rise was shared vicariously by thousands of Irish-Americans. Where their grandfathers dreamed of wakening as Yankee overlords, now they might dream of becoming Kennedys."

Goodwin views Kennedy's victory in a slightly different light. In *The Fitzgeralds and the Kennedys: An American Saga* (1987), she argues that the campaign was a "great triumph" for the entire Kennedy family. For the earlier Senate loss of Kennedy's grandfather, former Boston mayor John "Honey Fitz" Fitzgerald, to Henry Cabot Lodge Sr. in 1916 had at last been avenged. Parmet, in his fair-minded work *Jack: The Struggles of John F. Kennedy* (1980), emphasizes the primacy of the Kennedy campaign organization. "In a state with a chaotic conglomeration of factions loosely gathered under the Democratic umbrella," he wrote, "Jack's people established their own machine."

The following is a list of the principal sources used for this work.

Manuscript Collections

Boston University, Boston, Massachusetts
　　Ralph Martin Collection, Department of Special Collections (RMC)
John F. Kennedy Library, Boston, Massachusetts (JFKL)
　　Pre-Presidential Papers
　　Arthur Schlesinger Jr. Papers
Massachusetts Historical Society, Boston, Massachusetts (MHS)
　　Nigel Hamilton Papers
　　Henry Cabot Lodge Papers
　　Henry Cabot Lodge II Papers
　　Henry Cabot Lodge II Papers GC 166
University of Wyoming, Laramie, Wyoming
　　Joan and Clay Blair Papers (JCBP)

Personal Interviews

Dick Early
Robert Healy
Jeremiah Murphy
Dave Powers
Maxwell Rabb
James J. Sullivan
William Sutton

Books and Articles

Barbrook, Alec. *God Save the Commonwealth: An Electoral History of Massachusetts.* Amherst, Mass., 1973.
Beatty, Jack. *The Rascal King: The Life and Times of James Michael Curley.* Reading, Mass., 1992.
Buckley, Steve. "The Other Joe Russo." *Boston Magazine,* June 1993.
Burns, James MacGregor. *John F. Kennedy: A Political Profile.* New York, 1960.
Blagden, Ralph. "Cabot Lodge's Toughest Fight." *The Reporter,* September 30, 1952.
Blair, Anne E. *Lodge in Vietnam.* New Haven, Conn., 1995.
Blair, Joan, and Clay Blair. *The Search for J.F.K.* New York, 1976.
Hatch, Alden. *The Lodges of Massachusetts.* New York, 1973.
Hilty, James W. *Robert Kennedy: Brother Protector.* Philadelphia, 1997.
Kennedy, Rose Fitzgerald. *Times to Remember.* 1974.
Kenny, Herbert A. *Newspaper Row: An Anecdotal History of the Flamboyant Age of Boston Journalism, 1890–1956.* Chester, Mass., 1987.
Koskoff, David E. *Joseph P. Kennedy: A Life and Times.* Englewood Cliffs, N.J., 1974.
Lodge, Henry Cabot. *The Storm Has Many Eyes.* New York, 1973.

Matthews, Christopher. *Kennedy and Nixon: The Rivalry That Shaped Postwar America*. New York, 1996.

Miller, William J. *Henry Cabot Lodge: A Biography*. New York, 1967.

O'Brien, Lawrence F. *No Final Victories: A Life in Politics from John F. Kennedy to Watergate*. Garden City, N.J., 1974.

O'Connor, Thomas H. *The Boston Irish: A Political History*. Boston, 1994.

O'Donnell, Kenneth, and David F. Powers with Joe McCarthy. *Johnny, We Hardly Knew Ye: Memories of John F. Kennedy*. Boston, 1972.

Parmet, Herbert S. *Jack: The Struggles of John F. Kennedy*. New York, 1980.

Patterson, James T. *Mr. Republican: A Biography of Robert A. Taft*. Boston, 1972.

Pierce, Charles. "Nobody Ever Loses Money with John Fox." *New England Monthly,* March 1986.

St. John, Seymour, and Richard Bode. " 'Bad Boy' Jack Kennedy." *Good Housekeeping,* September 1985.

Index